The Growth and Structure
of Human Populations

A Publication of
the Office of Population Research
Princeton University

THE GROWTH
AND STRUCTURE OF
HUMAN POPULATIONS

A Mathematical Investigation

ANSLEY J. COALE

Princeton, New Jersey
Princeton University Press
1972

Publication of this book has been aided by a grant
from the Office of Population Research
of Princeton University
This book has been composed in Times Roman.

Printed in the United States of America by
Princeton University Press
Princeton, New Jersey

Preface

ANY self-renewing aggregate that generates new members ("births") and loses existing members ("deaths") is governed by certain logical relationships; for example, each surviving member becomes one year older with the passage of each calendar year, and annual increase equals births during the year minus deaths. The subject of this book is the mathematical analysis of relationships of this sort in human populations. Some of the results could easily be extended to other aggregates such as industrial equipment or free neutrons in an atomic reactor, but many are tied to socially or biologically based characteristics common to all (or most) large human populations, and not shared by other aggregates.

From the author's point of view, this book is the third of a trilogy to which he has contributed—the third of three books dealing with mortality schedules, fertility schedules, and age composition. One of these books ("Regional Model Life Tables and Stable Populations") is derived from empirical observation, and expresses essentially the full range of age distributions implicit in combinations of human fertility and mortality schedules; the second ("Methods of Estimating Basic Demographic Measures from Incomplete Data") is an application of age distribution analysis (and other techniques) for the pragmatic purpose of supplementing incomplete data and correcting inaccurate data; and the present book is a theoretical statement of how fertility and mortality schedules combine to determine age composition and growth. The principal difference between this book and other theoretical treatments of the same subject is its greater emphasis on dynamics: the changing age composition of a population as it evolves to a stable form, and the age composition resulting from constantly changing fertility and mortality.

The use of mathematics in this book will be unsatisfactory to readers at virtually every level of mathematical competence. The author's formal instruction in mathematics was limited to undergraduate courses completed more than 30 years ago, and a major part of his experience in applying mathematics was in electronics and radio engineering: specifically in studying radar and teaching radar at the training school for Army and Navy officers operated during World War II at M.I.T. This experience explains why Fourier series and what might be called a "circuit analysis" approach appear in Chapters 6 and 7. The text is not understandable by a person who lacks training in differential and integral calculus, or to someone without a smattering of differential equations and functions of complex variables. On the other hand, to a

v

person with an extensive mathematical background, and above all to a mathematician, the mathematics will seem primitive, old-fashioned, and probably inexact.

My greatest intellectual debt is to A. J. Lotka. It should be noted that in addition to his impressively full development of stable population theory, Lotka also analyzed the birth sequences and age compositions of populations following certain curves of overall population increase, especially the logistic. I am also grateful to Frank Notestein for his role in introducing his students to age distribution theory, to George Stolnitz and Norman Ryder for having helped the author in the development of his ideas on mortality and fertility respectively, and to Jean Bourgeois-Pichat, Nathan Keyfitz, John Hajnal, Alvaro Lopez, and Leo Goodman for ideas on stable populations that I found useful. Collaboration with Paul Demeny was not only instrumental in producing two books, but an enjoyable experience in interchanging and developing ideas. Alvaro Lopez provided the cornerstone for this book in proving the theorem on "weak ergodicity," and conversations with him have helped clarify points on which I was uncertain, and opened new avenues for thought as well as prevented my entering certain blind alleys. A majority of the computations in this book were programmed by Mrs. Erna Harm, a research assistant at the Office of Population Research. Without her skill and patience, the book could not have been completed. The general research program at the Office of Population Research, of which this book is a product, has enjoyed the generous support of the Milbank Memorial Fund, the Rockefeller Foundation, and the Ford Foundation.

Princeton
July, 1971

Contents

viii

CONTENTS

X

List of Figures

xiv

List of Tables

The Growth and Structure
of Human Populations

Fertility, Mortality, and Age Distributions: Introduction

THE age composition of a population that neither gains nor loses by migration is determined by the recent sequence of fertility and mortality risks at each age to which it has been subject. Its overall birth rate, death rate, and rate of increase at each moment are determined by the current age composition and the current age schedules of fertility and mortality. In principle, then, both age composition and vital rates can be determined from knowledge of the history and present value of fertility and mortality schedules. Consider a female population in which the annual death rate of persons at age a and time t is $\mu(a,t)$, and the annual rate of bearing a female child at age a and time t is $m(a,t)$. If these schedules are specified for a sufficient time interval — in practice no more than a century — the age composition, birth rate, death rate, and rate of increase can all be calculated. If an age distribution in the past is among the available data, the calculation of current age composition and vital rates can be made by standard methods of population projection. If no past age distribution is stipulated, it appears at first that knowledge of past fertility and mortality schedules is not sufficient to calculate the current age distribution. However, Alvaro Lopez has proven a conjecture made by the author in 1957: that two arbitrarily chosen age distributions no matter how different, subject to identical sequences — whether varying or constant — of fertility and mortality, ultimately generate populations with the same age composition (Coale [2], Lopez [8, 9], also McFarland [10]). Age distributions gradually "forget" the past. It is therefore possible to reproduce the age composition of a given population by projecting an arbitrarily selected initial population from many years in the past, employing the age schedules of fertility and mortality that the population actually experienced in the interim. If the period of projection is long enough, the effect of the arbitrary initial age composition wholly disappears, and the current age composition ($c(a,t_0)$) is seen to be entirely a function of $\mu(a,t)$ and $m(a,t)$ during a substantial interval before t_0. Moreover, if $c(a,t)da$ is the proportion of the female population between age a and $a + da$, $b(t)$ is the birth rate and $d(t)$ the death rate, and ω is the highest age attained,

(1.1)
$$b(t) = \int_0^\omega c(a,t)m(a,t)da,$$

3

$$(1.2) \qquad\qquad d(t) = \int_0^\omega c(a,t)\mu(a,t)da.$$

The rate of increase of the population at time $t - r(t)$ — is the difference between $b(t)$ and $d(t)$, and the proportionate increase in numbers from t_1 to t_2 is $e^{\int_{t_1}^{t_2} r(t)dt}$

The principal purpose of this book is to analyze the relation of levels, age patterns, and time patterns of fertility and mortality to the growth and age composition of populations. If our minds could readily visualize the outcome of the large number of multiplications and additions that constitute a population projection, the book could be terminated right here, or at most would need to include a brief description of how a population projection is made and a recapitulation of Lopez' proof. But in view of our incapacity to visualize elaborate calculations, what has been presented is enough to enable a demographer merely to *calculate* an age distribution, a birth rate, a death rate, and a rate of increase from a long sequence of fertility and mortality schedules without providing him the basis for *understanding* what features of mortality, fertility, and their changes account for particular characteristics of the age structure, for changes in the birth and death rates, etc. In trying to explain how age structures are formed, and vital rates determined, we shall consider the age distributions produced by schedules of fertility and mortality that do not change with the passage of time (Chapters 2 and 3); and then the age distributions produced by changing fertility and mortality (Chapters 4 to 7).

Fertility and Mortality Schedules in Human Populations

FERTILITY SCHEDULES

The variation of the rate of childbearing with age depends partly on biological factors. The capacity to conceive and bear children normally begins at about age 15 (following menarche), attains a broad maximum beginning at about age 20, falls slightly by age 30, and then follows an accelerated pace of decline after age 35. A typical mean age at the birth of the last child among married women not practicing birth control is about 40 years; only a small minority can bear children after age 45 and practically none after age 50.

The actual curve of childbearing as a function of age of course depends not only on the varying capacity to conceive and bear live issue, but on variations with age in exposure to intercourse with a fertile

4

partner, and on whether or not measures are taken in different degree at different ages to prevent conception or to cause an early termination of pregnancy. The rise of fertility with age is strongly affected by laws and customs that determine when women enter fertile unions. Among societies in which marriage is ordinarily a prerequisite for fruitful intercourse, there are wide variations in mean age at marriage, from less than 15 to nearly 30 years. The decline of fertility with age is influenced by the rising incidence of widowhood, divorce, and perhaps of abstinence, as well as by declining fecundability. The practice of contraception and abortion could in principle reduce fertility at any age in the fertile span and thus produce an essentially arbitrary modification of the age structure of fertility; but, in fact, voluntary control seems always to cause a greater proportionate reduction of fertility among older women (i.e., women 30 to 45) than among younger.

Figure 1.1 shows schematically how the principal factors that determine the shape of fertility schedules operate. In panel A the variations in the shape of age-specific fertility schedules of cohabiting women that occur with and without contraception are shown. The schedules have been adjusted so that the maximum of each is 100; otherwise the schedule of women practicing contraception would ordinarily have a lower maximum. In panel B can be seen variations in the proportion of women cohabiting, again with the maximum proportions set at 100. With very early marriage — as in India, Pakistan, and much of Africa — the highest proportions are reached in the early twenties, while in nineteenth century northern Europe, the peak occurs well in the thirties. In each panel, the curves are based on recorded values; almost all recorded experience would be matched by these curves, or by intermediate ones.

The combined effect of variations in fecundability, cohabitation rates, pregnancy wastage, and contraception with age is to produce age schedules of childbearing that vary quite substantially, both in overall level (as indicated by total fertility, or by the gross reproduction rate if referring to female births)[1] and in the shape of the fertility schedule, in the sense of the proportion of childbearing that occurs in different segments of the fertile span. Nevertheless, age schedules of fertility in human populations have a number of general features in common. All rise smoothly from zero at an age in the teens to a single peak in the twenties or thirties, and then fall continuously to near zero in the forties and to zero not much above age 50. The lowest mean age of fertility I have found is a little less than 26 years (in recent years in Hun-

5

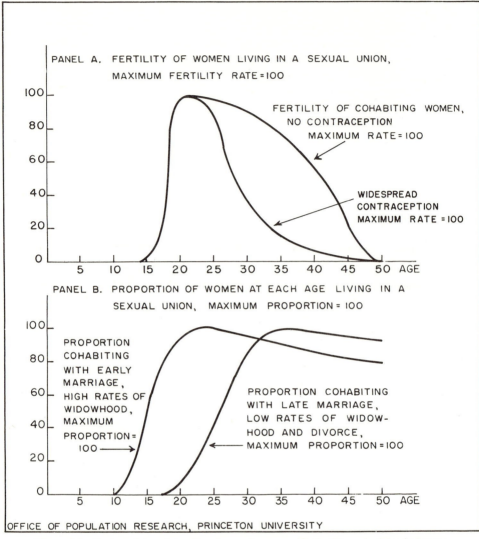

PANEL A. FERTILITY OF WOMEN LIVING IN A SEXUAL UNION, MAXIMUM FERTILITY RATE = 100

FERTILITY OF COHABITING WOMEN, NO CONTRACEPTION MAXIMUM RATE = 100

WIDESPREAD CONTRACEPTION MAXIMUM RATE = 100

PANEL B. PROPORTION OF WOMEN AT EACH AGE LIVING IN A SEXUAL UNION, MAXIMUM PROPORTION = 100

PROPORTION COHABITING WITH EARLY MARRIAGE, HIGH RATES OF WIDOWHOOD, MAXIMUM PROPORTION = 100 →

PROPORTION COHABITING WITH LATE MARRIAGE, LOW RATES OF WIDOWHOOD AND DIVORCE, ← MAXIMUM PROPORTION = 100

OFFICE OF POPULATION RESEARCH, PRINCETON UNIVERSITY

Figure 1.1. Factors determining the shape of age-specific fertility schedules in human female populations: The shape is determined by the product of a curve from panel A and one from panel B.

gary); the highest a little over 33 years (in nineteenth century Sweden). In all but a few fertility schedules, 75% of total fertility occurs within a span of 16 years, and in every case I have examined within a span of 20.

The area under the fertility schedule—*total fertility* if the schedule refers to all live births, and the *gross reproduction rate* if to female births only — *could* range from zero (in a celibate or sterile population) to a maximum that would be attained by constant exposure to intercourse from menarche to menopause, the prohibition of contraception, abortion, and breastfeeding, by medical treatment for the sterile, etc. However, no actual population on record approaches such a maximum, and certainly no large population closed to migration has ever had zero fertility.

Variations in the gross reproduction rate can be described in terms of the two components of age-specific fertility shown in panels A and B of Figure 1.1. The highest fertility that can be realistically imagined would result from a combination of early and continued cohabitation — the left curve in panel B modified to remain near its peak in the early twenties — and the absence of contraception or abortion — the right curve in panel A. This combination would provide the *shape,* or age structure, of a very high fertility schedule. In Figure 1.1 the maximum vertical ordinate of each curve has been set at 100, but in fact the maximum differs from one population to another. There are large differences in fertility rates at the same ages even among different groups of cohabiting women who do not practice "controlled fertility" as defined by Louis Henry,[2] the highest rates being at least 50% above the lowest at almost every age. The existence of control in this sense can lower the whole schedule of fertility, including its maximum, well below the level that would otherwise exist. The proportion cohabiting sometimes approaches a peak of 100%. In many populations virtually every woman by her mid-twenties *has been* married, or *has been* a partner in a consensual union of some sort, but widowhood, divorce, and separation usually reduce the proportion currently cohabiting at any given age noticeably below 100%, and to progressively lower levels in the thirties and forties. In societies characterized by late marriage, there is often a substantial proportion (as high as 30%) who remain single at age 50 (Hajnal [5]).

The highest gross reproduction rate based on complete and reliable records is 4.17 for the women in the Cocos-Keeling Islands (Smith [11]).[3] The high fertility in this population results from the combination of a favorable age structure of fertility (because cohabitation proportions follow the left curve in panel B of Figure 1.1) and the absence of fertility control as defined earlier. However, the fertility of the married women in this population is surpassed by nearly 50% at every age by marital fertility among the Hutterites (Eaton and Mayer [4]) and among the French population of Canada in the eighteenth century

7

(Henripin [6]); and therefore a population with the age pattern of co-habitation characteristic of the Cocos-Keeling Islands and the fertility at each age of married Hutterites or eighteenth century French Canadians would have a gross reproduction rate of over six.

The lowest gross reproduction rates for a national population were recorded in Europe during the 1930s—a level of about 0.80 in Austria and Sweden. Very much lower fertility has occurred within smaller geographical units—0.30 in Vienna at the time the Austrian GRR was 0.80, for example.

MORTALITY SCHEDULES

In almost every accurately recorded schedule of death rates by age, mortality declines sharply during the first year from a high value immediately after birth, falls more moderately after age 1 to a minimum between age 10 and 15, increases gradually until about age 50, then increases ever more steeply until the highest age for which a rate is given. There are exceptions to this pattern: When tuberculosis is a major cause of death there may be a broad peak of mortality in the twenties and thirties followed by a slight decline centered on age 35 or 40 (before the accelerated rise with age beginning at 45 or 50); when diarrhea and enteritis are major causes of deaths under age 5 there may be a minor rise in mortality at about age 6 months, breaking the usual pattern of rapid decline from age 0 to 2 or 3.

There is a remarkable general similarity in the age schedules of mortality among today's highly industrialized countries. In all such countries (Australia, New Zealand, Canada, the United States, the Soviet Union, almost all of the countries of Europe, and Japan) current mortality schedules would produce an average duration of life for women of more than 70 years. Infant mortality among females varies from about 12 to about 40 per thousand live births; the death rate falls to an extremely low minimum between ages 10 and 15 of from .2 to .9 per thousand; then increases gradually until the fifties; and rises sharply by age 65 to 70, lying between 14 and 27 per thousand in this age interval. There is also a broadly similar age pattern of mortality among populations with high death rates. When the expectation of life at birth is 30 years or less, mortality in the first year of life is more than 200 per thousand, falls to a minimum at or soon after age 10 of 5 to 10 per thousand, and by 65 to 70 is over 70 per thousand, and rising rapidly with age.

These generally similar patterns found in high and low mortality schedules are a manifestation of an interrelation that exists among the mortality risks experienced by different age segments of the population: If mortality at a particular age in one population is 10 times as high as in another, one normally expects higher mortality at every other age as well. Such an interrelationship is caused by the fact that persons of different ages in the same population share conditions that affect the health of all: the state of medical technology and the organization of medical practice and public health services, environmental sanitation, standards of diet and housing, etc. At the Office of Population Research, after examining all of the national mortality tables based on high quality data we could assemble, we found four characteristic sets of age patterns of mortality. Within each set the intercorrelations among mortality rates at different ages are extremely high—over .90 from age 0 to age 70 in each set, and over .95 in most instances. In other words, if the mortality rate is known at one age within one of these sets of schedules, the rate at other ages can be accurately estimated. One of these age patterns characterizes the mortality experienced in Norway, Sweden, and Iceland; another the mortality schedules of central and parts of eastern Europe; a third the schedules of Spain, Portugal, and southern Italy; and a fourth encompasses mortality in western Europe, northern America, Oceania, Japan, and Taiwan. Twenty-four model life tables have been calculated for each of these age patterns of mortality at levels of mortality ranging from a life expectation of 20 years to one of 77.5 (Coale and Demeny [3]). Each set of model life tables provides age schedules of mortality at every level of mortality from close to the lowest to close to the highest of peacetime, nonepidemic human experience—age schedules conforming in pattern to the recorded experience of a particular group of populations. These model tables will be used frequently in this book to illustrate the effect of differences in, or changes in, mortality.

Figure 1.2 shows two typical schedules of female mortality—one at a high overall level ($e_0^0 = 30$ years), and the other at a low level ($e_0^0 = 65$ years).

Age Distribution and Birth and Death Rates

The birth and death rates in a population are the result of the interaction of the age schedules of fertility and mortality on the one hand and of the age composition on the other, as indicated by Equations (1.1) and (1.2). Sometimes the same schedule of fertility or mortality can produce quite different birth or death rates in populations with differing

9

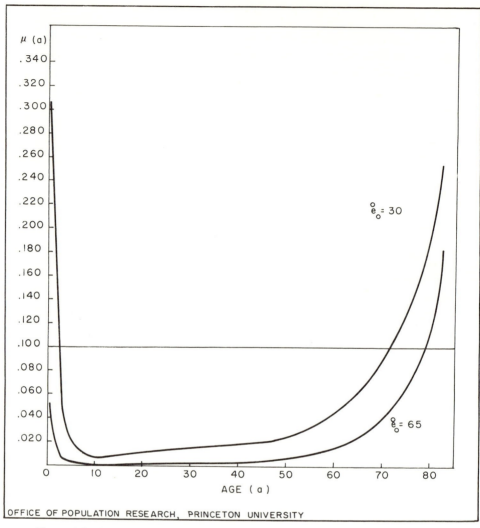

Figure 1.2. Age-specific mortality ($\mu(a)$) for females ("West" model life tables) at indicated expectations of life at birth.

age composition. Because age composition has an important influence, birth and death rates are not satisfactory summary indexes of age schedules of fertility and mortality. For example, Austria had lower mortality rates at every age in 1961 than Mexico (less than half the Mexican rates at all ages less than 50) but had a higher death rate; and the Japanese birth rate of 1956 was higher than the birth rate in the United Kingdom in 1961, although Japanese fertility rates at every age were lower. In each instance, of course, the source of the anomaly is the difference in age distribution in the populations compared: Austria (when compared to Mexico) had nearly four times as large a proportion over 65, a part of life with high mortality rates in every schedule, and Japan had a higher birth rate with a lower fertility schedule because of larger proportions at the childbearing ages than in the United Kingdom.

Because fertility rates are zero below an age in adolescence (about 15) and virtually zero above an age in the mid-forties, the only values of the age composition that help determine the birth rate are the proportions at ages from 15 to 44. Demographers have introduced the *general fertility rate* — births per woman 15 to 45 — as a measure of the fertility of those members of the population who produce the births. The general fertility rate multiplied by the ratio women 15–44/total population equals the birth rate, a relation that encompasses an important part — but not all — of the influence of age distribution on the birth rate. Two populations with the same fertility schedule have different general fertility rates if one has higher proportions of the women within the childbearing ages concentrated at the ages of highest fertility. This effect can be expressed in terms of the *covariance* between the proportions at each age from the lower limit (α) to the upper limit (β) of childbearing, and the fertility rates at these ages. This covariance ($\mu_{c \cdot m}$) is given by:

$$(1.3) \qquad \mu_{c \cdot m} = \frac{\displaystyle\int_\alpha^\beta m(a)c(a)da}{\beta - \alpha} - \frac{\displaystyle\int_\alpha^\beta m(a)da \int_\alpha^\beta c(a)da}{(\beta - \alpha)^2}.$$

On the right hand of Equation (1.3) the numerator of the first term is the birth rate, the numerator of the second term is the product of the gross reproduction rate and the proportion of the female population that is in the childbearing ages, and $\beta - \alpha$ is the number of years in the childbearing span. Rearranging terms,

$$(1.4) \qquad b = \frac{\text{GRR}}{\beta - \alpha} \int_\alpha^\beta c(a)da + \mu_{c \cdot m}(\beta - \alpha)$$

where b is the birth rate of the female population. Also,

$$(1.5) \qquad G = \frac{\text{GRR}}{\beta - \alpha} + \mu_{c \cdot m} \frac{\beta - \alpha}{\displaystyle\int_\alpha^\beta c(a)da}$$

11

where G is the female general fertility rate—female births per woman of childbearing age. Thus general fertility equals the area under the fertility schedule (GRR) divided by the width of the childbearing span, plus a term expressing the effect of the interaction between the form of the age distribution from α to β and the form of the fertility schedule. Note that this second term is zero whenever (1) proportions at every age from α to β are essentially constant, or (2) there is no linear correlation between the proportion at each age and fertility at each age.

The relations expressed in Equations (1.4) and (1.5) are illustrated by the changing circumstances in the United States in the 1950s. A comparison of various parameters for 1950 and 1959 is given in Table 1.1. The gross reproduction rate increased by 20% from 1950 to 1959, although the female birth rate rose by less than 1%. Part of this difference in relative increase can be attributed to the reduced proportion of women 15 to 44, which accounts for the fact that the increase in general fertility was more than 13% while the birth rate rose less than 1%. In 1950 general fertility was greater than $GRR/(\beta - \alpha)$ because of a bulge in the age distribution that coincided, approximately, with the peak ages of childbearing, while in 1959 G was *less* than $GRR/(\beta - \alpha)$ because of a conspicuous hollow at ages 20 to 24 and 25 to 29, the age intervals of highest fertility. (See Figure 1.3.) In 1950 the covariance term in Equation (1.5) added 3.2% to general fertility; in 1959 it subtracted 3.6%. Hence general fertility rose only 13% while GRR rose 20%.

Although the relationship between age composition and the death rate can be quantitatively important, it does not lend itself to a treatment analogous to Equations (1.4) and (1.5). Fertility is confined to a rather narrow portion of the life span (almost all fertility occurs within 30 years, and 75% within 15 to 20 years); while the highest age attained is in the order of 100 years. Moreover, the age schedule of fertility rises to a maximum near the center of the span within which its

Table 1.1. Measures of fertility in the United States, 1950 and 1959

	Gross repro-duction rate	Female births / Females 15–44	Female births / Female pop.	Females 15–44 / Female pop.
1950	1.505	.05180	.02327	.4492
1959	1.812	.05863	.02341	.3993
1959/1950	1.204	1.132	1.006	.889

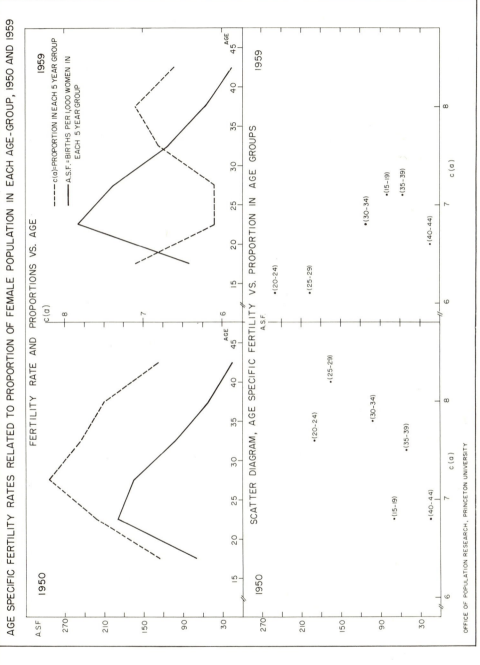

Figure 1.3. Relationship between fertility and the age distribution within the childbearing span for the United States, 1950 and 1959.

values are nonzero, so that its effect can be approximated (with a suitable adjustment as in Equations (1.4) and (1.5)) by employing a mean value such as $GRR/(\beta - \alpha)$. In contrast mortality occurs at *all* ages and $\mu(a)$ has a typically U-shaped pattern, an asymmetrical pattern, moreover. In consequence we shall limit our discussion of the role of the age distribution in determining the death rate to noting one or two features of $\mu(a)$ that affect this role, and shall not attempt to develop additional formulae.

Figure 1.2 shows typical age schedules of mortality, one at a moderately high and the other at a moderately low level. With either schedule it is possible to stipulate age distributions that would produce a wide range of death rates. With a life expectation at birth of 30 or 65 years, a population with very high proportions in the later years of childhood, in adolescence, and in the younger adult ages would have a much lower death rate than a population heavily weighted with persons over 65 or 70. With a low average duration of life (i.e., a high schedule of mortality) a population containing a large proportion of young children tends to have a higher death rate than one with a smaller proportion, whereas with more favorable mortality conditions this tendency has much less force. The reason that large proportions at very early ages have an especially adverse effect on the death rate at high levels of mortality is the characteristic shape of high age schedules of mortality. When high mortality and low mortality schedules are compared, the biggest differences in $\mu(a)$ are always at ages within the first year or two of life. As a result, there is a much lower death rate in a population that has a steep gradient with age in its general structure (and therefore high proportions at all young ages, and small proportions at older ages) than in a population with a "flatter" age structure and the same mortality schedule, *provided* the mortality schedule is at a moderate or low level. But if the mortality schedule in question is a high mortality schedule, the sharply tapering age distribution with high proportions in early childhood may have a death rate as high as or higher than the flatter age distribution, which has a much higher proportion of the aged. With a high mortality schedule, the presence of many infants to experience high infant mortality can produce more deaths than are avoided by the small proportion of old persons, hence a very young age distribution may have a higher death rate than an older distribution.

NOTES

[1] Total fertility is the total number of children that would be born per woman among a group passing through life subject to the given fertility rates at each age. The gross

14

reproduction rate is the number of *female* children per woman. Since the sex ratio at birth varies remarkably little from an average value of about 105 male births per 100 female births, TF is approximately 2.05 GRR.

[2] "Control can be said to exist when the behavior of the couple is bound to the number of children already born and is modified when this number reaches the maximum which the couple does not want to exceed; it is not the case for a taboo concerning lactation, which is independent of the number of children already born" (Henry [7]).

[3] Because high fertility often occurred in the past (or is now occurring) in areas with incomplete records, it is possible that a GRR of more than 4 has not in fact been uncommon, but is rather only rarely recorded. According to somewhat unreliable estimates, there are several areas in tropical Africa with a gross reproduction rate over 4 (Brass et al. [1]).

REFERENCES

[1] Brass et al., *The Demography of Tropical Africa,* Princeton, Princeton University Press, 1968.
[2] Coale, A. J., "How the Age Distribution of a Human Population Is Determined," *Cold Spring Harbor Symposia on Quantitative Biology,* Vol. 22, 1957, pp. 83–89.
[3] Coale, A. J., and Demeny, P., *Regional Model Life Tables and Stable Populations,* Princeton, Princeton University Press, 1968.
[4] Eaton, J. W., and Mayer, A. J., "The Social Biology of Very High Fertility Among the Hutterites," *Human Biology,* Vol. 25, No. 3, 1953, pp. 206–264.
[5] Hajnal, J., "European Marriage Patterns in Perspective," Glass, D. V., and Eversley, D. E. C. (Eds.), *Population in History,* London, Arnold Press, 1964, pp. 101–143.
[6] Henripin, J., *La population canadienne au début du xviiie siècle,* Paris, Presse Universitaire, 1954.
[7] Henry, L., "Some Data on Natural Fertility," *Eugenics Quarterly,* Vol. 8, June 1961, pp. 81–91.
[8] Lopez, A., *Problems in Stable Population Theory,* Princeton, Office of Population Research, 1961.
[9] Lopez, A., "Asymptotic Properties of a Human Age Distribution Under a Continuous Net Fertility Function," *Demography,* Vol. 4, 1967, pp. 680–687.
[10] McFarland, D. D., "On the Theory of Stable Populations: A New and Elementary Proof of the Theorems Under Weaker Assumptions," *Demography,* Vol. 6, 1969, pp. 301–322.
[11] Smith, T. E., "The Cocos-Keeling Islands: A Demographic Laboratory," *Population Studies,* Vol. 14, November 1960, pp. 94–130.

The Stable Population

Characteristics of Stable Populations

WE SAW in Chapter 1 that the age distribution of any closed population is wholly determined by the recent history of its fertility and mortality. A helpful device in understanding how age compositions are determined is to imagine a history of fertility and mortality schedules that have not changed for many years. If fertility and mortality have been fixed, and remain so, the recent history of the population is unchanging from year to year, and since according to Lopez' theorem two populations with the same histories have the same age composition, it follows that the age structure must be fixed when fertility and mortality are constant. Suppose age-specific fertility (the annual rate, assumed unchanging with time, at which women bear female children at age a) is $m(a)$, age-specific mortality is $\mu(a)$, and the proportion of women from age a to $a + da$ is $c(a)da$. The birth rate is $\int_0^{\omega} c(a)m(a)da$ and the death rate is $\int_0^{\omega} c(a)\mu(a)da$; therefore, with fixed age composition birth and death rates are constant; and the difference between them, which in a closed population is the rate of increase, is also constant. Thus the total number of persons, $N(t)$, follows a simple exponential curve $(N(0)e^{rt})$, and because of constant birth and death rates the annual number of births and deaths follow similar paths: $B(t) = B(0)e^{rt}$, and $D(t) = D(0)e^{rt}$.

The population that is established by a prolonged regime of unchanging fertility and mortality schedules is called the stable population; it is characterized, as we have just seen, by a fixed age composition, constant birth and death rates, and a constant rate of increase. In the remainder of this chapter we shall analyze the characteristics of the stable population, and show how these characteristics are related to the fertility and mortality schedules that establish it.

We shall first show that the age distribution of a stable population is given by the following equation:

$$(2.1) \qquad\qquad c(a) = be^{-ra}p(a),$$

where b is the birth rate, r the annual rate of increase, and $p(a)$ is the proportion surviving from birth to age a, given the mortality schedule $\mu(a)$. The relation of $p(a)$ to $\mu(a)$ is given in Equation (2.2).

(2.2) $$p(a) = e^{-\int_0^a \mu(x)dx}.$$

Equation (2.2) is an alternative expression of the relationship $\mu(a) = -(dp(a)/da)/p(a)$, the validity of which is seen by visualizing $N \cdot p(a)$ as the number of survivors in a cohort of N births subject to the mortality rates $\mu(a)$; the death rate in this cohort at exact age a would be $-N(dp(a)/da)/Np(a)$.

Equation (2.1) can be verified as follows: by noting first that $c(a)$ is defined as the number at age a relative to the total number of females N; that the number at age a equals births a years ago times $p(a)$; that births a years ago equaled the total number of females a years ago times the birth rate b, and that the total number a years ago was Ne^{-ra}. Thus:

$$c(a) = \frac{n(a)}{N} = \frac{(Ne^{-ra})(b) \cdot p(a)}{N} = be^{-ra}p(a).$$

If r and $p(a)$ are known, b can be calculated as:

(2.3) $$b = \frac{1}{\int_0^\omega e^{-ra}p(a)da}$$

since $\int_0^\omega c(a)da = 1$. The value of $p(a)$ can be calculated directly from $\mu(a)$ by means of Equation (2.2); there remains the determination of r, which must have a value that satisfies Equation (2.4):

(2.4) $$\int_0^\omega e^{-ra}p(a)m(a)da = 1.$$

Equation (2.4) is obtained by substituting the expression for $c(a)$ given in Equation (2.1) into the equation that defines the birth rate in any population: $b = \int_0^\omega c(a)m(a)da$.

There are a number of ways of finding the value of r that satisfies this equation, and hence of determining the rate of increase in the stable population. Before discussing any of them we shall consider a pair of simpler measures—the gross reproduction rate (GRR) and the net reproduction rate (NRR)—that deal with the increase in population every *generation*. GRR is the total area under the maternity schedule. It is the number of daughters born per woman who passes through the entire childbearing span giving birth to female offspring according to the schedule $m(a)$. NRR is the number of daughters per

17

female who from birth is subject to the maternity schedule $m(a)$ and the survivorship schedule $p(a)$.

$$(2.5) \qquad \qquad \mathrm{GRR} = \int_{\alpha}^{\beta} m(a)da$$

and

$$(2.6) \qquad \qquad \mathrm{NRR} = \int_{\alpha}^{\beta} m(a)p(a)da,$$

where α and β are the lower and upper limiting ages of childbearing. Since $p(a)$ in most life tables follows a very nearly linear course from α to β, especially over the central years of this span,[1]

$$(2.7) \qquad \mathrm{NRR} \doteq p(\bar{m}) \int_{\alpha}^{\beta} m(a)da = p(\bar{m}) \cdot \mathrm{GRR},$$

where $\bar{m}$ is the mean age of the fertility schedule.

THE MEAN LENGTH OF GENERATION IN THE STABLE POPULATION

The average number of daughters per woman subject to the given schedules (NRR) is a measure of the proportionate increase *per generation* in the stable population. But a generation is not a specific time interval that is the same for all populations. The concept of the NRR as a measure of multiplication for each generation in fact provides a definition of length of generation: The mean length of female generation (T) is the number of years required to multiply the stable population by the average ratio of daughters to mothers (NRR).

$$(2.8) \qquad \qquad e^{rT} = \mathrm{NRR},$$

where r is the annual rate of increase.

Equation (2.8) provides a basis for estimating r, the annual rate of increase of the stable population, if the mean length of generation can be estimated. The NRR can be calculated from the given mortality and fertility schedules (Equation 2.6). It seems intuitively clear that T depends on the ages at which childbearing is concentrated. The mean length of generation is greater in a population where childbearing occurs late in the fertile ages than in one where childbearing is early. But T is not, somewhat surprisingly, equal to any of the several mean ages of childbearing that can be defined. There are three mean ages of fertility of interest in this context: (1) the mean age ($\bar{m}$) of the fertility schedule, or the mean age of childbearing in a cohort subject to no mortality; (2) the mean age (μ_1) of the net fertility schedule (i.e., of

$\phi(a) = p(a)m(a))$, or the mean age of childbearing in a cohort; and (3) the mean age $(\bar{A})$ of childbearing in the stable population. The three formulae are:

$$(2.9) \qquad \bar{m} = \frac{\int_{\alpha}^{\beta} am(a)da}{\int_{\alpha}^{\beta} m(a)da},$$

$$(2.10) \qquad \mu_1 = \frac{\int_{\alpha}^{\beta} am(a)p(a)da}{\int_{\alpha}^{\beta} m(a)p(a)da},$$

and

$$(2.11) \qquad \bar{A} = \frac{\int_{\alpha}^{\beta} ae^{-ra}p(a)m(a)da}{\int_{\alpha}^{\beta} e^{-ra}p(a)m(a)da}.$$

In most life tables, especially those at higher levels of mortality, $p(a)$ is approximately linear from α to β, particularly in the central ages of childbearing. If $p(a)$ is approximated by a straight line ($p(a) = u - va$) from α to β, the following relation emerges:

$$(2.12) \qquad \mu_1 = \bar{m} - \frac{\sigma^2 v}{p(\bar{m})}$$

where σ^2 is the age variance of $m(a)$, $-v$ is the slope of $p(a)$, and $p(\bar{m})$ is the proportion surviving to the mean age of $m(a)$.[2] The value of $v/p(\bar{m})$ can be approximated by $\mu(\bar{m})$ since $-v \doteq dp(a)/da$ when $a = \bar{m}$.

When the expression for $\bar{A}$ in Equation (2.11) is expanded in a MacLaurin series, it is found that $(d^n(\bar{A})/dr^n)_{r=0} = (-1)^n \mu_{n+1}$, where μ_n is the nth cumulant of the net fertility function. Hence

$$(2.13) \qquad \bar{A} = \mu_1 - \mu_2 r + \mu_3 \frac{r^2}{2!} \cdots .$$

It can also be shown that $T = (\int \bar{A} dr)/r,$[3] or that

$$(2.14) \qquad T = \mu_1 - \frac{\mu_2}{2!}r + \frac{\mu_3}{3!}r^2 \cdots .$$

Thus, T is very close to $(\mu_1 + \bar{A})/2$, to the average of the mean ages of childbearing in the stationary and the stable populations. Because

19

of properties common to all fertility schedules, the terms in Equation (2.14) beyond the second are negligible.[4] The coefficient of the second term is one-half the variance (μ_2) of the net fertility function ($\phi(a) = p(a)m(a)$); the greatest observed variance is less than 60, so the maximum difference between T and μ_1 (the mean age of $\phi(a)$) is (30)(.05) or about 1.5 years. In other words, μ_1 is a close approximation to T for small values of r, and $\mu_1 - (\mu_2/2)r$ is extremely close to T, even at the largest value r attains. Finally, T can be related to $\bar{m}$ (the mean age of the fertility schedule) by combining Equations (2.12) and (2.14), first noting that μ_2 (the variance of the net fertility function, $p(a)m(a)$) is nearly the same as σ^2 (the variance of the fertility function, $m(a)$). Thus

$$(2.15) \qquad T \doteq \bar{m} - \sigma^2 \left(\frac{v}{p(\bar{m})} + \frac{r}{2} \right) \doteq \bar{m} - \sigma^2 \left(\mu(\bar{m}) + \frac{r}{2} \right).$$

Equation (2.15) can be simplified by incorporating two further approximations: $r/2 \doteq (\log \text{GRR} + \log p(\bar{m}))/2\bar{m}$ (which is valid within $0.05 \cdot r/2$, producing a trivial error in the estimate of T), and $\mu(\bar{m}) \doteq -(\log p(\bar{m})/2\bar{m})$. The latter relation is observed to hold with only slight discrepancy in a large number of life tables. Specifically, a comparison of $\mu(30)$ with $\log (p(30)/60)$ in four families of model life tables, each family embodying a distinctive age pattern of mortality, reveals an average difference of less than .001 in 24 comparisons (Coale and Demeny [3]). The life tables in which the comparison was made covered in each family a range of life expectation at birth from 20 to 70 years, at 10 year intervals. In individual life tables, of course, the difference may be greater, and Equation (2.15) in such instances will give a somewhat better estimate of T than Equation (2.16) below. As a result of the relation between $\mu(\bar{m})$ and $\log p(\bar{m})/2$, the two contributions of mortality to the difference between $\bar{m}$ and T (namely $\sigma^2\mu(\bar{m})$ and $\sigma^2(\log p(\bar{m})/2)$) are approximately equal and opposite in sign, so T is nearly independent of $\mu(a)$ (provided the mortality schedule is of the usual sort). Hence,

$$(2.16) \qquad\qquad T \doteq \bar{m} - \sigma^2 \frac{\log \text{GRR}}{2\bar{m}}.$$

THE RATE OF INCREASE IN A STABLE POPULATION

Since $r = \log \text{NRR}/T$, we have arrived at two approximate formulae relating r to parameters of mortality and fertility, by using an approximation (Equation (2.7)) for NRR, and two alternative approximations for T.

(2.17)
$$r \doteq \frac{\log (\text{GRR} \cdot p(\bar{m}))}{\bar{m} - \sigma^2 \left(\mu(\bar{m}) + \dfrac{\log (\text{GRR} \cdot p(\bar{m}))}{2\bar{m}} \right)}.$$

This approximation is very close (maximum error in estimating r is about .0002; the principal source of error being the imprecision with which $\text{GRR} \cdot p(\bar{m})$ approximates NRR). Somewhat less exactly,

(2.18)
$$r \doteq \frac{\log (\text{GRR} \cdot p(\bar{m}))}{\bar{m} - \sigma^2 \cdot \dfrac{\log \text{GRR}}{2\bar{m}}}.$$

Noting that $\bar{m}$ is never far removed from age 30, and assuming that $\mu(a)$ in the neighborhood of 30 is constant and equal to $\mu(30)$, we arrive at the approximation $p(\bar{m}) \doteq p(30)e^{-(\bar{m}-30)\mu(30)}$. Here we introduce again the empirically based relation, $-\mu(\bar{m}) \doteq \log p(\bar{m})/2\bar{m}$. Hence $\log p(\bar{m}) \doteq \log p(30) + ((\bar{m} - 30)/60) \log p(30) = ((\bar{m} + 30)/60) \log p(30)$. This expression for $\log p(\bar{m})$ leads to still another formula for r:

(2.19)
$$r \doteq \frac{\dfrac{\bar{m} + 30}{60} \log p(30) + \log \text{GRR}}{\bar{m} - \sigma^2 \dfrac{\log \text{GRR}}{2\bar{m}}}.$$

Note that in Equation (2.19) mortality enters in the form of a term that explicitly distinguishes the effect of $\bar{m}$ and the effect of the mortality schedule itself.

It can be seen from Equations (2.17) through (2.19) that the characteristics of fertility that influence r are the area under $m(a)$, its mean age, and—for large values of GRR—its variance.

Mortality affects the rate of increase of a stable population by helping to determine NRR, and sometimes (rarely) by affecting T. Different sequences of $\mu(a)$ before age α that produce the same $p(\alpha)$ do not produce different values of r. Differences in $\mu(a)$ above age β have no effect on r, which, given the same $m(a)$, is exactly the same even with mortality schedules (alike to age β) wherein on the one hand all women die at age β, or on the other all alive at β survive to 1,000. Most mortality schedules follow a form, producing an approximately linear $p(a)$ from α to β, and having $\mu(\bar{m}) \doteq -(\log p(\bar{m})/2\bar{m})$, that insures the validity of Equation (2.19) in which the only mortality term is $p(30)$. In other words, the feature of $\mu(a)$ that usually determines NRR is simply $p(30)$, or $e^{-\int_0^{30} \mu(a)da}$, and usually the contributions of mortality to a difference between $\bar{m}$ and T are self-canceling.

We shall now comment on the typical range of the terms that appear in Equation (2.19). It was noted in Chapter 1 that a GRR as low as .30 has been recorded, and as high as about 4.20 (Cocos-Keeling Islands). The low value was in an urban population (Vienna in the 1930s); the lowest recorded value in a national population is about .80. A GRR over 6.0 would result if cohabitation were usual from age 15 until the end of childbearing, and if cohabiting women equaled the highest recorded schedules of marital fertility.

The lowest recorded mean ages of the fertility schedule (under 26 years) have occurred in populations combining moderately early marriage with the widespread practice of birth control, for example in the United States in the late 1950s, and in Hungary, Rumania, and Yugoslavia in the 1960s. One can picture a still lower $\bar{m}$ if effective contraceptive practices were combined with the *very* early marriage characteristic of southern Asia and much of Africa. In the absence of the control of fertility, $\bar{m}$ is about 28 years when cohabitation begins very early, and has been as late as 33 years with the high age at marriage characteristic of parts of western Europe in the nineteenth century.

The minimum observed variance of the age schedule of fertility is about 18.0, the result (in Japan, 1962) of moderately late marriage that produced low fertility under age 25, and widespread effective birth control that produced moderate fertility over age 30 and low fertility over 35. Such a low variance can occur only in a fertility schedule with a low GRR (in this instance less than 1.0). The maximum observed variance in a fertility schedule based on data not biased by age misreporting is more than 55, the result (in the Cocos-Keeling Islands) of early cohabitation and little control of fertility. Other schedules, for which parameters have been calculated by Keyfitz and Flieger [7], yield a σ^2 as high as 60, but age misreporting — especially the exaggeration of the age of women at the upper ages of childbearing — tends to overstate σ^2, and it is prudent to accept 55 or 56 as a probable upper limit. In the large number of calculations made under Keyfitz' direction, all schedules with a GRR of more than 3.0 had a σ^2 of 43 or more, with an average σ^2 of about 50. The existence of high variance when total fertility is large is virtually a logical necessity: Given the observed maximum age-specific fertility rates, a GRR of 3.0 or more can be achieved only if fertility begins early and finishes late. On the other hand, low values of GRR do not necessarily imply a small value of σ^2. Low variance can occur only at low values of GRR, but a low GRR can also be accompanied by a large σ^2 (e.g., a σ^2 of over 44 with GRRs of 1.10, 1.26, and 1.32 in the United States, 1930; Finland, 1930; and France, 1904). Such a combination is the consequence of heterogeneity in the completed size of family within the population in question, so the low GRR is the result of *very* low fertility in part of the population combined with moderate fertility in another segment, or of large variance in the age at marriage when family size is fairly uniform.[5]

The mortality schedule with the lowest proportion surviving to $\bar{m}$ would prevail in a period of disaster—a war, famine, or great epidemic —in an area with primitive medical facilities and generally poor material conditions: under such circumstances $p(\bar{m})$ might be close to zero, or actually zero if the disaster killed all members of any age segment below $\bar{m}$. The lowest value of $p(30)$ in a published life table for a national population (about .31) is for India during the decade 1911–21 ($e_0^0 = 20.9$ years) (Davis [4]). The highest is nearly .98 (Sweden, 1965, $e_0^0 = 75.9$ years).

Equation (2.19) and the preceding remarks about the range of the relevant fertility and mortality parameters provide the basis for visualizing clearly the relative importance of the various parameters in determining r. First, we can see the outline of the forces at work by considering the basic equation $r = \log \text{NRR}/T$. A larger GRR has its principal effect by increasing NRR; the principal (virtually the sole) effect of mortality is to help determine NRR. If NRR is greater than one, the stable population has a positive rate of increase, if equal to one, a zero rate, and if less than one, a negative rate. If NRR is one, the value of T has no effect on the rate of increase; if NRR is other than one, the absolute value of r is less the greater the value of T. Thus if NRR is greater than one, the annual rate of increase for a given NRR is greater, the less the length of generation; if NRR is less than one, the population diminishes more each year the less is T, hence r is greater for larger values of T. The effect of T on r is more important the farther removed is NRR from one. The value of T is predominantly determined by $\bar{m}$, the maximum discrepancy between T and $\bar{m}$ reaching only about 5% of the latter (when GRR is at its largest value).

We shall now examine the influence of GRR, $p(30)$, $\bar{m}$, and σ^2 on r in more detail. A convenient device is to examine the partial derivatives of r with respect to the log of each parameter in Equation (2.19),[6] with the following results, after simplification:

$$(2.20) \qquad \frac{\partial r}{\partial \log \text{GRR}} = \frac{1 + r\sigma^2/2\bar{m}}{T},$$

$$(2.21) \quad \frac{\partial r}{\partial \log p(30)} = \frac{(\bar{m} + 30)/60}{T},$$

$$(2.22) \quad \frac{\partial r}{\partial \log \bar{m}} = \frac{-\bar{m}[\mu(\bar{m}) + r(1 + (\sigma^2/2\bar{m}^2) \log \text{GRR})]}{T},$$

and

$$(2.23) \quad \frac{\partial r}{\partial \log \sigma^2} = \frac{\sigma^2 r \log \text{GRR}}{2\bar{m} \cdot T}.$$

Table 2.1 illustrates the application of Equations (2.20) to (2.23) by showing the difference in r that would result from a 10% difference in each parameter, at various values of GRR. (In all instances $\bar{m}$ is taken as 28, $p(30)$ as .85, and σ^2 as 45.) Note that at values of GRR from 0.80 to 4.00 a 10% difference in GRR always implies a difference of about 3.5 per thousand in r. The increment in r is somewhat greater at higher values of GRR because r itself is greater and T less. (Cf. Equation (2.20).) The difference in r caused by a 10% difference in $p(30)$ is essentially the same as that caused by a 10% difference in GRR. (The difference in r varies less because the partial derivative with respect to $\log p(30)$ [Equation (2.21)] does not contain r.) The effect of a 10% difference in $\bar{m}$ is a moderate difference (1.5 per thousand in the same sense) when GRR is 0.80, but becomes a substantial difference in the opposite sense (minus 4.5 per thousand) when GRR is 4.00. In fact, this is a larger increment than from the same relative change in GRR or $p(30)$, showing that at high values of the net reproduction rate, the effect of a difference in T on the rate of increase is large. The maximum difference in r caused by a 10% difference in σ^2 is hardly important (less than 0.2 per thousand when GRR is 4.00); the difference is wholly negligible at low or moderate GRRs. In interpreting the sensitivity of r to differences in these parameters (as indicated in Equations (2.20) to (2.23) and Table 2.1) it is essential to bear

Table 2.1. The difference in r (per thousand) resulting from a 10% difference in specified parameter, at various values of GRR

Parameter subject to 10% difference	Level of GRR			
	0.80	1.00	2.00	4.00
GRR	3.35	3.40	3.53	3.68
$p(30)$	3.28	3.30	3.36	3.43
$\bar{m}$	1.53	0.79	−1.68	−4.46
σ^2	0.01	0.00	0.04	0.18

in mind the degree of variation to which each parameter is subject. GRR has a maximum at least five times its minimum; for $p(30)$ the equivalent ratio is more than 3; for $\bar{m}$, 1.25 or 1.30; and for σ^2, about 3. However, because very large values of GRR require that fertility begin at an early age and continue to a late one, the ratio of the maximum to the minimum $\bar{m}$ is no more than about 1.15 when GRR is very large, and max σ^2/min σ^2 is no more than 1.20 for large values of GRR. In fact, σ^2 can be assigned a fixed value of 50 in Equation (2.19) when estimating r without introducing an important error; 50 is within about 10% of the true σ^2 when GRR is large and makes very little difference (see Table 2.1) when GRR is small.

Two final comments on the determination of r: (1) If second order effects are ignored, $\partial r/\partial \log$ GRR and $\partial r/\partial \log p(30)$ can both be considered approximately equal to $1/\bar{m}$. Thus, the *absolute* difference in r is the same for the same *relative* difference in GRR or $p(30)$; the difference in r in comparing GRRs of 0.80 and 1.00 is about the same as in comparing GRRs of 4.00 and 5.00. (2) The expression in brackets in Equation (2.22) contains two terms: $\mu(\bar{m})$, and r multiplied by a factor differing from unity by less than 5%. These two terms express the two ways in which variations in $\bar{m}$ affect r: by exposing women to more or less mortality (at the rate $\mu(\bar{m})$), thus affecting the value of the net reproduction rate, and by spreading the increase per generation over a longer or shorter interval, an effect that is important only for large absolute values of r.

THE AGE DISTRIBUTION OF THE STABLE POPULATION

The stable population illustrates the effect of fertility and mortality on age composition in a simple and direct way; it has the unique age distribution that is inherent in the fertility and mortality schedules themselves. The two schedules determine r, as noted in the preceding section, and r and $p(a)$ (which equals $e^{-\int_0^a \mu(x)dx}$) are all that is needed to stipulate the proportion at every age in the stable population, since

$$c(a) = be^{-ra}p(a) \quad \text{and} \quad b = 1 \bigg/ \int_0^\omega e^{-ra}p(a)da.$$

We shall now consider the two functions of age into which $c(a)$ may be factored: $p(a)$ and e^{-ra}.

Figure 2.1 shows four alternative examples of $p(a)$ when $p(30) = 0.90$, and four when $p(30) = 0.40$. In Figure 2.2 e^{-ra} is plotted for $r = -0.01$, 0.00, 0.01, and 0.02. A stable age distribution is formed by combining a "life table" ($p(a)$) and an exponential (e^{-ra}) with the

25

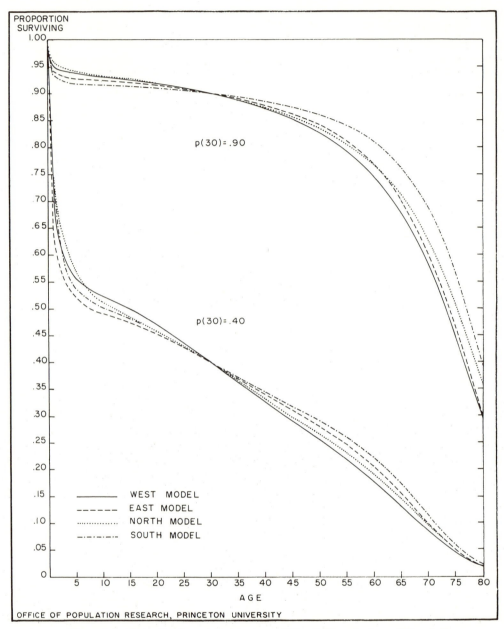

PROPORTION SURVIVING

p(30)=.90

p(30)=.40

WEST MODEL
EAST MODEL
NORTH MODEL
SOUTH MODEL

AGE

Figure 2.1. Alternative forms of $p(a)$ when $p(30) = 0.90$, and when $p(30) = 0.40$.

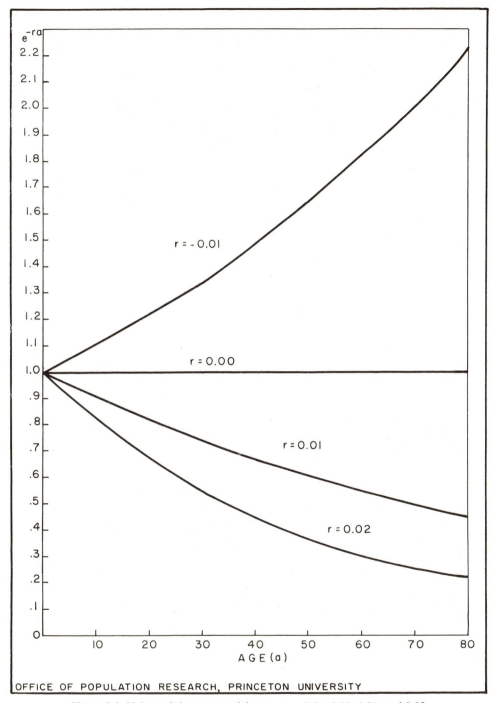

Figure 2.2. Values of the exponential e^{-ra}, $r = -0.01$, 0.00, 0.01, and 0.02.

vertical scale of the resultant product adjusted so that the proportions sum to one. If r is zero, the exponential is simply a constant, and the age distribution is the same as the life table, with a suitable adjustment of scale. This special case of a stable population with zero growth is called the stationary population. Its age distribution is given by:

$$(2.24) \qquad c(a) = \frac{p(a)}{\displaystyle\int_0^\omega p(a)da} \qquad \text{(when } r = 0\text{)}.$$

The denominator of Equation (2.24) is the average duration of life of persons subject to $\mu(a)$; a consequence is the well known fact that the birth rate in a stationary population is the reciprocal of the expectation of life at birth.

Figure 2.3 shows the result of combining e^{-ra} for alternative values of r with the same $p(a)$. Higher values of r create stable age distributions that taper more rapidly with age. One way of expressing this "taper" is by calculating the relative slope of the age distribution:

$$(2.25) \qquad \frac{1}{c(a)} \frac{dc(a)}{da} = -(\mu(a) + r).$$

The relative slope at age a is, with sign reversed, the sum of r and age-specific mortality at a; hence a stable population with a higher rate of increase but the same mortality schedule has the same increment to its relative slope at every age when compared to the slower-growing population. The faster-growing stable population consequently has higher proportions at every age up to the point of intersection, and lower proportions above this age. When the difference in r is very small, the point of intersection is the mean age $\bar{a}$ of the stable population, as can be shown by finding the age at which $c(a)$ does not change with r, or for which $dc(a)/dr = 0$. $(dc(a)/dr = (db/dr)(e^{-ra}p(a)) - bae^{-ra}p(a) = c(a)[((1/b)(db/dr)) - a].)$ But,

$$(2.26) \qquad \frac{db}{dr} = \frac{d}{dr}\frac{1}{\displaystyle\int_0^\omega e^{-ra}p(a)da} = \frac{\displaystyle\int_0^\omega ae^{-ra}p(a)da}{\left(\displaystyle\int_0^\omega e^{-ra}p(a)da\right)^2} = \bar{a}b,$$

where $\bar{a}$ is the mean age of the stable population. Hence,

$$(2.27) \qquad \frac{dc(a)}{dr} = c(a)(\bar{a} - a),$$

28

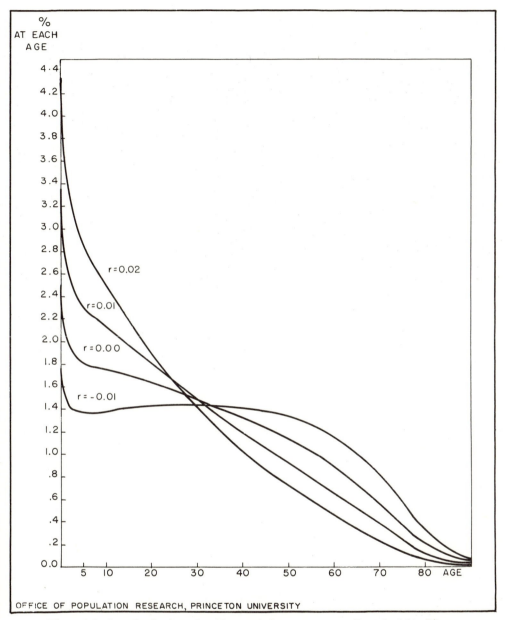

Figure 2.3. Age distribution of stable populations, same mortality schedule, different rates of increase ($e_0^0 = 40$ years).

29

and $dc(a)/dr = 0$ when $a = \bar{a}$. When one stable population has a very slightly higher rate of increase than another, both sharing the same mortality schedule, both have the same proportion at $\bar{a}$; the faster-growing population has a relatively higher $c(a)$ at ages below $\bar{a}$ to an extent proportional to the distance from $\bar{a}$, and a relatively lower $c(a)$ at ages above $\bar{a}$, again to an extent proportional to the distance from $\bar{a}$. Lotka describes this relation between stable age distributions with different growth rates as a "pivoting" action on the mean age. The stable population with a higher rate of increase of course has a lower mean age, so the intersection of the two distributions can be considered equal to the mean age only for very small differences in r. For moderate differences, the intersection occurs, to a close approximation, at the average of the mean ages of the two stable populations.[7]

Since a stable population with a higher rate of increase and a given mortality schedule has a higher relative slope at every age than one with a lower rate of increase, the proportion under *any* specified age is greater. The *ogives* of the two age distributions never intersect between ages 0 and ω; the ogive of the population with the greater r is everywhere higher. In fact, if $C(a)$ is the proportion under age a in the stable population,

$$(2.28) \qquad \frac{dC(a)}{dr} = C(a)\{\bar{a} - a'\},$$

where a' is the mean age of the stable population from age zero to age a. Since a' is always less than $\bar{a}$ (until $a = \omega$), $dC(a)/dr$ is positive at all ages, proving that the ogive of the stable population with the higher growth rate is everywhere higher.

The exponential factor in the stable age distribution thus transforms the life table or survival function ($p(a)$) by everywhere increasing or diminishing its relative steepness — a transformation that can be visualized as a sort of pivoting action on the mean age. Whatever the value of r, certain basic features of the stable age distribution are determined by $p(a)$, or by $\mu(a)$ from which $p(a)$ can be derived. The eight schedules of $p(a)$ in Figure 2.1 represent two life tables (one with $p(30) = 0.90$ and one with $p(30) = 0.40$) from each of four families of model life tables, each family embodying the typical age patterns of mortality shared by a group of national populations (Coale and Demeny [3]). Thus these two "nests" of $p(a)$ curves illustrate some, but far from all, of the variability in the form of $p(a)$ at the same level of mortality, in the sense of yielding the same r when combined with a given fertility schedule.

As was noted in Chapter 1, most mortality schedules share certain very general properties: a rapid fall in infancy and childhood from a relatively high value at age zero; a minimum at about age 10; a gradual increase from the minimum; an increase that accelerates after age 40 or 50, and that continues with ever more rapidly rising death rates until the highest age is attained, at which point mortality may be assumed infinite. (See Figure 1.2.) Genuine centenarians are very rare in all populations, sometimes contrary to official data, since their number is often greatly exaggerated by age misreporting. The highest age attained so far is probably not much over 110.

The variety of stable populations generated by combining alternative fertility schedules with empirically based mortality schedules is circumscribed by these typical properties of $\mu(a)$. Note in Figure 2.1 that "regional" model stationary populations with the same $p(30)$ are by no means identical, yet have many similar structural features. Stable age distributions with a basically different structure would be generated by hypothetical mortality schedules that did *not* share these typical properties — for example, a $\mu(a)$ that was constant at all ages, or that declined continuously with age, or that remained at a minimum level from age 10 to age 80.

Differences in Fertility and Differences in the Age Distribution of Stable Populations

Fertility affects only the rate of increase in a stable population; if we consider the two variable factors in $c(a)$, $p(a)$ and e^{-ra}, we can see immediately that fertility helps to determine the gradient of the exponential component, but does not enter $p(a)$. We can define higher *effective fertility* in the context of stable populations as fertility that produces a higher rate of increase when combined with a given mortality schedule. As was noted in an earlier section, effective fertility is not wholly determined by the gross reproduction rate, but also depends — sometimes strongly — on the mean age of childbearing, and (to a much lesser degree) on the age variance of fertility.

Consider two stable populations both incorporating the same mortality schedule, but subject to different fertility schedules. If the two schedules are equally effective (e.g., $GRR = 3.36$ and $\bar{m} = 28$ in one, and $GRR = 4.02$, $\bar{m} = 32$ in the other, both combined with a mortality schedule where $p(30) = .957$) the two stable populations are the same; otherwise the two age distributions differ, but only in r. If one distribution is $c_1(a)$ and the other $c_2(a)$,

31

(2.29)
$$\frac{c_2(a)}{c_1(a)} = \frac{b_2}{b_1} e^{-\Delta r a} = e^{-\Delta r(a-\hat{a})},$$

where $\Delta r = r_2 - r_1$ and $\hat{a}$ is the point of intersection of the two distributions, approximately $(\bar{a}_1 + \bar{a}_2)/2$.

A stable population with higher effective fertility thus differs from one with lower fertility in an obvious and simple manner: The higher fertility population has an age distribution with a greater relative slope at every age, a higher proportion at age zero (higher birth rate), and a higher proportion below every age from just after birth until the very upper limit of the age distribution.

Differences in Mortality and Differences in the Age Distribution of Stable Populations

The influence of differences in mortality on the age distribution of the stable population is more subtle and complex than the influence of differences in fertility, and the effects of mortality differences include some surprising features, such as the fact that a mortality schedule embodying lower risks of dying at every age and consequently a greater average duration of life usually connotes a stable population with a higher proportion of children, a lower mean age, and often a lower proportion of the aged.

The greater complexity of the influence of the mortality schedule has two sources:

(1) In the basic formula for the stable age distribution $[c(a) = be^{-ra}p(a)]$, the complement of mortality, survival, appears explicitly as a function of age, so the stable age distribution necessarily reflects directly any idiosyncrasies in the age pattern of mortality. Consequently, the effect of different schedules of mortality on differences in the stable age distribution depends on the particular age pattern of differences in mortality. Differences in the age pattern of fertility can only determine whether and to what extent the age distribution "pivots" on the mean age; differences in age pattern of mortality determine the very nature of the differences in stable age distributions.

(2) Higher fertility by causing a greater rate of increase causes all age groups below the mean to be increased, and all above the mean to be diminished. A high fertility age distribution always slopes more steeply, and always has a lower mean age than a low fertility distribution. In contrast, higher rates of survival (lower mortality) influence the steepness of the age distribution in two opposing ways: By permitting more

women to survive to maternal ages, lower mortality causes a greater rate of increase, thereby tending to make the age distribution slope more steeply and to have a lower mean age; but lower mortality means a schedule of survival ($p(a)$) which slopes *less* steeply, thereby tending to produce an age distribution that slopes less steeply and has a higher mean age. Hence, without knowledge of the age pattern of mortality differences, it is impossible to specify even the gross effect of these differences on the stable age distribution.

In exploring the effect of different mortality schedules we shall again employ the device of dividing one stable age distribution by another. Thus,

$$(2.30) \qquad \frac{c_2(a)}{c_1(a)} = \frac{b_2}{b_1} e^{-\Delta ra} \frac{p_2(a)}{p_1(a)}.$$

We begin by considering a special case of differences in mortality schedules.

A DIFFERENCE IN MORTALITY THAT WOULD HAVE NO EFFECT ON THE STABLE AGE DISTRIBUTION

If the difference between two mortality schedules were such that $\mu_2(a) = \mu_1(a) - k$ (i.e., if the difference in mortality rates were the same at all ages), then $\mu_1(a)$ and $\mu_2(a)$ would produce the same stable age distribution when combined with any given fertility schedule. Recall that $p(a) = e^{-\int_0^a \mu(x)dx}$; hence $p_2(a) = p_1(a)e^{ka}$. Since $\int_0^\omega e^{-r_1 a}p_1(a)m(a)da = 1$, it is apparent that $\int_0^\omega e^{-r_2 a}p_2(a)m(a)da = 1$ if and only if $r_2 = r_1 + k$. Thus $c_2(a)/c_1(a) = (b_2/b_1)e^{-ka}e^{ka} = 1$ at all a.

Under these hypothetical circumstances, the effect of faster growth in making the stable population taper more rapidly is exactly offset by the effect of lower mortality in making it taper more slowly. Actually a difference in mortality of this nature—the same difference in $\mu(a)$ at every age—leaves the age distribution unaffected whether the population is stable or not. Consider two populations otherwise identical, one of which experiences a decline, k, in mortality at every age, the other experiencing no change in mortality. One year later, the population with reduced mortality will have e^k times as many survivors to every age as the other, and with the same fertility, will have e^k times as many births. The number at every age in the larger population has the same multiplier relative to the smaller, hence the populations have identical age compositions.

In fact, no actual instances of mortality differences of this form can be found. The hypothetical case is nevertheless relevant because it helps to explain why genuine mortality differences that cause substantial increments in the rate of increase of stable populations may cause relatively inconspicuous differences in the stable age distribution.

TYPICAL DIFFERENCES IN MORTALITY SCHEDULES

Figure 2.4 shows two examples of the typical difference between mortality schedules of the same female population at different times. The pattern is very often roughly U-shaped as in this figure, especially when the mortality schedules compared have widely different expectations of life at birth. In Figure 2.4 the mortality schedules compared are two from "regional" model life tables and two from Sweden, but the generally U-shaped pattern is very common, subject to these comments and qualifications:

(1) The mortality schedules compared are drawn from peacetime experience of large populations not subject to an unusual epidemic. To ensure with more certainty that the pattern will not prove exceptional, the two schedules should be drawn from the experience of the same area, or at least from areas not characterized by different idiosyncrasies in mortality by age.

(2) The *left arm* of the U represents a difference in mortality rates that falls from a high value at age 0 to a near minimum by age 5, and a genuine minimum before age 15. This feature is very nearly universal in comparisons of mortality schedules experienced until now. However, the prominence of the left arm of the U relative to the base, and especially relative to the right arm, varies. When the comparison involves a high mortality schedule (low expectation of life) and a very low mortality schedule, the left arm of the U is always pronounced, because of the universal prevalence of high infant and child mortality rates under primitive health conditions, and the universal success in achieving low or moderate rates at these ages under better conditions.

(3) The base of the U is not flat, or symmetrical, but typically slopes upward gradually after a minimum at age 5 to 15, rising with only slight acceleration until age 45 to 60, where a markedly steeper rise may occur, forming the right arm of the U. Irregularities in the lower portion of the U may produce a small local maximum, with a succeeding decline before age 45 or 50. A common source of such irregularities is high death rates either from tuberculosis or in childbirth. Each of these causes of death has an age incidence with a peak in the span of 5 to 50.

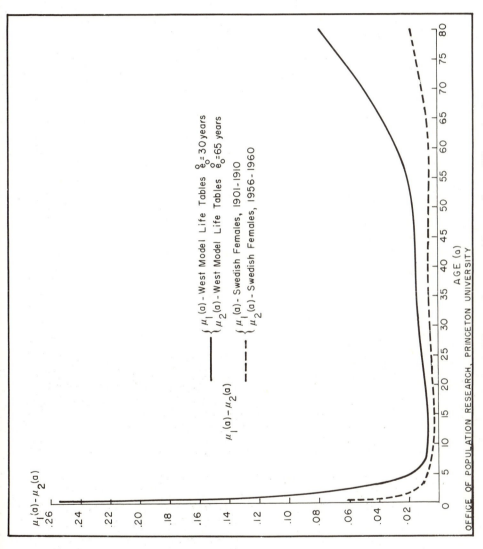

Figure 2.4. Typical differences in age-specific mortality at different levels.

(4) The prominence of the right arm of the U — representing large and rising differences in the mortality rates at older ages — is quite different among different pairs of mortality schedules. It usually, though not always, characterizes the experience of the same area at different times. But in the most recent experience of countries with low mortality risks, age-specific death rates among older persons, especially males, have failed to decrease to any marked extent and in some instances have actually risen although mortality rates for younger persons have continued to fall. Hence, the extent (and even the existence) of the right arm of the U is its most uncertain feature. The common-sense basis for the U shape of differences in mortality rates is simply that the rates in high mortality schedules themselves follow a roughly U-shaped pattern, and as death rates move toward zero, a U-shaped pattern of change is inevitable. The lesser steepness and uncertain existence of the right arm reflect the more modest progress attained in reducing mortality rates at older ages.

In the future of low mortality populations, if further major additions to the average duration of life occur, they must result from increased survivorship at ages above 45, since in the lowest mortality schedules the distance to zero mortality rates under age 5 is modest, and from 5 to 45, virtually negligible. Major changes (if they occur) will thus form a U with a very small left arm and a large right arm.

DIFFERENCES IN STABLE AGE DISTRIBUTION CAUSED BY TYPICAL DIFFERENCES IN MORTALITY SCHEDULES

The effect of a U-shaped pattern of differences in age-specific death rates on the age composition of the stable population can be described by the consecutive consideration of three components:

(1) The bottom of the U, approximated by a horizontal line at the average value of $\mu_1(a) - \mu_2(a)$ for $5 < a < 45$.

(2) The left arm, in excess of the bottom, that is, $\mu_1(a) - \mu_2(a)$ from 0 to 5 *less* the average from 5 to 45.

(3) The right arm, in excess of the bottom.

If $\mu_1(a) - \mu_2(a)$ from 5 to 45 is approximated by an average value and we assume for the moment that this average prevailed at every age from 0 to ω, there would be no resultant difference in age distribution at all, since a uniform value of $\mu_1(a) - \mu_2(a)$ implies no difference in $c(a)$. Thus we can subtract the minimum value (approximated by the mean value of the base of the U) from $\mu_1(a) - \mu_2(a)$ and consider only the residual. The subtracted portion contributes a difference in rate of

36

increase in the two stable populations, but no difference in age composition.

The left arm of the U−values of $\mu_1(a) - \mu_2(a)$ from $a = 0$ to $a = 5$ in excess of the average from 5 to 45−causes the same difference above age 5 in the two age distributions as would higher fertility in the population that in fact has higher survivorship. This point can be readily appreciated by imagining a convention in which the existence of a child is not recognized until it is exactly five years old. Suppose that reaching the fifth anniversary were by this convention defined as "birth," and that the age distribution were considered to begin at age five. Then an increased "birth rate" (in fact a faster flow past the fifth anniversary) would result equally well from an increased rate of "conceptions" (the events we call births) or from increased survival from "conception" to "birth"−from a lower rate of fetal mortality (in fact, from lower mortality at ages zero to five). Within the age distribution past age five, differences in childhood survival are indistinguishable from differences of an appropriate magnitude in fertility. In fact, since the main elevation of the left arm usually occurs below age one, its effect closely resembles that of a difference in fertility in the age distribution above age one rather than above age five.

Within the region where $\mu_1(a) - \mu_2(a)$ has exceptionally high values, that is, within the region of the left arm itself, the difference in age distribution is, of course, *not* the same as would be caused by a difference in fertility. Specifically, the birth rate−the proportion at age zero−is not the point of maximum $c_2(a)/c_1(a)$, as it is when the source of difference in the age distributions is different fertility. Indeed, since in examining mortality differences fertility is assumed to be the same, b_2/b_1 differs from unity only because of what differences there may be in the proportions at childbearing ages. Hence, $c_2(a)/c_1(a)$ in the first five years, instead of falling from a maximum at zero as it does when fertility differs, rises from a value which may be above or below one to a maximum at about age five. From age five, however, it falls exactly as if fertility rather than mortality had differed.[8] Figure 2.4 shows $\mu_1(a) - \mu_2(a)$ for two Swedish life tables, and Figure 2.5 the resultant $c_2(a)/c_1(a)$. The right arm is not very prominent, so at most ages $c_2(a)/c_1(a)$ reflects the influence of the left arm only. Note the similarity from age 5 to 55 or 60 to the effect of a 12% increase in GRR (Coale [1]).

The different effect under age five, implying $c_2(a)/c_1(a)$ at those ages less than would result from a difference in fertility, means that in the

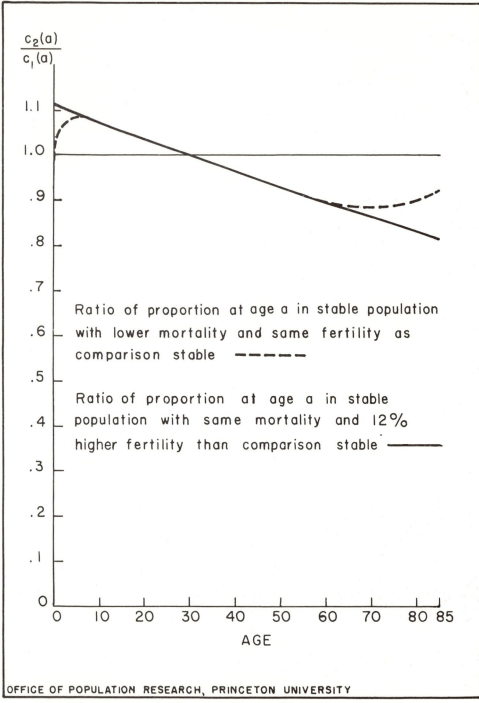

Figure 2.5. Comparison of stable age distributions differing (1) because of difference of mortality schedule in Sweden, 1896–1900 and 1950; (2) because of 12% difference in GRR, same mortality.

lower mortality population the proportions *above* age five are all slightly greater than if fertility differences had been the operating factor. However, this qualification is of negligible magnitude, and the effect of the left arm may to a close approximation be summarized as follows:

(1) Values of $\mu_1(a) - \mu_2(a)$ for $a < 5$ in excess of the average for $5 < a < 45$ cause a difference in age distribution nearly identical (except at ages under five) to that caused by a difference in fertility. The equivalent difference in fertility is one that would yield the same difference in five-year-olds.

(2) The resultant difference in age distribution can be described as a "pivoting" action on the mean age, and the population with higher survivorship has higher proportions up to the mean age, and lower proportions thereafter.

(3) Statement (2) holds only for ages above five: $c_2(a)/c_1(a)$ departs from the form that "pivoting" causes in the range from zero to five, and $c_2(0)/c_1(0) = b_2/b_1$ may be less than, equal to, or greater than one; but except when fertility is very low, stable populations with lower mortality rates have lower birth rates. (See pp. 46–47.)

The effect of the right arm of the U-shaped $\mu_1(a) - \mu_2(a)$ is to cause $c_2(a)/c_1(a)$ at ages above 45 or 50 to be higher than it would be without the right arm. Since, however, these ages are beyond the reproductive span, the right arm produces no differences in growth rate, and influences $c_2(a)/c_1(a)$ at younger ages only because increased $c_2(a)/c_1(a)$ at the older ages implies a slight uniform reduction over the rest of the age span in order that the age distributions total 100%.

The gross effects of the three components acting simultaneously are to produce a $c_2(a)/c_1(a)$ above unity at ages from slightly above zero until short of the mean age, and below unity from this point until age 50, 60, or sometimes until the oldest age attained. Often, but not always, $c_2(a)/c_1(a)$ is above one from 50, 60, or higher until the end of the age distribution. The intersection of $c_1(a)$ and $c_2(a)$ that would occur at about $(\bar{a}_1 + \bar{a}_2)/2$ if only the left arm were operating is moved to a younger age because the right arm increases the proportions in $c_2(a)$ at the older ages, and therefore depresses the proportions at younger ages.

A surprising facet of the effects of mortality differences is that lower mortality has a nearly universal tendency to produce a stable population with a lower mean age.[9] Most of us would assume, and many casual observers have written, that reduction in mortality produces an older population. Examination of stable age distributions shows that this is an instance where common sense, or at least merely casual thought, leads to erroneous conclusions. Common sense tells us that lower mortality, by permitting more to survive to old age, tends to produce an older population. In other words, our intuition readily leads us to the $p(a)$ factor in the stable age distribution. What common sense does not so readily reveal is the fact that higher rates of survival produce more persons at *all* ages, so the effect on the mean age cannot be easily discerned. Our intuition does not lead us to consider the e^{-ra} factor. Since the greatest differences in survival are almost always in infancy and early childhood, the proportion of children is nearly always higher, and the mean age somewhat less universally lower, with a more favorable life table.

Comparison of the Effects on the Stable Age Distribution of Differences in Fertility on the One Hand and Differences in Mortality on the Other

The *qualitative* difference in implications for the stable age distribution between variations in fertility schedules and variations in mortality schedules is that fertility differences make the whole distribution steeper or flatter, whereas mortality differences have partially self-canceling effects on the steepness of the age distribution, and operate on the details of the age distribution rather than on an overall property such as relative slope. Because of this qualitative difference, it is possible to judge the approximate level of fertility from a simple visual inspection of a stable age distribution — a rapidly tapering distribution must have high fertility, for example — but it is much more difficult to infer the mortality level. Perhaps the best clue to the level of mortality is the change in the slope of the age distribution between the proportion under age one on the one hand and from five to nine on the other. A very large decline in steepness in this range is a sign of high mortality.

A quantitative comparison of the effects of mortality and fertility differences on stable age distributions can be obtained by examining differences in age composition resulting from *equal* differences in fertility and mortality. Such a comparison requires an acceptable definition of "equal differences." In this context, a difference in mortality will be considered equal to a difference in fertility if the two would cause an equal change in r.

Table 2.2 and Figure 2.6 show differences in stable age distributions created by mortality and fertility differences equal in this sense. All of

Table 2.2. Differences in various characteristics of stable populations associated with (a) mortality differences and (b) fertility differences causing the same difference in r [a]

Δr	Area between stable populations		Difference in mean age		Difference in proportion under 15		Difference in proportion over 65	
	(a)	(b)	(a)	(b)	(a)	(b)	(a)	(b)
.010	.064	.160	1.2	3.7	.029	.068	.0006	.017
.020	.125	.306	2.4	6.9	.058	.146	.0011	.028

[a] All data are from "West" model stable populations. "Reference" stable population is that with $e_0^0 = 27.5$ years, $r = 0$.

the differences examined (the total area between the two stable populations, the difference in mean age, the proportion of children (less than 15), the proportion of the aged (over 65)) are more than twice as great when the source of difference in r is fertility.

The Birth Rate in the Stable Population

The expression for the birth rate in a stable population that provides the basis for the usual numerical calculation of b is the equation $b = 1 / \int_0^\omega e^{-ra} p(a) da$. However, this equation does not show explicitly the interplay of fertility and age composition in the determination of b, and it is more convenient to take as a point of departure for our discussion the general relation $(b = \int_0^\omega c(a) m(a) da)$ that holds for all populations, stable or otherwise. In Chapter 1 this relation was expanded into a form $(b = (\text{GRR}/(\beta - \alpha)) \int_\alpha^\beta c(a) da + (\beta - \alpha) \mu_{c \cdot m})$ that shows the effect on the birth rate of the gross reproduction rate, the proportion of the population in the fertile age span, and the interaction between the shape of the fertility function and the age structure *within* the fertile span. This approach could be followed in considering the birth rate of a stable population, but it would be an unnecessary and slightly artificial complication to introduce the covariance of $c(a)$ and $m(a)$ in this context. The covariance term is strongly influenced by large bumps and hollows in the age distribution between α and β, and helps provide an understanding of how the birth rate is determined in populations with such irregularities. However, stable populations are intrinsically free of such bumps and hollows, and because of the form $p(a)$ usually has in the ages of childbearing, stable populations usually have an approximately linear distribution by age from α to β, or at

41

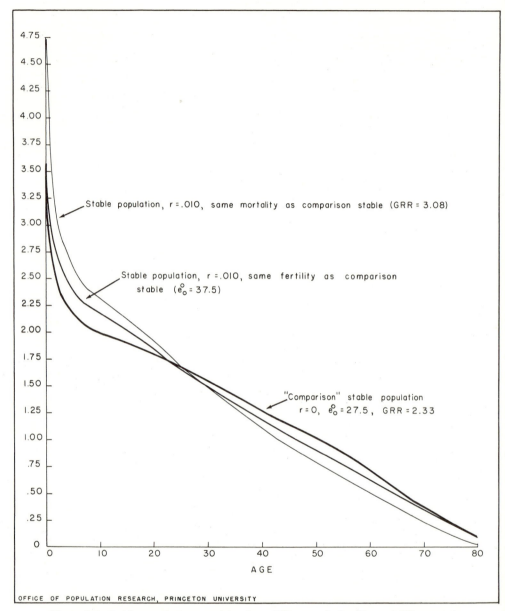

Figure 2.6. Stable populations resulting from differences in fertility and differences in mortality that produce the same difference in *r*.

least over the central span between α and β where childbearing is concentrated.

The near-linearity of $c(a)$ in the principal childbearing ages means that a particularly simple formula for the birth rate in the stable population is valid to a very close approximation, namely

(2.31) $$b \doteq \text{GRR} \cdot c(\bar{m}),$$

where $\bar{m}$ is the mean age of the fertility schedule. Equation (2.31) is exact if $c(a)$ is linear from α to β, as the following argument shows: Suppose $c(a) = L + Ma$. Then $b = \int_{\alpha}^{\beta} (L + Ma)m(a)da$, or $b = L \int_{\alpha}^{\beta} m(a)da + M \int_{\alpha}^{\beta} am(a)da = L \cdot \text{GRR} + M \cdot \text{GRR} \cdot \bar{m}$ or $b = \text{GRR} \cdot c(\bar{m})$. Stable populations are so nearly linear (except at high rates of increase) that in the "West" model stable populations, when GRR is less than 2.75, the maximum error in this estimate of b is less than 1 per thousand. (When GRR is less than 2.0, the greatest error in the estimate of b is less than 3 per 10,000.)

If $c(\bar{m})$ were the same in all stable populations, the birth rate would be a fixed multiple of GRR; therefore the effect of age composition on the birth rate depends on the variations of $c(\bar{m})$. Figure 2.7 shows how $c(\bar{m})$ varies with $\bar{m}$, GRR, and e_0^0 in the "West" model stable populations. Fertility helps determine the birth rate directly through GRR in Equation (2.31), and combines with mortality in determining $c(\bar{m})$.

DIFFERENCES IN $c(\bar{m})$ WITH DIFFERENT VALUES OF $\bar{m}$

In the discussion of how r is determined, the effect of $\bar{m}$ on r was explained in the following terms: A higher value of $\bar{m}$ exposes women to the risk of dying for a longer time, on the average, before births take place, thus reducing NRR for a given value of GRR. Also, a higher value of $\bar{m}$ means a higher value of T, and thus a longer time to multiply the population by NRR, implying a smaller r with larger T if NRR > 1, and a larger r if NRR < 1. The relationship given in Equation (2.31) provides an alternative view of the effect of differences in $\bar{m}$. It is clear that different values of GRR can yield the same b (and, with a given $p(a)$, the same stable population) if on the one hand $\bar{m}$ is low (e.g., 27 years) or on the other is high (e.g., 33 years). If b is the same with different values of $\bar{m}$, we have:

(2.32) $$\frac{\text{GRR}(\bar{m}_1)}{\text{GRR}(\bar{m}_2)} = \frac{c(\bar{m}_2)}{c(\bar{m}_1)}.$$

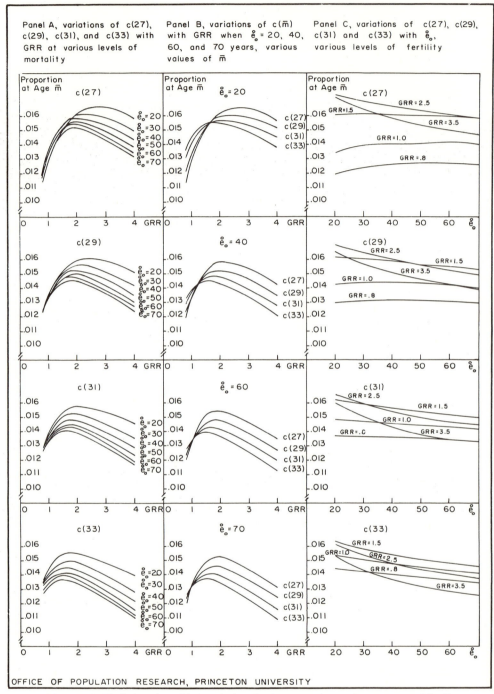

Figure 2.7. Variations in stable populations in the proportion at the mean age of fertility schedule ($c(\bar{m})$), for various levels of fertility and mortality.

If the age distribution is horizontal over the central ages of childbearing, $c(\bar{m}_1)$ and $c(\bar{m}_2)$ are equal, and the difference in $\bar{m}$ does not matter; if the age distribution slopes steeply downward, $c(27)$ may be substantially greater than $c(33)$, and hence a much larger GRR is required to produce a given stable population with the greater mean age of fertility; conversely, if the age distribution slopes steeply upward, a much smaller GRR is required with a greater mean age of fertility.

Because of the approximate linearity of the age distribution in this neighborhood, we may write

$$(2.33) \qquad \frac{c(\bar{m} + \Delta\bar{m}) - c(\bar{m})}{c(\bar{m})} = \frac{\Delta\bar{m}}{c(\bar{m})} \cdot \left(\frac{dc(a)}{da}\right)_{a = \bar{m}}.$$

But $(1/c(a))(dc(a)/da) = -(\mu(a) + r)$ (cf. Equation (2.25)). Hence

$$(2.34) \qquad \frac{c(\bar{m} + \Delta\bar{m})}{c(\bar{m})} = \frac{\text{GRR}(\bar{m})}{\text{GRR}(\bar{m} + \Delta\bar{m})} = 1 - (\mu(\bar{m}) + r)\Delta\bar{m}.$$

It follows from Equation (2.34) that in a stable population where $r = -\mu(30)$, $c(29) = c(31)$, and the GRRs in two fertility schedules (each compatible with the given stable population, with $\bar{m}$'s of 29 and 31 respectively) are the same, as is readily confirmed by specific examples. In other words, when $r = -\mu(30)$, the stable age distribution from 29 to 31 is horizontal.

Equation (2.34) shows how the sensitivity of $c(\bar{m})$ to differences in $\bar{m}$ is affected by mortality ($\mu(\bar{m})$) and the rate of increase (r). To show more directly how this sensitivity is influenced by pertinent fertility and mortality parameters, we shall use the rough approximation $r \doteq (\log \text{GRR} + \log p(\bar{m}))/\bar{m}$ and $\log p(\bar{m})/\bar{m} \doteq -2\mu(\bar{m})$. Substituting, we get:

$$(2.35) \qquad \frac{c(\bar{m} + \Delta\bar{m})}{c(\bar{m})} = \frac{\text{GRR}(\bar{m})}{\text{GRR}(\bar{m} + \Delta\bar{m})} \doteq 1 - \left(\frac{\log \text{GRR}}{\bar{m}} - \mu(\bar{m})\right)\Delta\bar{m}.$$

Equation (2.35) is scarcely precise, but it does indicate correctly how the sensitivity of "effective fertility" to $\bar{m}$ is affected (i.e., how the relative steepness of the stable age distribution in the neighborhood of $\bar{m}$ is affected) by different values of GRR and $\mu(\bar{m})$. The greatest sensitivity (i.e., the greatest relative slope of $c(a)$) occurs at very high fertility and low mortality. Thus when e_0^0 is 75 years a GRR(27) of 3.65 and a GRR(31) of 4.41 produce the same stable population.

DIFFERENCES IN $c(\bar{m})$ WITH DIFFERENT VALUES OF GRR

With any given schedule of mortality $c(\bar{m})$ follows the same general pattern of variation with different levels of fertility: a low point when

GRR is very small, a relatively rapid increase as moderate values of GRR are reached, a broad maximum, and a gradual decline as very high fertility is approached (Figure 2.7). This pattern of variation is a consequence of the "pivoting" action of the stable age distribution as effective fertility varies with the point of pivoting at the mean age, $\bar{a}$, of the stable population. If $\bar{m} < \bar{a}$, the "pivoting" of $c(a)$ increases the proportion at age $\bar{m}$ as fertility is increased, and if $\bar{m} > \bar{a}$, pivoting decreases the proportion at $\bar{m}$ as fertility is increased; hence, the maximum value of $c(\bar{m})$ occurs at a level of fertility where the mean age of the stable population is the same as the mean age of fertility. Consequently the maximum value of $c(27)$ occurs at higher effective fertility than the maximum value of $c(29)$. Since $b \doteq c(\bar{m}) \cdot \text{GRR}(\bar{m})$, the birth rate in a higher fertility stable population is a larger multiple of the birth rate in a lower fertility stable population than the ratio of the two GRRs, provided that $\bar{m} < \bar{a}$, because when $\bar{m}$ is below the age of pivoting higher fertility increases the proportion at the childbearing ages. More precisely,

$$\frac{db}{b} \bigg/ \frac{d\text{GRR}}{\text{GRR}} = \frac{\text{GRR}}{b} \cdot \frac{db}{d\text{GRR}} = \frac{\text{GRR}}{b} \cdot \frac{db}{dr} \cdot \frac{dr}{d\text{GRR}}.$$

But $db/dr = \bar{a}b$; $dr/d\text{GRR} \doteq 1/(\bar{m}\text{GRR})$; hence

$$(2.36) \qquad \frac{db}{b} \bigg/ \frac{d\text{GRR}}{\text{GRR}} = \frac{\bar{a}}{\bar{m}}.$$

For small differences in fertility, the relative increase in the birth rate is $\bar{a}/\bar{m}$ times the relative increase in GRR.

DIFFERENCES IN $c(\bar{m})$ WITH DIFFERENT VALUES OF e_0^0

Variations in $c(\bar{m})$ with different mortality schedules are determined by the age pattern of mortality differences in the schedules. We shall consider briefly the effect of mortality differences that take an approximately "U-shaped" form, as discussed earlier. The left arm of the U is the large difference between mortality schedules that is usually found in early childhood. If it operated alone (i.e., if there were no right arm), the effect of lower mortality (higher survival) on $c(\bar{m})$ would be much the same as higher fertility: namely to increase $c(\bar{m})$ when $\bar{a} > \bar{m}$, to leave it unchanged when $\bar{a} = \bar{m}$, and to diminish it when $\bar{a} < \bar{m}$. The effect of the right arm—rising differences in mortality above age 45 or 50—is always to cause a lower $c(\bar{m})$ in the lower mortality stable population, because the right arm causes higher proportions than would otherwise exist at older ages in the lower mortality population, thus diminishing the proportion at all ages below 45 or 50. The extent of this effect depends on the prominence of the right arm and also on the proportion at higher ages in the higher mortality stable population. The right arm tends to inflate the proportion at older ages by a factor that depends on the magnitude of the arm, and the effect of such an inflation on the proportion at younger ages (including $\bar{m}$) depends on the relative size of the segment subject to inflation. When fertility is low, the stable population has high proportions at advanced ages, and the inflation of this segment by the right arm of the U tends to cause a substantially lower $c(\bar{m})$ with a lower mortality schedule.

The net effect of these forces can be seen in the four right-hand panels of Figure 2.7. When fertility is high (GRR = 2.50 or 3.50)$c(\bar{m})$ falls more steeply with lower mortality than at intermediate fertility levels for all $\bar{m}$ from 27 to 33 years, because the pivoting effect caused by the left arm acts in the same direction as the effect of the right arm. Note that $c(33)$ is less at higher expectation of life at birth even when GRR is 0.800, because when $\bar{m}$ is so high the positive effect on $c(\bar{m})$ of pivoting on the mean age is small, and slightly more than offset by the effect of the right arm. In fact, higher expectation of life at birth always diminishes $c(\bar{m})$ in the "West" model stable populations, except when fertility is very low and the mean age of fertility moderately young. With this exception, in other words, lower mortality produces a stable population with a lower birth rate in the "West" family of model life tables.

The Death Rate in a Stable Population

The relation between the mortality schedule and the stable age distribution has a different geometry from the relation between the fertility schedule and the age distribution; the difference is such that no simple formula for the stable death rate can be found equivalent to the expression $b = \text{GRR} \cdot c(\bar{m})$. The birth rate can be expressed as the product of an aggregate measure of fertility and a single parameter of the age distribution, because fertility is concentrated in a central portion of the life span, a portion where the stable age distribution does not depart much from linearity. In contrast, the typical form of mortality schedules is an asymmetrical U, with death rates that fall steeply with age from 0 to a minimum at about age 10, gradually increasing rates to age 45 or 50, and more steeply increasing rates to the end of life.

One of the effects of the different topography of fertility and mortality

47

schedules is that there is typically less variation in the birth rate among stable populations with the same fertility schedule than in the death rate among stable populations with the same mortality schedule. When e_0^0 ranges from 20 years to 77.5 years (implying, with fertility fixed, a difference in r of about 4%), the highest birth rate is no more than 1.2 times the lowest. But when GRR ranges from 0.800 to 2.500 (implying, with mortality fixed, a difference in r of about 4%), the highest death rate is nearly five times the lowest.

The most important features of the age distribution in helping to determine the death rate are the proportion in early childhood (when mortality is above the valley occurring in later childhood and early adult years) and the proportion who are aged. With a given mortality schedule, age distributions of alternative stable populations differ by the familiar pivoting on the average of their mean ages: a high fertility population has high proportions in childhood and low proportions at old ages relative to a low fertility population.

The effect of this pivoting action is quite different in stable populations embodying high and low mortality schedules, respectively. Figure 1.2 showed typical schedules at high and low levels of mortality. A conspicuous difference in form is the much greater relative importance of mortality early in life in the higher mortality schedule. The pivoting action differentiating a higher from a lower fertility stable age distribution produces higher proportions at all ages below the mean — with the greatest relative difference at age 0, and lower proportions above the mean — with an increasing relative difference as age increases. With a high mortality schedule the effect of the high proportion near age 0 in a high fertility population is a much more powerful offset to the effect of a low proportion over age 50 than with a low mortality schedule. As a result, the variation in stable death rates with GRRs ranging from .800 to 4.000 is much greater (2.5 to 1) when e_0^0 is 60 years than it is (1.3 to 1) when e_0^0 is 30 years. The contrast is still greater at more extreme levels: The ratio of the highest to the lowest death rates in stable populations with GRRs ranging from .80 to 4.00 is 6.8 to 1 when e_0^0 is 70 years, and only 1.2 to 1 when e_0^0 is 20 years.

Because mortality schedules have a downward slope departing from age 0, and a rising portion that extends to ω, and because of the pivoting effect of fertility differences, for every mortality schedule there is a level of fertility yielding a stable population with a minimum death rate, that is, higher or lower fertility than at the minimum would make the death rate higher. When infant mortality is very low (as for example in contemporary Sweden where $_1q_0$ for females is no more than 12 per thousand) the minumum death rate would occur at a GRR above 7.0, beyond the plausible limit for any large population. However, when e_0^0 is 70 years, the minimum occurs when GRR($\bar{m} = 29$ years) is a little less than 6.00. When e_0^0 is 30 years, the minimum death rate occurs when GRR is about 2.3 (and r very nearly zero); when e_0^0 is 20, d_{min} occurs when GRR is about 2.0, and r about $-.0016$.

Variation in the Overall Rate in Stable Population of Any Age-Specific Characteristic

The effect of age composition of the stable population on the death rate is a particular instance of a more general question: How is the overall proportion (or rate) of any characteristic (or event) affected by differences in age composition among stable populations with different rates of increase? Suppose that there is a specific pattern of variation with age in the proportion of persons with a given characteristic, or in the proportion of persons who experience a given event. Suppose $g(a)$ is the rate (or proportion) at age a, and G is the overall rate or proportion in the stable population. Then,

$$(2.37) \qquad G = \int_0^\omega g(a)c(a)da.$$

To examine the effect on G of different values of r, we calculate:

$$(2.38) \quad \frac{dG}{dr} = \int_0^\omega g(a) \cdot \frac{dc(a)}{dr} \cdot da = \int_0^\omega (\bar{a} - a)g(a)c(a)da = G(\bar{a} - \bar{a}_g),$$

where $\bar{a}_g$ is the mean age of persons with the given characteristic. The maximum (or minimum) value of G occurs in that stable population where $\bar{a} = \bar{a}_g$. The value of G is a maximum if d^2G/dr^2 is negative (when $\bar{a} = \bar{a}_g$), and a minimum if the second derivative is positive. Taking the derivative of $G(\bar{a} - \bar{a}_g)$, and simplifying, we find

$$(2.39) \qquad \frac{d^2G}{dr^2} = G(\bar{a} - \bar{a}_g)^2 + G(\sigma_g^2 - \sigma^2).$$

Hence when $\bar{a} = \bar{a}_g$, G is a maximum if $\sigma_g^2 < \sigma^2$, and a minimum if $\sigma_g^2 > \sigma^2$. Thus if $g(a)$ is age-specific labor force participation, and is confined primarily to ages 15 to 65, overall labor force participation is a maximum in the stable population where the mean age is the same as the mean age of labor force participants (the form of $g(a)$ in this instance insures that $\sigma_g^2 < \sigma^2$). Note that the value of r that maximizes

G is that same value that minimizes $(1 - G)$; when the proportion participating in the labor force is a maximum, the proportion *not* participating is a minimum. At this point the mean age of participants and nonparticipants is the same.

CALCULATION OF G

Equation (2.38) can be rewritten as:

$$(2.40) \qquad \frac{dG}{G} = d \log G = (\bar{a} - \bar{a}_g)dr.$$

Hence

$$(2.41) \qquad G = G_0 e^{\int_0^r (\bar{a} - \bar{a}_g)dr},$$

where G_0 is the value of G in the stationary population. But

$$(2.42) \qquad \bar{a} = \frac{\int_0^\omega ae^{-ra}p(a)da}{\int_0^\omega e^{-ra}p(a)da} = \lambda_1 - \lambda_2 r + \frac{\lambda_3}{2}r^2 - \frac{\lambda_4}{3!}r^3 \cdots,$$

and

$$(2.43) \qquad \bar{a}_g = \frac{\int_0^\omega ae^{-ra}p(a)g(a)da}{\int_0^\omega e^{-ra}p(a)g(a)da} = \delta_1 - \delta_2 r + \frac{\delta_3}{2}r^2 - \frac{\delta_4}{3!}r^3 \cdots,$$

where λ_i is the ith cumulant of the stationary population, and δ_i is the ith cumulant of $p(a) \cdot g(a)$. Hence

$$(2.44) \qquad G = G_0 e^{(\lambda_1 - \delta_1)r - ((\lambda_2 - \delta_2)/2)r^2 + ((\lambda_3 - \delta_3)/3!)r^3 \cdots}.$$

Since the birth rate in the stable population is given by:

$$(2.45) \qquad b = b_0 e^{\lambda_1 r - (\lambda_2/2)r^2 + (\lambda_3/3!)r^3 \cdots},$$

$$(2.46) \qquad G = G_0 \cdot \frac{b}{b_0} e^{-\delta_1 r + (\delta_2/2)r^2 - (\delta_3/3!)r^3 \cdots}.$$

VARIATION OF THE INTRINSIC DEATH RATE

The death rate in a stable population is

$$(2.47) \qquad d = \int_0^\omega c(a)\mu(a)da,$$

where $\mu(a)$ is the age-specific mortality rate, and $c(a) = be^{-ra}p(a)$.

50

It follows that

(2.48)
$$\frac{dd}{dr} = d(\bar{a} - \bar{a}_d),$$

and that the minimum death rate with a given life table occurs in the stable population where $\bar{a} = \bar{a}_d$. (Cf. Equation (2.38).) It can also be shown that $dd/dr = \bar{a}b - 1$ (since $d = b - r$), and that in the stable population with the minimum death rate, $\bar{a} = 1/b$ (Lotka [8]). Also

(2.49)
$$d = d_0 e^{(\lambda_1 - \delta_1)r - ((\lambda_2 - \delta_2)/2)r^2 \cdots},$$

where d_0 is the death rate in the stationary population, λ_i the ith cumulant of the age distribution of the stationary population, and δ_i the ith cumulant of the distribution of deaths in the stationary population. Note that λ_1 is the mean age of the stationary population, and $\delta_1 = e_0^0$ is the mean age of the deaths in the stationary population. If $\lambda_1 = \delta_1$, the stationary population has the lowest death rate among the stable populations associated with the given life table. (The lowest death rate occurs with a zero rate of increase in female life tables with a mean duration of life of about 30 years (Coale and Demeny [3]).) When λ_1 is less than δ_1, the lowest death rate occurs with a negative r. In general, the larger the difference in λ_1 and e_0^0, the greater is the difference between the life table death rate and the minimum stable death rate. For example, when $e_0^0 = \delta_1 = 70.0$, $\lambda_1 = 38.0$, and $d_{\min}$ is about 0.0041, some 0.0102 less than d_0. (In this instance, a growth rate well above 6% is required to produce the minimum death rate.)

Equation (2.49) does not provide a very rapidly convergent series for determining d, especially at large values of r. To obtain an approximation to d within 0.0002 of the correct figure for all values of r no greater than 0.030 and of b no greater than 0.060, it is necessary to include the term in r^4.

Some Uses and Limitations of the Stable Population

THE HYPOTHETICAL NATURE OF STABLE POPULATIONS

The stable population, as noted earlier, is the population that is established by a prolonged regime of unchanging schedules of fertility and mortality. Since actual schedules always change, the stable population must be regarded as hypothetical: It is the population that *would* result if specified schedules of fertility and mortality were to persist. Perhaps the most useful view of the concept is as a particularly elaborate set of implications of any pair of schedules.

The earliest extended exposition of the stable population, in a classic article by Dublin and Lotka [5], emphasized the fact that the "true" rate of increase of the female population (i.e., the rate of increase of the stable population) in the United States in the early 1920s was much less than the difference between the current birth and death rates. In the years between the appearance of this article and World War II, many demographers pointed out that in certain populations the "true" rate of increase was negative, although the populations in question were still growing. In retrospect it appears that the use of the term "true rate of increase" and the general tone of the discussion gave an inappropriate flavor of prediction to the characteristics of the stable population. It is always unlikely, and often logically impossible, for specific schedules of fertility and mortality to remain unchanged for a long time. However, it would not be wise to conclude from the observed changeability of fertility and mortality that the concept of a stable population is useless. The proper conclusion is that the stable population should rarely (if ever) be interpreted as a prediction. A reading of 60 mph on a speedometer means that the automobile bearing it would travel 60 miles in an hour if velocity were held constant. Because cars usually travel at varying speeds, a reading of 60 would only rarely be a valid prediction; nevertheless, the speedometer is a useful instrument, and so is the stable population if properly used.

Demographers and actuaries have long been aware of the hypothetical nature of the *stationary* population, which, hypothetical or not, is a valuable framework of analysis. The knowledgeable user never makes the mistake of thinking that the expectation of life at birth in a "period" life table is the mean age at death of any actual population. It is the average age at death only in the hypothetical population defined by the mortality schedule.

Similarly, $c(a)$, r, b, and d are characteristics of a hypothetical population and do not ordinarily describe any real population, past, present, or future. These characteristics illustrate, in pure form, the influence of fertility and mortality on growth, birth and death rates, and age composition.

Because the discussion of detailed aspects of this influence in the earlier part of this chapter is sometimes extended and complex, the principal effects of fertility and mortality on the characteristics of stable populations have very likely been obscured. These principal effects are summarized in Table 2.3. The stable populations characterized in this table are based on schedules of fertility and mortality ranging from very high to very low levels, and embodying the typical age patterns of observed fertility and mortality at these levels.

MALE AND FEMALE STABLE POPULATIONS

The stable populations most frequently calculated are those implied by schedules of fertility and mortality for one sex; in particular, the fer-

Table 2.3. Parameters of stable age distribution based on "West" model life tables at various levels of mortality and a standard fertility schedule ($\bar{m} = 29$ years) at various levels

Expectation of life	Gross reproduction rate						
	0.80	1.00	1.50	2.00	2.50	3.00	4.00
	Proportion at ages 0 to 14						
20	.099	.129	.198	.257	.308	.351	.420
30	.117	.152	.230	.294	.348	.393	.464
40	.129	.167	.251	.319	.374	.420	.491
50	.138	.178	.266	.336	.393	.439	.510
60	.144	.186	.277	.349	.407	.453	.524
70	.148	.192	.286	.359	.417	.464	.534
	Proportion at ages 65 and over						
20	.168	.135	.086	.059	.042	.032	.020
30	.180	.143	.088	.058	.041	.031	.018
40	.189	.149	.090	.059	.041	.030	.018
50	.198	.155	.091	.059	.041	.030	.017
60	.206	.160	.093	.060	.041	.029	.017
70	.215	.166	.096	.061	.042	.030	.017
	Mean age						
20	44.6	41.6	35.7	31.6	28.5	26.1	22.7
30	43.9	40.5	34.2	29.9	26.7	24.4	21.0
40	43.5	39.9	33.2	28.8	25.7	23.3	20.0
50	43.4	39.5	32.6	28.1	24.9	22.6	19.4
60	43.4	39.3	32.2	27.6	24.4	22.0	18.9
70	43.6	39.3	32.0	27.2	24.0	21.7	18.5
	Birth rate						
20	.0096	.0133	.0223	.0315	.0399	.0476	.0613
30	.0098	.0134	.0225	.0310	.0388	.0458	.0581
40	.0098	.0134	.0223	.0305	.0379	.0445	.0558
50	.0097	.0133	.0221	.0300	.0371	.0434	.0542
60	.0097	.0133	.0219	.0297	.0366	.0426	.0529
70	.0096	.0131	.0217	.0293	.0360	.0419	.0518
	Death rate						
20	.0570	.0532	.0488	.0478	.0483	.0495	.0528
30	.0437	.0398	.0350	.0335	.0333	.0338	.0356
40	.0349	.0309	.0258	.0239	.0233	.0233	.0242
50	.0284	.0244	.0191	.0169	.0160	.0157	.0158
60	.0234	.0194	.0139	.0115	.0103	.0098	.0094
70	.0194	.0154	.0097	.0072	.0058	.0057	.0044

tility schedule normally utilized indicates (for males or for females) the rate of production of ŏffspring of the same sex, as a function of age.

It is a simple matter to extend the stable population to two sexes, provided that fertility is considered a function of the age of members of one sex only. Suppose the fertility schedule of females is defined as $m_1(a)$ for female offspring, and $m_2(a)$ for male offspring; then r can be determined as the real root of Equation (2.4), with $m_1(a)$ written in place of $m(a)$. If $m_2(a)/m_1(a)$ were constant, it would be the sex ratio at birth in the population. If the ratio $m_2(a)/m_1(a)$ varies with age of women, the overall sex ratio at birth in any population depends on age composition. Even when the masculinity of births varies with age of mothers, there is a unique SRB in the stable population, namely:

$$(2.50) \qquad \text{SRB (stable)} = \int_0^\beta e^{-ra} p_f(a) m_2(a) da,$$

since $e^{-ra}p_f(a)$ is a female stable population that would produce one female birth annually and Equation (2.50) gives the number of male births such a population would have. (The subscript f means that $p_f(a)$ is the proportion of females surviving from birth to age a.) The male stable population defined by female fertility schedules has a male birth rate,

$$(2.51) \qquad b_m = \frac{1}{\displaystyle\int_0^\omega e^{-ra} p_m(a) da};$$

and a male stable age distribution, defined by female fertility schedules and mortality schedules for females and males,

$$(2.52) \qquad c_m(a) = b_m e^{-ra} p_m(a).$$

The principal parameters of the total stable population implied by fertility schedules (producing female and male offspring) of women, and survival schedules for each sex, are as follows:

overall birth rate: $b_t = \dfrac{(1 + \text{SRB}) b_f b_m}{\text{SRB } b_f + b_m}$

overall death rate: $d_t = \dfrac{b_m d_f + \text{SRB } b_f d_m}{\text{SRB } b_f + b_m}$ \quad (where $d_m = b_m - r$)

sex ratio of population (males/female): $\text{SR} = \text{SRB}\left(\dfrac{b_f}{b_m}\right).$

A complete stable population (again including both sexes) could equally well be based on fertility schedules for the *male* population (schedules for the production of male and female offspring as a function of age of males), and mortality schedules for both sexes. However, the two stable populations derived from the same mortality schedules, but in one instance from female and in the other from male fertility schedules (as observed in an actual population), are not necessarily the same, and in fact normally differ, sometimes substantially. The basic difference is the different intrinsic rates of increase (r_f and r_m) associated with the current fertility and mortality of the two sexes, a difference originating in the fact that the balance of the sexes in the reproductive ages is often not the same in the actual population as in either of the two stable populations. The fertility schedules of the two sexes in the same population are inevitably linked by the fact that every birth is identified with one father and one mother; thus, by necessity,

$$(2.53) \qquad \int_0^\omega N_m(a) f_1(a)\, da \equiv \int_0^\omega N_f(a) m_1(a)\, da.$$

Equation (2.53) could equally well be written with $f_2(a)$ and $m_2(a)$ substituted for $f_1(a)$ and $m_1(a)$. ($N_m(a)$ is the number of males at age a; $f_1(a)$ the age-specific paternity rate for female offspring; $N_f(a)$ the number of females at age a; and $m_1(a)$ the age-specific maternity rate for female offspring.) Equation (2.53) states the obvious fact that in a closed population the number of daughters sired by fathers and the number born to mothers are the same. Suppose $N'_m(a)$ and $N'_f(a)$ are the numbers of males and females at age a in a stable population (based on the fertility schedules of one sex) with an arbitrary total of, say, one million persons. In general, Equation (2.53), which must hold for N_m and N_f, will not hold when these numbers are replaced by N'_m and N'_f. Equality would be preserved only if the balance of the sexes in the principal reproductive ages were the same in the actual population as in the stable. The "balance of the sexes" can be so defined as to ensure the equality of the relative fertility of males and females on the one hand and of the balance of the sexes on the other; so that, in short, an imbalance of the sexes must be offset by an equal imbalance of fertility. Suppose TF_m is $\int_{\alpha_1}^{\beta_1} f_1(a)\, da$ and TF_f is $\int_{\alpha_2}^{\beta_2} m_1(a)\, da$, where the α's and β's are the earliest and latest ages of parenthood for each sex. Then Equation (2.53) can be rewritten as

$$(2.54) \qquad TF_m \int_{\alpha_1}^{\beta_1} N_m(a) \frac{f_1(a)}{TF_m}\, da \equiv TF_f \int_{\alpha_2}^{\beta_2} N_f(a) \frac{m_1(a)}{TF_f}\, da.$$

55

Thus the ratio of male to female total fertility must be the inverse of the ratio of the number of males of parental age to the number of females — when "number of females" and "number of males" are calculated as the weighted sum of the number at each age, with the proportion of total fertility at each age as weight. The balance of the sexes in the reproductive ages in the actual population and in the stable population have very different sources. The balance in the latter depends on the current sex ratio at birth, on the relative survival rates to the principal fertile ages in the current life table and the difference in the mean age of the current fertility schedules of the two sexes, and (especially if the last mentioned difference is large) on the rate of increase of the stable population. The balance of the sexes in the actual population depends, in contrast, on recent history, often including differential gains or losses of one sex or the other through migration, and episodic sex-selective mortality, especially as a result of war.

If in the actual population the numbers of males and females in the principal reproductive ages are very unequal, this imbalance will be matched by very unequal total fertility among males and females. If, for example, there are only half as many males as females in the ages of parenthood, male fertility must be about twice as high as female fertility. Twice as high a proportion of the men of parental age must be fathers than women of parental age are mothers each year. If the imbalance has resulted from historical events (a war in which males suffered exceptional mortality, or sex-selective migration) rather than from special features such as a continuing unusual sex ratio at birth or persistent sex-selective mortality, the higher male fertility would imply a substantially higher rate of increase in the male-based than in the female-based stable population; that is, a larger r_m than r_f. A difference between r_m and r_f need not be viewed as paradoxical, but merely as an indication of an imbalance of the sexes at parental ages as compared to the balance inherent in the current sex ratio at birth, and the relative survival of the sexes in the current mortality schedules. In fact, when $r_m > r_f$, multiplying the number of males at every parental age by a factor $e^{(r_m - r_f)T_m}$ (with the number of births unchanged) would make $r_m = r_f$. (T_m is the mean length of generation in the male-based stable population. Alternatively, multiplying the number of females by $e^{-(r_m - r_f)T_f}$ would make $r_f = r_m$.) The greatest imbalance of the sexes found in a search of recent Demographic Year Books of the U.N. was in West Berlin in 1950, where $r_m = -0.0001$, and $r_f = -0.0115$.[10] In this instance the number of males in each age interval would require

56

multiplication by 1.43 ($e^{(r_m - r_f)T_m}$) with the number of births in each interval unchanged, to produce an r_m of -0.0115. At the most prolific childbearing ages (20 to 35), the ratio of females/males was precisely 1.43.

It is evident that a single stable population cannot be derived (without introducing further assumptions) from the fertility schedules of both sexes, since the schedules of each sex provide the basis for calculating a complete stable population, and the two complete stable populations differ. Some writers have concluded that the concept of the stable population is on this account self-contradictory, because if (for example) female fertility schedules were to remain fixed, male schedules would inevitably have to change. Hence — so this argument runs — the stable population is not based on genuinely fixed schedules. One resolution of this apparent contradiction is to calculate a "female-dominant" stable population based on female fertility schedules and on the assumption that changes in proportions cohabiting among males will take place; a "male-dominant" population based on corresponding assumptions about adjustments in female fertility; and finally, various intermediate stable populations on the assumption that *both* fertility schedules will be modified as the balance of the sexes is altered. A recent exposition by Goodman [6] summarizes earlier efforts to construct stable populations based on the fertility of males and females, and offers the most general version yet constructed of a stable population based on the fertility of both sexes. Goodman shows how the age and sex distribution of a stable population can be derived with any degree of dominance of males or females in determining cohabitation.

A more elaborate approach would construct a stable population by postulating the age-and-sex incidence of entry into and departure from procreating couples, making appropriate allowance for the availability by age of eligible individuals of each sex. In such a model, the age schedule of fertility of each sex would change as age and sex composition was modified. Ultimately the age and sex composition would stabilize, and each sex would arrive at a fertility schedule compatible with the final stable population. There would be a single r, somewhere intermediate between r_f and r_m (if the procreation of current couples is consistent with the rules underlying the computations). However, computations of this sort could not be based on observed schedules. It would be necessary to make assumptions about the influence of the age and sex distribution on fertility. That there is such an influence no one can doubt, but by its nature it cannot be observed directly, as can fertility and mortality schedules. Hence a stable population derived from the fertility of both sexes is *not* a population inherent in observed fertility and mortality schedules, and is therefore different in concept from the stable population as we have defined it in this chapter.

USE OF THE STABLE POPULATION TO ILLUSTRATE THE LIMITS OF THE BIRTH RATE, THE DEATH RATE, AND THE RATE OF NATURAL INCREASE

The highest birth rate that a human population could attain would occur when a schedule of maximum fertility rates would be combined with the most favorable possible age composition. The fertility schedule would have a high gross reproduction rate, and presumably early childbearing, so the highest fertility would coincide with high proportions of women within the childbearing span. If the effects of migration are ruled out, the maximum birth rate can be calculated in a stable age distribution because a history of rising fertility would produce a less favorable age distribution, and it is scarcely plausible in calculating the maximum birth rate obtainable to assume that fertility has been declining. The proportion in the childbearing ages is enhanced by high mortality.

If the age-specific fertility schedule of the Cocos-Keeling Islands — the highest recorded fertility schedule for a whole population — is combined with the model life tables that the Office of Population Research has calculated, a birth rate of about 63 per thousand is found when the expectation of life at birth is 20 years. If the expectation of life at birth were 71 years, the birth rate would be about 53 per thousand. However, it is at least imaginable that a still higher level of fertility could occur. If the synthetic schedule obtained by combining the highest observed marital fertility rates at each age is employed (gross reproduction rate 6.1), the stable birth rate is 84 when e_0^0 is 20 years and 67 when e_0^0 is 71 years. Even the higher of these two rates is not the maximum birth rate because it occurs in a population growing steadily at about 2.5% per year. If the population were stationary, the birth rate would be over 90 — and the expectation of life at birth about 11 years!

The minimum intrinsic death rate consistent with observed mortality and fertility schedules would result from a combination of the fertility of the Cocos-Keeling Islands with a recent Swedish mortality schedule. The death rate of this stable population is about 2.5 per thousand. The lowest reliably recorded death rate to date is in Hong Kong, 1965: 4.8 per thousand.

The maximum growth rate would result from a combination of high fertility and low mortality. Cocos-Island fertility combined with Swedish mortality (GRR 4.17, e_0^0 75 years) would produce a rate of increase of about 5.0% per year. A gross reproduction rate of 6.1 (combination of highest observed rates at each age) would lead to a growth of about 6.5% per year. Still lower mortality would, surprisingly enough, add very little to these growth rates. A death rate of zero (immortality for all) would add only about 0.1% to the long-run growth rate (Coale [2]). To be sure, the death rate would fall from 2.5 per thousand to 0, but the slight increase in the proportion of older persons would reduce the birth rate by about 1.5 per thousand. Mankind has not closely approached the biologically feasible fertility schedule that would maximize growth, but has come very near to the ultimate in growth-producing mortality schedules.

NOTES

[1] Equation (2.7) would be exact if $p(a)$ were linear from α to β. An empirical check of its accuracy (in model stable populations with precisely calculated values of NRR and GRR, at mortality levels ranging from $e_0^0 = 20$ years to 77.5 years, and $\bar{m}$ from 27 to 33 years) shows that NRR is estimated with a maximum error of about .5% and a typical error of less than .3%.

[2] Substituting $u - va$ for $p(a)$ in Equation (2.11), one obtains $\mu_1 = [u \int_\alpha^\beta am(a)da - v \int_\alpha^\beta a^2m(a)da]/[u \int_\alpha^\beta m(a)da - v \int_\alpha^\beta am(a)da]$. But $\int_\alpha^\beta m(a)da = $ GRR, $\int_\alpha^\beta am(a)da = \bar{m}$ GRR, and $\int_\alpha^\beta a^2m(a)da = $ GRR$(\sigma^2 + \bar{m}^2)$. Hence $\mu_1 = (u\bar{m} - v\bar{m}^2 - v\sigma^2)/(u - v\bar{m}) = \bar{m} - v\sigma^2/p(\bar{m})$.

[3] Let $Y(s) = \int_0^\omega e^{-sa}p(a)m(a)da$; $dY(s)/ds = -\int_0^\omega ae^{-sa}p(a)m(a)da = -\bar{A}(s) \cdot Y(s)$. Then $(1/Y(s))(dY(s)/ds) = -\bar{A}(s)$, where $\bar{A}(s) = \mu_1 - \mu_2s + \mu_3(s^2/2!) \cdots$, and $\log Y(s) = -\int \bar{A}(s)ds + \log Y(0)$ or $Y(s) = Y(0)e^{-\int \bar{A}(s)ds}$. But $Y(0) = $ NRR, as is seen by letting $s = 0$ in the definition of $Y(s)$. Also if r is the rate of increase in the stable population, $Y(r) = 1$. Hence: NRR $= e^{\int \bar{A}(r)dr}$, but since NRR $= e^{rT}$ we see that $T = (\int \bar{A} dr)/r$.

[4] If the largest recorded value of r (.05) is combined with the largest calculated value of μ_3 (120), the third term would be $20(.05)^2 = .05$, very small compared to a typical value of 28 years for T.

[5] As a rule of thumb for estimating r from Equation (2.19) without calculating σ^2, I suggest the following: Assume σ^2 is 50 if GRR is greater than 3.0; 45 for $2.5 < $ GRR $ < 3.0$; 42 for $2.0 < $ GRR $ < 2.5$; and 38 for GRR $ < 2.0$. The suggested values are least reliable for the smaller GRRs, but when GRR is small, the error introduced by a wrong estimate of σ^2 is unimportant. Since GRR and $\bar{m}$ can be calculated very easily with pencil and paper from a fertility schedule by five-year age intervals, these assumed approximate values of σ^2 make it possible to calculate r very quickly using no more than a natural log table or a slide rule to determine log GRR and log $p(30)$.

[6] The partial derivative is taken with respect to the log of each parameter so as to com-

pare the increment in r resulting from a *relative* increase in each; otherwise the difference in units among the different parameters presents difficulties of interpretation.

[7] For larger differences in r, the intersection occurs at an age somewhat above $(\bar{a}_1 + \bar{a}_2)/2$. Lotka [8] shows that the point of intersection is: $\hat{a} = \lambda_1 - (\lambda_2/2!)(r_1 + r_2) + (\lambda_3/3!) \times [r_1^2 + r_1 r_2 + r_2^2] - (\lambda_4/4!)[r_1^3 + r_1^2 r_2 + r_1 r_2^2 + r_2^3] \cdots$ whereas, $\bar{a}_1 + \bar{a}_2 = \lambda_1 - (\lambda_2/2)[r_1 + r_1] + (\lambda_3/2 \cdot 2!)[r_1^2 + r_2^2] - (\lambda_4/2 \cdot 3!)[r_1^3 + r_2^3] \cdots$, where λ_i is the ith cumulant of the stationary age distribution. The difference in the third term between these expressions (the first two terms are identical) is $(\lambda_3/12)(r_1 - r_2)^2$. The maximum calculated value of $\lambda_3/12$ in a large number of life tables is less than 400, so when the difference in r is less than 0.02, $\hat{a}$ differs from $(\bar{a}_1 + \bar{a}_2)/2$ by at most .16 years. However, for a difference in r of 0.06, $\hat{a}$ would exceed $(\bar{a}_1 + \bar{a}_2)/2$ by as much as 1.4 years.

[8] The reader must bear in mind that we are here discussing the effect of the left arm only. The rising ratio of survival at older ages that exists in many mortality differences is not compatible with the statement in the text.

[9] Exceptions are normally found in comparisons of schedules of mortality for the same population at different dates only when a low mortality schedule is compared with a *very* low mortality schedule.

[10] Births by age of father and age of mother taken from DYB, 1959, Tables 12 and 14. Only *legitimate* births are tabulated by age of father; legitimate births in each age interval were multiplied by the ratio (all births at all ages)/(legitimate births at all ages) before r_m was calculated.

REFERENCES

[1] Coale, A. J., "The Effects of Changes in Mortality and Fertility on Age Composition," *Milbank Memorial Fund Quarterly,* Vol. 34, No. 1, January 1956, pp. 79–114.

[2] Coale, A. J., "Increases in Expectation of Life and Population Growth," International Union for the Scientific Study of Population, *Proceedings* (Vienna, 1959), pp. 36–41.

[3] Coale, A. J., and Demeny, P., *Regional Model Life Tables and Stable Populations,* Princeton, Princeton University Press, 1966.

[4] Davis, K., *The Population of India and Pakistan,* Princeton, Princeton University Press, 1951.

[5] Dublin, L. I., and Lotka, A. J., "On the True Rate of Natural Increase," *Journal of the American Statistical Association,* Vol. 20, No. 151, September, 1925, pp. 305–339.

[6] Goodman, L. A., "On the Age-sex Composition of the Population That Would Result from Given Fertility and Mortality Conditions," *Demography,* Vol. 4, No. 2, 1967, pp. 423–441.

[7] Keyfitz, N., and Flieger, W., *World Population,* Chicago, University of Chicago Press, 1968.

[8] Lotka, A. J., *Théorie Analytique des Associations Biologiques,* Part II, Paris, Hermann et Cie, 1939.

CHAPTER 3
Convergence of a Population to the Stable Form

IN DISCUSSIONS of the stable population from Lotka's pioneering work to the present, and in the related literature on self-renewing aggregates, little attention has been given to analyzing the *process* of convergence from arbitrary initial circumstances to the stable form. Renewal theory, as well as Lotka's proof that under stipulated conditions a population becomes stable, is concerned with proofs of existence — with the proof of ultimate convergence, not with intermediate states, nor with the duration of the process. The literature on the use of stable population concepts for estimation and other pragmatic purposes has not included a systematic study of convergence (Bourgeois-Pichat [1], Coale and Demeny [3]).

This chapter is intended to fill at least some part of this gap in the theory of stable populations. The process of convergence is obviously an important aspect of the theory of stable populations: if the stable form were closely approached only after several million years, for example, the stable population would be an abstract concept indeed.

The basic theorem of stable populations states that a closed population of one sex subject to unchanging fertility and mortality schedules ultimately attains a fixed age composition and a constant rate of increase. The ultimate age composition and rate of increase are wholly determined by the specified fixed mortality and fertility schedules and are independent of the age composition of the initial population, provided only that it includes some members who have not yet passed the highest age of nonzero fertility.

The stable population is established from the moment the proportion at every age falls within some arbitrarily small margin of the proportion stipulated in the well-known equation $c(a) = be^{-ra}p(a)$, where $c(a)$ is the proportion at age a, b the constant birth rate in the stable population, r the constant rate of increase, and $p(a)$ the proportion surviving to age a. Since the stable age distribution is a consequence (when mortality is fixed) of a sequence of births in which the number constantly changes at a fixed rate, the stable population is established no more than ω years after the number of births last deviates by an arbitrarily small proportionate amount from a pure exponential sequence, where ω is the highest age attained under the given mortality regime.

The path followed as the sequence of births approaches the form stability requires can be calculated to any desired degree of precision

61

by two quite different procedures. One possibility is to apply the standard techniques of population projection, recording the initial population in small age intervals, and calculating the development of the population in equally small time intervals. If the chosen interval of age and time is Δ, the population at each age above Δ at the end of the first time interval is calculated by applying appropriate survival rates to the initial population, and the population under age Δ calculated by determining the number of survivors from the births occurring during the interval according to the given fertility schedule. The other possibility is to decompose the birth sequence beginning at $t = 0$ into the exponential term that ultimately constitutes the births of the stable population plus a series of oscillatory terms of different frequencies. The oscillatory terms diminish in magnitude with time, at least relative to the exponential term, until relative deviations from the exponential are less than the arbitrarily small criterion.

The two procedures correspond to two methods of proving the stable population theorem — a method in which population dynamics are defined in terms of the product of a sequence of matrices, and a method in which the sequence of births is defined by means of an integral equation (Lopez [6], Chapters 1 and 2).

The calculation by population projection of the sequence of births from $t = 0$ until stability is approached is readily accomplished on a modern computer, and someone interested in the convergence to stability of a particular population subjected to particular schedules of fertility and mortality can explore the process at modest cost in time and effort by projection. The difficulty with such an approach is that it reveals little about the factors that make convergence slow or fast, or about the factors causing the transient deviations from the stable birth sequence to be large or small.

The calculation of the sequence of births as the sum of a real exponential term and a series of relatively diminishing oscillatory terms is quite laborious, even with the help of an electronic computer. However, it is possible by this approach to show how salient features of the process of convergence are determined by certain characteristics of the fertility and mortality schedules on the one hand, and certain properties of the initial age distribution on the other. Thus, in spite of the difficulties of computation, the second approach — the decomposition of the birth sequence into one exponential and many damped oscillatory terms — is the one we shall follow here.

We shall be concerned in this chapter with four major topics: (1) how the sequence of births expressed as the sum of exponential functions (one real and an infinite number of complex exponentials) implies convergence, and how the exponents of the constituent functions can be calculated; (2) how specific characteristics of the fertility and mortality schedules govern the nature of the component exponential functions; (3) how characteristics of the initial age distribution interact with the fertility and mortality schedules to determine the coefficients of each exponential term; and (4) how the approach to stability can be visualized in some concrete examples.

The Sequence of Births as Sum of a Set of Exponential Functions, with Real and Complex Exponents

LOTKA'S PROOF THAT CONSTANT FERTILITY AND MORTALITY LEAD TO A STABLE POPULATION [1]

Lotka's proof of convergence provides a framework for exploring the factors that control the duration and nature of the transition from arbitrary initial conditions to the stable state. He first shows that a combination of a sequence of births that follows an exponential path [i.e., $B(t) = B(0)e^{rt}$] and an unchanging age schedule of mortality produces a population with a constant age distribution, birth rate, death rate, and rate of increase. He then proves that a fixed age schedule of fertility, combined with the fixed mortality schedule, leads eventually from arbitrary initial conditions to a birth sequence that is a real first order exponential function of time and therefore leads to a stable population. A brief outline of this part of the proof follows:

Suppose that a constant regime of fertility and mortality is imposed at $t = 0$, when there exists some arbitrary initial female age distribution. Subsequent female births will be the sum of two components — births occurring to women in the initial population, and births to women themselves born during the regime of constant fertility and mortality.

$$(3.1) \qquad B(t) = F(t) + \int_0^t B(t - a)p(a)m(a)da,$$

where $F(t)$ are births to the original population, $p(a)$ is the proportion surviving from birth to age a, and $m(a)$ is the annual rate of bearing female children at age a. After $t = \beta$ (the oldest age of nonzero fertility), $F(t) = 0$, and Equation (3.1) reduces to:

$$(3.2) \qquad B(t) = \int_0^\beta B(t - a)p(a)m(a)da \qquad (t \geqslant \beta).$$

63

Lotka solves the integral Equation (3.1) by finding a family of functions satisfying Equation (3.2) and selecting from this family members that satisfy Equation (3.1) for $t \leq \beta$. Equation (3.2) is satisfied by $B(t) = Qe^{rt}$, provided r is such that:

$$(3.3) \qquad \int_0^\beta e^{-ra} p(a)m(a)da = 1$$

as can be verified by substitution of $B(t) = Qe^{rt}$ in Equation (3.2). If $r_0, r_1, r_2 \cdots$ are values of r that satisfy Equation (3.3), then the birth sequence consists of the sum of exponentials, of which there are, in general, an infinite number.[2]

$$(3.4) \qquad B(t) = \sum_{i=0}^{\infty} Q_i e^{r_i t}.$$

The coefficients (Q_i) are chosen so that the birth sequence in Equation (3.4) conforms to Equation (3.1) for $t \leq \beta$.

The essence of Lotka's demonstration that the birth sequence becomes a real exponential function of time is to show that there is only one real (nonoscillatory) root of Equation (3.3), that it is larger than the real part of any complex root, and that consequently the nonoscillatory exponential term in the birth sequence defined by Equation (3.4) comes to exceed any preassigned multiple of the largest oscillatory term. The oscillatory terms become negligible relative to the one nonoscillatory exponential.

That there is only one real root of Equation (3.3) is easily seen. The left-hand side of Equation (3.3) is obviously a monotonically decreasing function of r along the real axis, since e^{-ra} and $p(a)m(a)$ are nonnegative, and e^{-ra} becomes smaller at every a as r is increased. Consequently, the integral can equal one for only one real value of r, which will be designated r_0.

Now consider a complex root $r = x + iy$. Substitution in Equation (3.3) leads to:

$$(3.5) \qquad \int_0^\beta e^{-xa-iya} \phi(a)da = 1 \quad \text{(where } \phi(a) = p(a)m(a)).$$

But $e^{-iya} = \cos(ya) - i \sin(ya)$. Hence

$$(3.6a) \qquad \int_0^\beta e^{-xa} \cos ya \phi(a)da = 1,$$

and

(3.6b)
$$\int_0^\beta e^{-xa} \sin ya\phi(a)da = 0.$$

Since $\cos ya = \cos(-ya)$, and since Equation (3.6b) is satisfied by $-y$ if by y, the complex roots occur in conjugate pairs. That the complex roots all have real parts smaller than r_0 is seen from a comparison of Equation (3.3) (satisfied by r_0) and Equation (3.6a) (which x must satisfy). The two integrals are the same, except that the one involving the real part of the complex root contains an additional factor, $\cos ya$. Cos ya has a maximum value of one, and must fall below one in any continuous interval of nonzero width, while $p(a)m(a)$ is above zero for an extended age range. Therefore, the presence of $\cos ya$ in the integral must serve to diminish it. Specifically, if x were equal to r_0, the integral in Equation (3.6a) would be less than one. In order to bring the integral up to one, the exponential term in Equation (3.6a) must be larger than in Equation (3.3), to make up for the diminishing effect of $\cos ya$. Therefore, e^{-xa} must be greater than e^{-r_0a} at every age, and x must be less than r_0.

CALCULATION OF THE ROOTS OF $\int_\alpha^\beta e^{-ra}\phi(a)da = 1$

A large number of roots of Equation (3.3) are readily calculated by the use of an electronic computer. The method is one of successive approximation starting with guessed values, as follows (Lotka [8], Coale [2]):

Let

(3.7)
$$Y = \int_0^\beta e^{-r_0a}\phi(a)da,$$

(3.8)
$$M_i = \int_0^\beta e^{-x_ia} \cos y_ia\phi(a)da,$$

(3.9)
$$N_i = \int_0^\beta e^{-x_ia} \sin y_ia\phi(a)da.$$

Then

(3.10)
$$\frac{dY}{dr_0} = -\int_0^\beta ae^{-r_0a}\phi(a)da = -\bar{A},$$

(3.11)
$$\frac{\partial M_i}{\partial x_i} = -\int_0^\beta ae^{-x_ia} \cos y_ia\phi(a)da = -G_i,$$

65

$$(3.12) \qquad \frac{\partial M_i}{\partial y_i} = -\int_0^\beta ae^{-x_ia} \sin y_ia\phi(a)da = -H_i,$$

$$(3.13) \qquad \frac{\partial N_i}{\partial x_i} = -\int_0^\beta ae^{-x_ia} \sin y_ia\phi(a)da = -H_i,$$

$$(3.14) \qquad \frac{\partial N_i}{\partial y_i} = \int_0^\beta ae^{-x_ia} \cos y_ia\phi(a)da = G_i.$$

Equations (3.7) and (3.10) are used to calculate the one real root; Equations (3.8), (3.9), and (3.11) through (3.14) to calculate complex roots. The real root (r_0) can be calculated by estimating an approximate value (r_0'), and substituting it in Equation (3.7) to determine $Y(r_0')$, and into Equation (3.10) to determine $\bar{A}(r_0')$. $Y(r_0') - 1$ is the "error" in the integral resulting from the "error" in r_0'. A second estimate can be calculated as:

$$(3.15) \qquad r_0'' = r_0' + \frac{Y(r_0') - 1}{\bar{A}(r_0')}.$$

Similarly, a guess of the value of a complex root, say $r_i' = x_i' + iy_i'$, can be substituted in the integrals given in Equations (3.8), (3.9), (3.11), and (3.12) to determine $M_i(r_i')$, $N_i(r_i')$, $G_i(r_i')$, and $H_i(r_i')$. Then, if r_i' is not too distant from r_i,

$$(3.16) \qquad M_i(r_i') - 1 \doteq -G_i(r_i')[x_i' - x_i] - H_i(r_i')[y_i' - y_i],$$

and

$$(3.17) \qquad N_i(r_i') \doteq -H(r_i')[x_i' - x_i] + G(r_i')[y_i' - y_i]$$

(because $dM = \dfrac{\partial M}{dx} dx + \dfrac{\partial M}{\partial y} dy$, and $dN = \dfrac{\partial N}{\partial x} dx + \dfrac{\partial N}{\partial y} dy$).

Solving Equations (3.16) and (3.17) for x_i and y_i leads to a second approximation r_i'', and the process can be repeated. If the initial guess is in an appropriate zone around one of the roots of Equation (3.3), convergent values of $r_i^{(n)}$ are obtained as is evident from a sequence of M's rapidly convergent on unity, and of N's convergent on zero. Other initial guesses, not located in a region of convergence in the neighborhood of a root, produce sequences that show no sign of converging even after a dozen steps.

To calculate the roots in this way, $\phi(a)$ must be approximated in a form that permits the evaluation of the integrals $y(r)$, $M(r)$, $N(r)$, etc. At the Office of Population Research, in finding the real root and the lowest frequency complex root of some 50 net fertility schedules, and in finding at least 50 complex roots of four of these, $\phi(a)$ was represented by a series of rectangles, one year in width, each rectangle equal to the recorded single-year age-specific fertility rate multiplied by survival factors — $p(a)$ — taken from a life table. In other words, net fertility was considered constant within each year of age, an assumption that made the approximate evaluation of the integrals simple.[3] At a later point we shall note the effect of alternative ways of representing $\phi(a)$ on the nature of the roots.

The IBM 7094 was programmed to try 12 successive steps in the sequence of approximations in each attempt to find a complex root. The lowest frequency pair of roots (roots with the smallest imaginary part; the roots occur in conjugate pairs) could always be found by beginning with $r'_1 = (r_0 - .08) + i(2\pi/\mu_1)$ where μ_1 is the mean age of net fertility. Subsequent roots were located by various systematic searching procedures. A method that missed only a few roots was to try increments in y (the imaginary part) of .05, and with each trial value of y to try x ranging from $(r_0 - .08)$ to $(r_0 - .26)$ in increments of .02. Procedures of this sort showed that roots above the 2nd or 3rd pair occurred at approximately constant increments in y, a fact that usually gave a clear signal — an unusually large gap — when a root had been missed in the preliminary search.

CALCULATION OF THE COEFFICIENTS (Q_i) IN $B(t) = \sum\limits_{i=0}^{\infty} Q_i e^{r_i t}$

An analytical expression for the sequence of births under a regime of constant net fertility requires a value of the coefficient (Q_i) for each exponential term whose exponent has been identified as a root of Equation (3.3) (see Equation (3.4)). Lotka has shown that:

(3.18)
$$Q_i = \frac{\displaystyle\int_0^\beta F(t) e^{-r_i t} dt}{\displaystyle\int_0^\beta a e^{-r_i a} \phi(a)\, da}.$$

The integral in the numerator of Equation (3.18) contains the product of $e^{-r_i t}$ and the number of births occurring at time t to the initial population of women. Equation (3.18) can be rewritten in a form that shows the separate roles in the determination of Q_i of the initial age distribution and of the net fertility function. Suppose $Q_i(a)$ is the value of Q_i that would be produced by a unit population element at age a, and $N(a)$ is the density at age a in the initial female population. Then

(3.19)
$$Q_i = \int_0^\beta Q_i(a)N(a)da,$$

where

(3.20)
$$Q_i(a) = \frac{\displaystyle\int_0^{\beta-a} e^{-r_i t}\phi(a+t)dt}{p(a)\displaystyle\int_0^\beta ae^{-r_i a}\phi(a)da},$$

which can be rewritten, after inserting $e^{-r_i a}$ inside the integral in the numerator of Equation (3.20) and $e^{r_i a}$ outside the integral, as:

(3.21)
$$Q_i(a) = \frac{e^{r_i a}\displaystyle\int_a^\beta e^{-r_i z}\phi(z)dz}{p(a)\displaystyle\int_0^\beta ae^{-r_i a}\phi(a)da},$$

where $z = a + t$. For the sole real root, Equation (3.21) becomes (Fisher [5], p. 27):

(3.22)
$$Q_0(a) = \frac{e^{r_0 a}\displaystyle\int_a^\beta e^{-r_0 z}\phi(z)dz}{\bar{A}p(a)},$$

where $\bar{A}$ is the mean age of childbearing in the stable population. For a complex root i, Equation (3.21) becomes:

(3.23)
$$Q_i(a) = \frac{\left\{e^{x_i a}(\cos y_i a + i \sin y_i a)\left[\displaystyle\int_a^\beta e^{-x_i z}\cos y_i z\phi(z)dz - i\int_a^\beta e^{-x_i z}\sin y_i z\phi(z)dz\right]\right\}}{p(a)\left[\displaystyle\int_0^\beta ae^{-x_i a}\cos y_i a\phi(a)da - i\int_0^\beta ae^{-x_i a}\sin y_i a\phi(a)da\right]},$$

or:

(3.24)
$$Q_i(a) = \frac{e^{x_i a}}{p(a)}\frac{(\cos y_i a + i \sin y_i a)(M_i(a) - iN_i(a))}{G_i - iH_i},$$

where

$$M_i(a) = \int_a^\beta e^{-x_i z}\cos y_i z\phi(z)dz, \quad \text{and} \quad N_i(a) = \int_a^\beta e^{-x_i z}\sin y_i z\phi(z)dz$$

and G_i and H_i are defined as in Equations (3.11) and (3.12).

If $Q_i(a)$ is expressed as $\bar{Q}_i(a)(\cos \theta_i(a) + i \sin \theta_i(a))$, where $\bar{Q}_i(a)$ is the absolute value of $Q_i(a)$,

$$(3.25) \qquad \bar{Q}_i(a) = \frac{e^{x_i a}}{p(a)} \left(\frac{M_i^2(a) + N_i^2(a)}{G_i^2 + H_i^2} \right)^{1/2},$$

and

$$(3.26) \qquad \theta_i(a) = y_i a - \arctan \frac{N_i(a)}{M_i(a)} + \arctan \frac{H_i}{G_i}.$$

As is evident from Equations (3.25) and (3.26), the conjugate roots $r_i = x + iy$ and $r_i' = x - iy$ have conjugate coefficients $Q_i(a) = A + iB$, and $Q_i'(a) = A - iB$. When $Q_i(a)e^{r_i t} + Q_i'(a)e^{r_i' t}$ is expressed in trigonometric form, the result is:

$$(3.27) \quad Q_i(a)e^{r_i t} + Q_i'(a)e^{r_i' t} = \frac{2e^{x_i a}}{p(a)} \left(\frac{M_i^2(a) + M_i^2(a)}{G_i^2 + H_i^2} \right)^{1/2}$$

$$e^{x_i t} \cos \left(y_i t + y_i a - \arctan \frac{N_i(a)}{M_i(a)} + \arctan \frac{H_i}{G_i} \right).$$

Thus the coefficients of the oscillatory component with a period $2\pi/y_i$ resulting from a population element at age a can be expressed as $2\bar{Q}_i(a)$, the initial magnitude of the component (the factor of 2 is occasioned by the complex conjugate roots), and $\bar{\theta}_i(a)$, the initial phase of the cosine. In short, Equation (3.27) can be rewritten simply as:

$$(3.28) \qquad Q_i(a)e^{r_i t} + Q_i'(a)e^{r_i' t} = 2\bar{Q}_i(a)e^{x_i t} \cos (y_i t + \theta_i(a)),$$

where $\bar{Q}_i(a)$ is defined by Equation (3.25), and $\theta_i(a)$ is defined by Equation (3.26). Note that when a is zero Equation (3.22) becomes:

$$(3.29) \qquad Q_0(0) = \frac{1}{A};$$

also:

$$(3.30) \qquad 2\bar{Q}_i(0) = \frac{2}{(G_i^2 + H_i^2)^{1/2}},$$

and

$$(3.31) \qquad \theta_i(0) = \arctan \frac{H_i}{G_i},$$

because $M_i(0) = 1$ and $N_i(0) = 0$ (cf. Equations (3.3), (3.6a), and (3.6b)).

If the oscillatory components of the birth sequence are expressed in trigonometric form, the term corresponding to the conjugate roots $x_i \pm y_i$ takes the form $2\bar{Q}_i e^{x_i t} \cos (y_i t + \theta_i)$, where

69

$$(3.32) \qquad \bar{Q}_i = \int_0^\beta N(a)\bar{Q}_i(a) \cos{(\theta_i(a) - \theta_i)}da,$$

and

$$(3.33) \qquad \theta_i = \arctan{\frac{\displaystyle\int_0^\beta N(a)\bar{Q}_i(a) \sin{\theta_i(a)}da}{\displaystyle\int_0^\beta N(a)\bar{Q}_i(a) \cos{\theta_i(a)}da}}.$$

Geometry of the Net Fertility Function and the Nature of the
Real and Complex Exponential Components of the Birth Series

The dependence of the real root of Equation (3.3) on the area under the net fertility function (the net reproduction rate, or the 0th moment) and on the mean length of generation (closely related to although not identical with the mean age of the net fertility function) is well known to demographers.

Moreover, the simple geometric argument by which Lotka proved convergence provides a basis for examining the factors that determine the frequency and rate of decay of the lowest frequency oscillatory term, and also for showing that all but the lowest frequency oscillation are subject to much more rapid attrition than this lowest frequency component. The proof of convergence shows that x_i must be smaller than r_0 because cos $y_i a$ diminishes the integral $\int_0^\beta e^{-x_i a} \cos{y_i a}\phi(a)da$. The rate of convergence depends on how much smaller x_i is than r_0, or on how great is the diminishing effect of cos $y_i a$ on the integral.

FACTORS GOVERNING THE FIRST (LOWEST FREQUENCY)
PAIR OF COMPLEX ROOTS

Suppose, initially, that there is a net fertility function that is symmetrical about its mean age, and that has an area (net reproduction rate) just large enough so that x_1 (the real part of the 1st conjugate pair of complex roots) is zero. Under these circumstances, the relative damping of the lowest frequency oscillations relative to the real exponential term is wholly embodied in the constant positive growth implied by a positive r_0, while the oscillations remain fixed in amplitude. Relative damping per year, $r_0 - x_1$, would of course equal r_0. It is always possible to multiply $\phi(a)$ by a scalar quantity (thus increasing or decreasing r_0) to make $x_1 = 0$. With net fertility symmetrical and x_1 equal to zero, what would be the period of lowest frequency oscillation, and how large would r_0 be?

It will be assumed that $\phi(a)$ has the general properties universally found in human net fertility schedules: a smooth departure from zero fertility beginning within a few years of age 15, a monotonic increase to a single maximum, followed by a monotonic decrease that reaches a small fraction of the maximum level by age 45 and zero a few years thereafter. Because of the assumption of symmetry, in this instance the maximum of $\phi(a)$ occurs at $(\alpha + \beta)/2$, where α and β are respectively the earliest and latest ages of childbearing.

The lowest frequency oscillation must satisfy Equations (3.6a) and (3.6b), which become, with $x_1 = 0$:

(3.34) $$\int_0^\beta \cos y_1 a \phi(a) da = 1$$

(3.35) $$\int_0^\beta \sin y_1 a \phi(a) da = 0.$$

The lowest frequency sine function that satisfies Equation (3.35) under the given conditions of symmetry is one that has a period equal to $2\mu_1$ (twice the mean of $\phi(a)$). Such a sine wave would have positive values from α to μ_1 and negative from μ_1 to β; the integral in Equation (3.35) would clearly be zero.

However, with $y_1 = \pi/\mu_1$, $\cos y_1 a$ would be negative over essentially all ages of nonzero fertility, and minus one at age of maximum fertility — clearly inconsistent with Equation (3.34). The lowest frequency satisfying *both* Equations (3.34) and (3.35) has a period equal to μ_1. At this frequency $\sin y_1 a$ is negative at ages below μ_1 and positive above, and symmetry assures that Equation (3.35) is exactly satisfied. $\cos y_1 a$ reaches plus one at the mean of the fertility function and is negative only below $3\mu_1/4$ and above $5\mu_1/4$. The ratio of

$$\frac{\int_0^\beta \phi(a) da}{\int_0^\beta \cos y_1 a \phi(a) da}$$

for the $\phi(a)$ shown in Figure 3.1 is 2.286, so if the vertical scale is adjusted to make $\int_0^\beta \cos y_1 a \phi(a) da = 1$, the net reproduction rate would be 2.286 and r_0 about .0263.

71

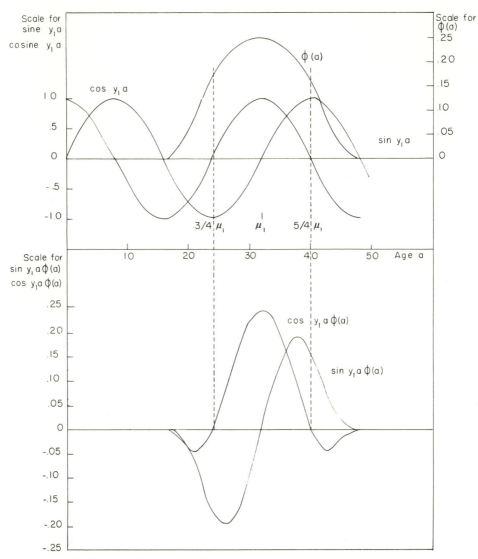

Figure 3.1. The constituent parts of:

$$\int_0^\beta e^{-x_1 a} \cos y_1 a \phi(a)da = 1$$

$$\int_0^\beta e^{-x_1 a} \sin y_1 a \phi(a)da = 0$$

when $\phi(a)$ is symmetrical, and $x_1 = 0$.

The quantity $\int_0^\beta \cos y_1 a\phi(a)da$ is less than $\int_0^\beta \phi(a)da$ because $\cos y_1 a$ is near unity only at ages near μ_1. The parts of $\phi(a)$ just inside $3/4\mu_1$ and $5/4\mu_1$ are multiplied by values of the cosine near zero, and the parts beyond $3/4\mu_1$ and $5/4\mu_1$ by negative values of the cosine. It is obvious that the relative decrement of the lowest frequency oscillatory root would be least when fertility is concentrated near the mean age of $\phi(a)$, and greatest when a high proportion of childbearing occurs near the extreme ages of the fertile span. Specifically, net fertility before $3\mu_1/4$ and after $5\mu_1/4$ contributes a *negative* area to the integral. This fact suggests that the relative annual decrement of the lowest frequency oscillations (i.e., $r_0 - x_1$) should be greater the greater the fraction of net fertility outside the limits $3\mu_1/4$ and $5\mu_1/4$, at least when $\phi(a)$ is symmetrical. In fact, because most observed net fertility schedules for large populations have positive values over roughly the same span of years, and are free of such irregularities as sudden fluctuations with age, those that have a larger fraction of net fertility before $3\mu_1/4$ and after $5\mu_1/4$ tend also to have a greater proportion of net fertility subject to attenuation because of multiplication by values of $\cos y_1 a$ near zero. In short, if all human net fertility schedules were symmetrical, the geometrical considerations just outlined (and illustrated in Figure 3.1) would suggest the likelihood of a close negative relationship between $r_0 - x_1$ and the fraction (F) of net fertility encompassed between $3/4$ and $5/4$ the mean age — at least when the level of fertility is such as to make x_1 equal to zero.

Asymmetry in $\phi(a)$ (in all observed net fertility schedules the mode and the median occur before the mean and in the majority markedly before) increases the tendency for $\int_0^\beta \cos y_1 a\phi(a)da$ to fall short of $\int_0^\beta \phi(a)da$. If as a first approximation y_1 is assumed, even with asymmetry, equal to $2\pi/\mu_1$, it is clear that the maximum value of $\phi(a)$ no longer occurs at an age where $\cos y_1 a$ equals one. In fact, the greater the asymmetry of $\phi(a)$, *ceteris paribus,* the greater the relative damping $(r_0 - x_1)$ that one would expect to find.

In these preliminary comments, it has been assumed that $\phi(a)$ has been adjusted in scale so that $x_1 = 0$, to simplify the geometry by eliminating the effect of the factor $e^{-x_1 a}$. Under this assumption, it appears plausible that $(r_0 - x_1)$ would be a closely defined monotonically decreasing function of F, the fraction of net fertility between $3\mu_1/4$

73

and $5\mu_1/4$, and also of V, the ratio median age of $\phi(a)$/mean age of $\phi(a)$, as an index of asymmetry.

An extensive empirical test of these relations has been made by calculating F, V, μ_1, y_1, and x_1 for 47 fertility functions that were recorded by single years of age, adjusted (by scalar multiplication) so that $r_0 = 0$. Exact values of x_1, y_1, G_1, and H_1 were calculated by the successive approximation procedure described earlier. The net fertility functions were recorded in the populations of Canada (4 dates from 1931 to 1961), Sweden (7 dates from 1891 to 1961), Norway (1930), the Ukraine (1926–27), Denmark (1950), Latvia (two dates in the 1930s), Finland (1950 and 1960), Belgium (7 dates from 1939 to 1960), the United States (1960), Hungary (1957 and 1960), France (five dates from 1925 to 1960), Portugal (4 dates from 1942 to 1960), Italy (1951), Poland (3 dates in the 1950s), Czechoslovakia (1930), Germany (1950 and 1960), Yugoslavia (1953 and 1960), and Cocos-Keeling Islands (1888–1947). The mean age of $\phi(a)$ ranges from 25.8 to 32.2 years, F ranges from .599 to .791, V from .956 to .995, and x_1 (when r_0 is held at zero) from −.053 to −.026.

First order, partial, and multiple correlations were calculated using these 47 schedules to see whether the postulated relations—that $r_0 - x_1$ should decrease as the fraction of fertility (F) between $3\mu_1/4$ and $5\mu_1/4$ increases, and also decrease as V (median/mode) increases toward unity—are strong and approximately linear. The partial correlation of $r_0 - x_1$ with F (V held constant) is −.917, and of $r_0 - x_1$ with V (F held constant) is −.970. (The multiple correlation of x_1 with V and F is .976.) Thus over the fairly extensive range of variation in age patterns of fertility in these schedules, the relationship of relative damping to the concentration of fertility within the range 3/4 to 5/4 of the mean age, and to an index of asymmetry, is remarkably close and linear.

The hypothesis that $r_0 - x_1$ is related to F and V arose out of a consideration of geometrical properties of net fertility schedules adjusted in scale so that x_1 is zero; and the hypothesis was confirmed by high correlation coefficients calculated for net fertility schedules adjusted in scale so that r_0 is zero. The relationships found under these artificially restricted conditions can be shown to have a broader validity by examining the change in $r_0 - x_1$ that occurs when the net fertility function is multiplied by a scalar $(1 + k)$. The change in $r_0 - x_1$ is easily found for small values of k by applying the method of calculating the roots r_0 and r_1 given in Equations (3.7) to (3.17). Suppose the real root of $\int_0^\beta e^{-ra}\phi(a)da = 1$ is r_0 and the lowest frequency pair of complex

74

roots is $x_1 \pm iy_1$. Now consider $\phi'(a) = (1 + k)\phi(a)$ where k is a small real number. The roots of $\int_0^\beta e^{-ra}\phi(a)da = 1$ can be used as the first approximation to $\int_0^\beta e^{-r'a}\phi'(a)da = 1$. We know that $Y(r_0) = 1$, $M_1(x_1,y_1) = 1$, and $N_1(x_1,y_1) = 0$ (Equations (3.7) to (3.9)). It is clear that multiplying $\phi(a)$ by $1 + k$ to produce $\phi'(a)$ implies that $Y'(r_0) = 1 + k$, $M'_1(x_1,y_1) = 1 + k$, and $N'_1(x_1,y_1) = 0$. Thus an approximation of r'_0 is $r_0 + k/\bar{A}(r_0)$ (Equations (3.10) and (3.15)), and of x'_1 is $x_1 + kG_1(r_0)/(G_1^2 + H_1^2)$ (an approximation of y'_1 is $y_1 + kH_1(r_0)/(G_1^2 + H_1^2)$). Thus for small values of k the ratio of the change in x_1 to the change in r_0 is given by:

$$(3.36) \qquad \frac{x'_1 - x_1}{r'_0 - r_0} = \frac{G_1\bar{A}}{G_1^2 + H_1^2}.$$

Among the 47 net fertility functions for which x_1, y_1, G_1, H_1, and $\bar{A}$ were calculated, $G_1\bar{A}/(G_1^2 + H_1^2)$ has a median value of .91, and 90% of the values fall between .84 and 1.02. Thus for small values of k the change in x_1 is ordinarily a little less than, but of the same order of magnitude as, the change in r_0. If the same relation holds for larger differences in the net reproduction rate (i.e., larger values of k), then the general magnitude of $r_0 - x_1$ established for $r_0 = 0$ could be considered representative of relative damping at other levels of r_0. Whether the relationship holds depends on whether $G_1\bar{A}/(G_1^2 + H_1^2)$ varies extensively or only slightly as $\phi(a)$ is multiplied by different scalars. To determine the variation of G_1, $\bar{A}$, and H_1 analytically would be complicated, but a simple empirical test with the 47 net fertility functions already referred to was performed as follows: (1) Each fertility function, normalized so that $\int_0^\beta \phi(a)da = 1$, was multiplied by $e^{.01972}\mu_1$ thus producing a $\phi'(a)$ such that $r'_0 = .020$.[4] (2) The exact value of x'_1 was calculated for each $\phi'(a)$ by the recursive method described earlier. (3) The expected value of x'_1 on the basis of Equation (3.36) was calculated, utilizing the values of $\bar{A}$, G_1, and H_1 associated with the original $\phi(a)$ (where $r_0 = 0$). Figure 3.2 shows the approximate calculations of $x'_1 - x_1$ plotted against the exact calculations. The fit is very close, although it is apparent that the estimates of the differences in x_1 are biased slightly downward. (The median error in the estimate of $x'_1 - x_1$ is only .0003; 90% of the errors are less than .001.) In short, Equation (3.36), which expresses the ratio of $(x'_1 - x_1)/(r'_0 - r_0)$ exactly when $\phi(a)$ is multiplied by a scalar that differs from one by a vanish-

75

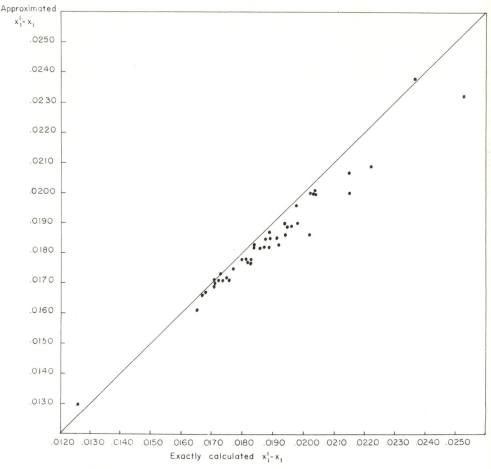

Figure 3.2. Difference in x_1 when $r_0 = 0.02$ and 0.00 in 47 net fertility schedules, estimated by $x_1' - x_1 = .02 G_1 \bar{A}/(G_1^2 + H_1^2)$ and calculated exactly.

ingly small quantity, is a very good approximation even for scalars of 1.7 to 1.9.

NUMERICAL ESTIMATION OF FIRST OSCILLATORY TERM BY REGRESSION

When the first complex roots of 47 net fertility functions (normalized so that $r_0 = 0$) were calculated on an electronic computer, the program provided for the calculation and print-out of x_1, y_1, G_1, H_1, $\bar{A}$ (or μ_1 when $r_0 = 0$), F (the fraction of net fertility function between $3\mu_1/4$ and $5\mu_1/4$, and V (median age of $\phi(a)$/mean age of $\phi(a)$). These printed values provided the basis for the multiple and partial correlations involving x, F, and V described earlier. The parameters of $\phi(a)$ that are readily computed on a desk calculator are μ_1 (the mean age of $\phi(a)$), V, and F. The multiple correlation of .976 between x_1 and (V, F) implies that x_1 can be closely determined by a regression equation from these readily computed quantities, when $r_0 = 0$. Multiple correlations of $2\pi/y_1$ (the period of the lowest frequency oscillation), and of G_1 and H_1 with $\mu_1 F$, and V are .997, .969, and .955 respectively, so that these parameters can be estimated from μ_1, F, and V also. The regression equations are:

$$(3.37) \quad x_1 = -.6260 + .09673F + .5319V,$$

$$(3.38) \quad \frac{2\pi}{y_1} = -34.626 - 12.9811F + 45.445V + 1.0047\mu_1,$$

$$(3.39) \quad G_1 = -302.5968 - 24.4936F + 345.1856V + .3788\mu_1,$$

$$(3.40) \quad H_1 = 96.6158 - 56.0747F - 62.2684V + .6393\mu_1.$$

With Equations (3.37) to (3.40) it is not difficult to calculate approximately the first complex root of any net fertility function. One determines the mean age μ_1 of $\phi(a)$ (which equals A when $r_0 = 0$), F, and V. Then from Equations (3.37) to (3.40) estimates of x_1, $2\pi/y_1$, G_1, and H_1 are obtained when $\phi(a)$ has been normalized to $\hat{\phi}(a)$ such that $\int_0^\beta \hat{\phi}(a)da = 1$. The value of r_0 for the given $\phi(a)$ can be estimated (Coale and Demeny [3], p. 31) from:

$$(3.41) \qquad r_0 = \frac{\log \int_0^\beta \phi(a)da}{\mu_1 - .7 \log \int_0^\beta \phi(a)da}.$$

Finally x_1 can be estimated, for the given $\phi(a)$, by Equation (3.37), and y_1 from Equation (3.42):

$$(3.42) \qquad \frac{y_1' - y_1}{r_0' - r_0} = \frac{H_1 \bar{A}}{G_1^2 + H_1^2}.$$

This procedure can be illustrated by employing it to estimate x_1 and y_1 for the net fertility of Swedish women, 1946–50. This schedule was not one of the 47 used to calculate the regression equations, but values for single years of age are available, so that exact values of x_1 and y_1 could be determined on the electronic computer. For this schedule $\mu_1 = 28.458$. $F = .7122$, $V = .9759$, $\int_0^\beta \phi(a)da = 1.1372$. From Equations (3.37) and (3.38) one can estimate the $\hat{x}_1$ and $\hat{y}_1$ for $\hat{\phi}(a) = \phi(a)/1.1372$. The estimates are: $\hat{x}_1 = -.0380$ and $\hat{y}_1 = .2135$. Then, approximating G_1 and H_1 from Equations (3.39) and (3.40), and applying Equations (3.36) and (3.41) to determine the difference in x_1 and y_1 when r_0 is (Equation (3.41)) $.00453$ instead of zero, one obtains estimates of: $x_1 = -.0344$ and $y_1 = .2154$. The exact values are $-.0349$ and $.2159$ respectively.

FACTORS GOVERNING THE SECOND AND THIRD PAIRS OF

COMPLEX ROOTS OF $\displaystyle\int_0^\beta e^{-ra}\phi(a)da = 1$

The relative decrement of the lowest frequency oscillatory component of $B(t)$ has been shown to depend on the symmetry of $\phi(a)$ and the fraction of fertility within the limits 3/4 to 5/4 the mean age on the basis of a consideration of the factors causing x_1 to be less than r_0. The period of this component can be seen, on similarly intuitive grounds, to be about equal to $2\pi/\mu_1$. These impressions are confirmed, and provide the basis for closely approximate numerical calculation of x_1 and y_1 by a combination of empirical relations (among 47 net fertility schedules) and mathematical analysis. We shall not examine in equal detail the factors affecting the nature of higher frequency terms in $B(t)$, but will comment briefly on the frequency and relative attenuation of the two oscillatory components next in frequency above y. Roots at the second and third lowest frequencies were calculated for 42 net fertility functions, and the following empirically based observations can be made as a result.

(1) The second pair of roots occur with a frequency of about one cycle every 20 years. The period $(2\pi/y_2)$ is related (multiple $R = .861$) to μ_1, to the proportion of fertility occurring between $3\mu_1/4$ and $5\mu_1/4$ (F), and to the ratio of the median to the mean (V). The period of the second oscillatory term is greater for higher mean ages of net fertility, for less symmetrical fertility functions, and for less concentrated fertility (smaller values of F). The period of the second oscillatory component shows less relative variation about its mean (standard deviation/mean $= .045$) than the first component (.062) in the 42 fertility functions for which both were calculated. The average annual decrement of the second component relative to the real exponential is $.097$. In all but one instance among the 42 fertility schedules, $r_0 - x_2$ was greater than twice $r_0 - x_1$. The relative decrement ($r_0 - x_2$) was very strongly correlated (multiple $R = .977$) with μ_1, F, and V. The

relative decrement was greater the more concentrated was net fertility (i.e., the greater the value of F), the less the mean age (μ_1), and the less the symmetry (the farther the mean from the median). The opposite relations of $r_0 - x_1$ and $r_0 - x_2$ to F follow from the fact that the period of the first oscillatory component approximately coincides with μ_1 so that the concentration of fertility near the mean diminishes the attenuating effect of cos $y_1 a$ whereas y_2 has a period neither equal to nor an integral submultiple of μ_1; in fact, typically cos $y_2 \mu_1$ is negative, and concentration of fertility near the mean *increases* the attenuating effect of cos $y_2 a$.

(2) The third pair of roots occur with an imaginary part (y_3) that is with few exceptions very close to $y_1 + .270$ (within .001 in more than 85% of the schedules), giving an average period of about 13 years to these oscillatory terms. The average annual decrement ($r_0 - x_3$) is about .099, only slightly greater than the average of ($r_0 - x_2$). In fact for about one third of the fertility schedules, the decrement of the third oscillatory component was less than of the second. ($r_0 - x_3$) is correlated, although much less strongly than ($r_0 - x_2$), with F, V, and μ_1 (multiple $R = .776$).

COMPLEX ROOTS OF $\int_0^\beta e^{-ra}\phi(a)da = 1$ AT FREQUENCIES
HIGHER THAN THE THIRD

What we can say about complex roots at frequencies higher than the third is based partly on abstract analysis, and partly on the calculation of many roots of several different net fertility schedules.

To calculate roots of the integral equation by the iterative procedure we have used, integrals of the product of the net fertility function and exponential and sinusoidal factors must be evaluated. The latter functions are of course precisely calculable at any age. If we suppose the population observed to be sufficiently large and age at death and at maternity to be recorded with sufficient precision, we can imagine determining net fertility for age intervals as narrow as we please. In finite populations, however, erratic fluctuations in fertility and mortality with age would be recorded if age intervals were very narrow. To circumvent problems arising from such considerations, continuous functions of fertility and mortality that would be experienced by an indefinitely large population are usually assumed to exist. The roots that are sought are the roots of an integral equation incorporating this continuous "true" net fertility function.

Suppose that the "true" net fertility function had been recorded in as fine detail as we please. We could approximate the integrals that must be evaluated by various procedures including:

(1) representing the exponential, the sine and cosine functions, and the net fertility function as rectangles over progressively narrower age intervals until further narrowing had a negligible effect;

(2) representing the net fertility function as a series of rectangles at progressively narrower intervals, calculating the area under the product of the exponential, the sinusoidal function, and this rectangle within each interval, until further narrowing had little effect; or

(3) representing the net fertility function as a series of progressively narrower trapezoids, the slope of each trapezoid representing the change in fertility from one interval to the next, and calculating the area under the product of the exponential, the sinusoidal function, and the trapezoid until further narrowing had little effect.

Recorded data on fertility are not in the form of continuous functions of age, but rather in the form of average values over intervals that at best are of one year's duration. The nature of the data thus precludes trying intervals of shorter and shorter duration — below one year, anyway. We have employed three systems of approximation in calculating the roots: (1) representing all functions as one-year-wide rectangles (equivalent to defining each function only at the mid-point of each year); (2) representing net fertility as a series of one-year-wide rectangles; and (3) representing fertility as one-year-wide trapezoids, in the latter two instances calculating the precise integral of the product of the three functions within each one-year interval. We cannot directly infer the result of progressively narrowing the intervals on the calculation of roots, but the fact that the three methods of calculation give virtually identical values for the ten to twelve pairs of complex roots of lowest frequency implies that finer subdivision would have no effects on these roots, and that they are valid figures for the roots of the "real" net fertility function. (Comparisons are seen in Figures 3.3 and 3.5.)

The roots calculated when net fertility is represented as a series of narrow rectangles and alternatively as a series of narrow trapezoids are best interpreted as the roots of two alternative (fictitious) sched-

80

ules, and differences in the roots do not reflect merely differences in technique of calculation, but genuine differences in two fertility functions. Specifically, if fertility consisted of a series of one-year trapezoids on the one hand or of one-year rectangles on the other, the birth sequence from certain initial populations would be different, requiring that the roots of the two integral equations differ. However the roots differ only for higher frequency terms and these are strongly damped. Hence after a generation the alternative net fertility schedules —and the "true" schedule—have the same birth sequence.

A particularly extensive set of calculations was made of the roots of a schedule combining the age-specific fertility of Swedish women in 1891–1900 and mortality from the "West" model life tables, $e_0^0 = 70$ years, the resultant net fertility normalized so that $NRR = 1$.

Roots were calculated for a version of net fertility in the form of one-year-wide rectangles equaling in height the recorded values of $\phi(a)$, and for a version in the form of a polygon formed by connecting successive annual values by straight lines. Figure 3.3 shows the resultant sequences of roots for these slightly different net fertility schedules. (Some of the roots were missed by the search procedures, especially for the trapezoidal schedule, but the relation between the two sets of roots is nevertheless clearly visible.) The most striking characteristic seen in Figure 3.3 is (for the "rectangular" net fertility function) the repetitious cycle of variation in the real part of the roots as frequency increases, superimposed on a gradually rising trend of $(-x_i)$ with frequency. Note that there is a large dip in attenuation for values of y_i in the neighborhood of multiples of 2π. These dips resemble points of "resonance" (reduced attenuation near critical frequencies) in an electrical network. Note that the frequencies when the dips occur are one cycle per year and its harmonics, suggesting that the dips are associated with the sharp changes at one-year intervals inherent in the "rectangular" fertility function. This explanation of the dips is confirmed in two ways: (1) the dip in the neighborhood of $y = 2\pi$ is much less pronounced in the trapezoidal fertility schedule (where it is associated merely with abrupt annual changes in the slope of $\phi(a)$, not in $\phi(a)$ itself); and (2) calculation of

$$\frac{1}{A} e^{r_0 t} + \sum_{i=1}^{266} \frac{2e^{x_i t}}{(G_i^2 + H_i^2)^{1/2}} \cos\left(y_i t + \arctan \frac{H_i}{G_i}\right)$$

—approximating the birth sequence with a rectangular fertility schedule and an initial population consisting of an element at age zero—

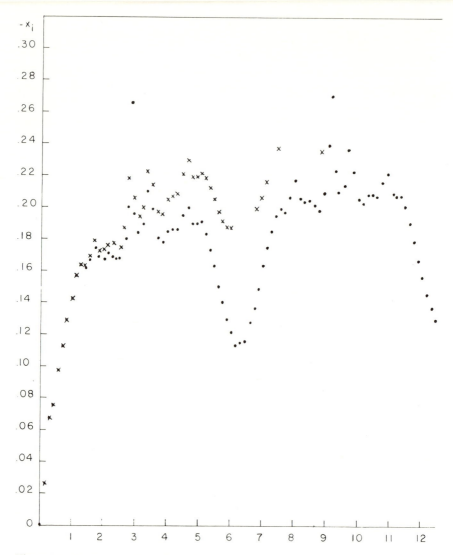

Figure 3.3. Components (x_1 and y_1) of complex roots of

$$\int_0^\beta e^{-r_i a}\phi(a)da = 1;$$

shows, when plotted at intervals of 0.1 year from age 16 to 35, a visible tendency to trace out (as it should) a rectangular $\phi(a)$ (Figure 3.4). Clearly the "spectrum" of frequencies and rates of attenuation for large values of y_i is strongly affected by the fine structure of the fertility schedule. For this reason the "true" spectrum at high frequencies could be calculated only by using an analytical representa-

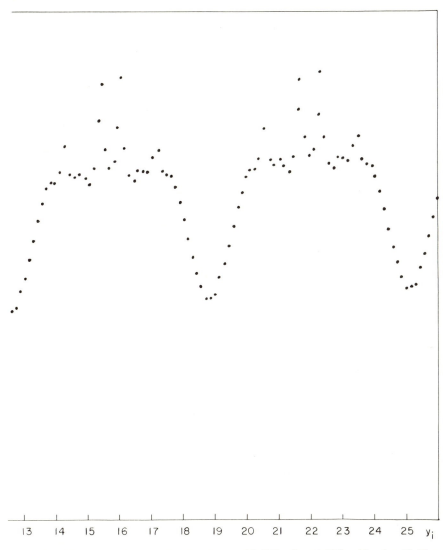

net fertility of Swedish females 1891–1900, with "West" model life table, $e_0^0 = 70$. Fertility represented as: rectangles one year in width at each age (• • •); trapezoids one year in width (x x x).

tion of the fertility function that fits the actual schedule in detail. Since, in fact, the net fertility schedule is not usually observed in greater detail than average values by single years of age, it might properly be said that "true" values of the roots beyond the first 10 or 15 cannot be determined.

At low frequencies, as noted earlier, the values of the roots are vir-

83

tually the same for fertility schedules that differ only in "fine structure." That this should be so is intuitively clear if one pictures the area
under a low frequency sine curve multiplied by various functions, each
with the same average value within each short interval, but differing
from each other within such intervals. The low frequency sine curve is
virtually constant within the short intervals; hence the alternative
functions would yield the same integrals. The integrals differ only when
the period of the sinusoidal function is of the same order of magnitude
as the interval within which the alternative functions differ.

Fifty or more pairs of complex roots were calculated for four different net fertility schedules. In each instance the intervals in frequency
between successive pairs of roots above the second or third were approximately constant, and not very different for the different schedules.
It can be shown that the average interval in the imaginary part between
pairs of roots in the first N roots, if N is a moderately large number,
must be $2\pi/\beta$, by the following argument: Suppose $\phi(a)$ is approximated by net fertility defined only at discrete ages — ages including the
integers $(15, 16, \cdots$ etc.$)$, and uniform-width subdivisions of the years
between the integers $(15 + 1/n, 15 + 2/n, 15 + (n - 1)/n, 16)$.

Then the fundamental equation $\int_0^\beta e^{-ra}\phi(a)da = 1$ is approximated
by

(3.43) $$\sum_{j=0}^{n\beta} Z^{-j/n}\phi(j/n) = 1.$$

Equation (3.43) has exactly $n\beta$ roots. One and only one is real and
positive. If $n\beta$ is even, there must be an odd number (usually one) of
real negative roots because the complex roots occur as complex conjugates.

All roots Z_i, whether real positive, real negative, or complex, can
be replaced by e^{r_i}, where r_i is chosen so that $e^{-r_i a} = Z_i^{-a}$ for those values of $a(j/n)$ for which $\phi(a)$ is defined. For the real positive root,
$r_0 = \log Z_0$. Any real negative root can be replaced by a conjugate pair
of complex roots $r = x \pm iy$, where $x = \log |Z|$ and $y = \pi$.

The term in $B(t)$ corresponding to a negative root of the form
$Q(Z)^{(j/n)t}$ is thus replaced by $Qe^{[\log |Z|]t} \cos(\pi jt/n)$. Complex conjugate
pairs of roots of Equation (3.43) $M + iN$ are replaced by $r = \log(M + iN)$ and $r' = \log(M - iN)$.

Now suppose $n = 1$ — that $\phi(a)$ is represented at intervals of one
year. Suppose β is odd, and there are no multiple roots. Then there

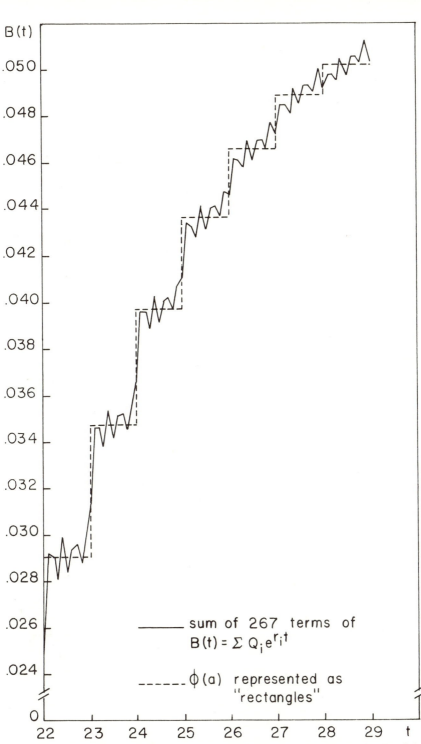

Figure 3.4. The real exponential birth sequence plus the sum of 267 terms, for Swedish fertility, 1891–1900, combined with mortality model "West" females, $e_0^0 = 70$, with initial age distribution an element at age zero. For $t = 22$ to $t = 29$, at intervals of 0.1 year.

will be $(\beta - 1)/2$ complex pairs of roots; or $(\beta - 1)/2$ components at frequencies other than zero. Let $x \pm iy$ be one pair of complex roots, then $x \pm iy'$ also satisfy the equation, where $y' = 2\pi - y$ because $\cos y_i' a = \cos y_i a$, and $\sin y_i' = -\sin y_i a$. Hence the roots all have "mirror images" around $i\pi$. Between zero and 2π, then, there will be $\beta - 1$ apparent values of y other than zero, or β altogether, for an average interval between consecutive values of y of $2\pi/\beta$. Because of symmetry, the spacing between the genuine roots is the same as in the "mirror image" roots.

If $n = 2, 3, 4, \cdots$ —if $\phi(a)$ is represented at half-years, one-third years, one-quarter years, etc.—there will be $(n\beta - 1)/2$ frequencies other than zero (if $n\beta$ is even, one of these will be associated with the negative root).

The "mirror image" roots now occur at $y' = 2n\pi - y$, symmetrical with $n\pi$. Hence there will be $n\beta$ frequencies in an interval of $2n\pi$ or again an average interval of $2\pi/\beta$ between consecutive values of y. As n grows larger, the approximation of the roots of the discrete $\phi(a)$ equation to the roots of the continuous version becomes closer, yet the average spacing remains exactly $2\pi/\beta$. Because of symmetry, the spacing of frequencies up to $n\pi$—where the genuine complex roots are found—is the same as to $2n\pi$. Thus the average spacing between consecutive values of y is always $2\pi/\beta$, and the average frequency increment is $1/\beta$.

As y_i increases—as the frequency of oscillation rises—there is a general tendency for the relative decrement to increase, or for x_i to diminish (become more negative). The increase in $r_0 - x_i$ with frequency can be understood intuitively as a natural effect of more cycles of $\cos y_i a$ between α and β—say 30 cycles instead of 10—causing a greater tendency for positive and negative half cycles to cancel, thus increasing the attenuating effect of $\cos y_i a$ on $\int_0^\beta e^{-x_i a} \cos y_i a \phi(a) da$.

It is, for example, readily evident why attenuation tends to be much less for the lowest frequency root than for any other. This is the only root creating values of $\cos ya$ that are positive throughout the central portion of $\phi(a)$, and values near one when $\phi(a)$ is a maximum. This general tendency becomes a rigorous asymptotic property of the roots as y_i becomes indefinitely large: as $y_i \to \infty$, $x_i \to -\infty$. At very high frequencies, adjacent positive and negative loops of $\cos y_i a (e^{-x_i a} \phi(a))$ would tend to cancel, unless x_i took on very large negative values. If x_i is given any finite preassigned value, y_i can be chosen so large that the ratio of adjacent positive and negative loops in every portion of $\cos y_i a (e^{-x_i a} \phi(a))$ is as close to unity as one pleases, and hence $\int_0^\beta \cos y_i a e^{-x_i a} \phi(a) da$ would be as close to zero as one pleases, and could not equal one. Only if $-x_i$ also increases without limit can a ratio of positive to negative areas differing from one by a finite amount be maintained, making it possible for $\int_0^\beta \cos y_i a e^{-x_i a} \phi(a) da$ to equal one.

As $y_i \to \infty$, the interval between adjacent frequencies approaches uniformity, at the average value (established above) of $1/\beta$. The approach of $y_{i+1} - y_i$ to a uniform value of $2\pi/\beta$ as $y_i \to \infty$, is related to the indefinite increase in $(-x_i)$ as frequency increases. The equality of $\int_0^\beta \cos y_i a e^{-x_i a} \phi(a) da$ to one and of $\int_0^\beta \sin y_i a e^{-x_i a} \phi(a) da$ to zero for large values of y_i is determined by relations in a small region adjacent to β, because as $-x_i$ increases, the area of $e - x_i a \phi(a)$ everywhere except in the neighborhood of β becomes negligible. Suppose y_i' is the imaginary part of a very high frequency (large y) root of $\int_0^\beta e^{r_i a} \phi(a) da =$ 1. Consider the relation of $\cos y_i'' a$ to $\cos y_i' a$, and of $\sin y_i'' a$ to $\sin y_i' a$ in the neighborhood of $a = \beta$, when $y_i'' = y_i' + 2\pi/\beta$. There will be exactly one more cycle of each sinusoidal function between zero and β for y_i'' than for y_i'; hence $\sin y'' \beta = \sin y' \beta$, and $\cos y'' \beta = \cos y' \beta$. At age $\beta - \Delta$, the phase difference in the sine and cosine of $y''(\beta - \Delta)$ and $y'(\beta - \Delta)$ is $(\Delta/\beta)2\pi$, which can be made as small as one pleases by choosing a small enough Δ. But because $-x_i$ approaches infinity as y_i does, high frequency roots ultimately become determined by relations within the region $(\beta - \Delta)$ to β, and $\Delta \to 0$ as $y_i \to \infty$. But as $\Delta \to 0$, $\sin y'' a \to \sin y' a$, and $\cos y'' a \to \cos y' a$ for all a in the interval $(\beta - \Delta)$ to β. Hence if y' is the imaginary component of a root, so is y'', and thus $y_{i+1} - y_i \to 2\pi/\beta$ as $y_i \to \infty$.

It was shown earlier that the average interval between successive values of y from zero to y_n is $2\pi/\beta$; yet in calculating the complex root of four net fertility functions expressed as rectangles, the average increment in y was always greater than $2\pi/\beta$—ranging from $2\pi/(\beta - 2)$ to $2\pi/(\beta - 7)(\beta \doteq 50)$. On reflection, and after experiment, it has become evident that the greater average spacing found in calculating these roots arose because some roots were missed—roots with unusually high attenuation.

The basis for this explanation is as follows: Calculation of roots when the net fertility function of Yugoslavia, 1960, is expressed as a series of points at exact ages 13.5, 14.5 · · · 50.5 should lead to exactly 101 roots: one real positive root, and 50 pairs of complex roots. A slight variation of an argument used earlier (p. 84) shows that these 50 frequencies will occur before $y_i = 2\pi$, so counting the real root (frequency equals zero), there should be β frequencies between zero and 2π —and, of course, $\beta = 51$. We have used the successive approximation procedure described earlier (Equations (3.11) to (3.17)) to search

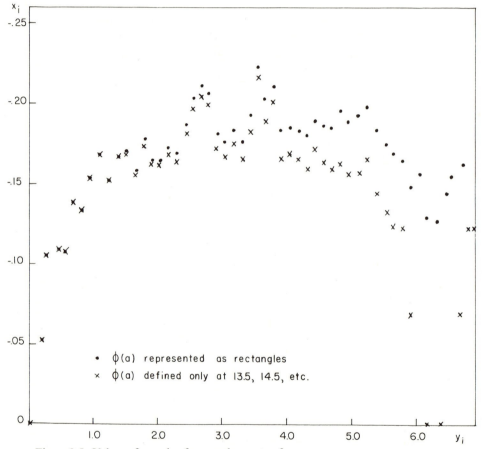

Figure 3.5. Values of x_i and y_i for complex roots of:

$$\int_0^r e^{-ra}\phi(a)da = 1$$

with an imaginary part less than 6.8; fertility of Yugoslavia 1960; mortality, "West" female model life table, $e_0^0 = 70$ years, net fertility normalized so that N.P.R = 1. $\phi(a)$ represented by "rectangles" one year in width; $\phi(a)$ represented by points at center of each single-year age interval.

for these roots, when $\phi(a)$ is taken as defined only at ages 13.5, 14.5 $\cdots$ 50.5, and the integral is approximated by a sum. The roots located in this way are virtually the same as those obtained by representing $\phi(a)$ as rectangles at low frequencies, but when $\phi(a)$ is considered as defined only at isolated points, x_i falls almost to zero in the neighborhood of $y_i = 2\pi$. (See Figure 3.5.) (If $\phi(a)$ were represented at 14.0, 15.0 $\cdots$ 51.0, instead of at midyear points, the "roots" would be symmetrical about $y_i = \pi$, and there would be a root exactly at $y = 2\pi$, $x = 0$.) However, the roots located in both instances — when $\phi(a)$ is represented as isolated points, and as rectangles — contain less than 51 frequencies; hence some roots have been missed in the search. A reason that some roots have been missed can be conjectured by imagining $\phi(a)$ to be extended to age $\beta + 1$ by adding a net fertility at age 51.5 of $\phi(50.5)/1,000$. In the discrete representation, we know that there must now be 51 pairs of complex roots, plus one real root, or 52 frequencies. Yet surely the previously calculated roots cannot be much affected by the addition of such a trivial net fertility at the next highest age. The additional pair of roots must be found somewhere between two previous pairs, and must be very "weak": with a large negative x_i, or a very large annual attenuation. In the recorded net fertility functions, the last age for which a nonzero value is recorded has a very small net fertility, and is by this argument associated with a pair of roots with a relatively high attenuation.

This line of reasoning led us to expect that missing roots might be found between previously located pairs with above average spacing in frequency, and with values of $r_0 - x_i$ above their neighbors, an expectation that led to locating roots previously missed. Hence the complex part of roots of exceptionally high attenuation, and the extent of this exceptional attenuation, are apparently determined by the way that $\phi(a)$ comes to zero in the neighborhood of $a = \beta$.

SUMMARY OF THE NATURE OF THE INFLUENCE OF $\phi(a)$ ON THE TERMS IN $B(t) = \Sigma_{t=0}^{\infty} Q_i e^{r_i t}$

The lowest frequency oscillations in the sequence of births that occur if net fertility is constant beginning with arbitrary initial conditions have a period approximately equal to μ_1, and are damped relative to the exponentially changing birth sequence by about 2.5% to over 5% annually, the degree of relative attenuation depending on asymmetry and on the proportion of net fertility occurring before $\tfrac{3}{4}$ and after $\tfrac{5}{4}$ the mean age. Among 47 empirical schedules examined, the least attenuation of low frequency oscillations would occur with late nineteenth century Swedish fertility, a schedule that is remarkably symmetrical, and that has a high proportion within $(^3/_4)\mu_1$ to $(^5/_4)\mu_1$, partly because of the high value of μ_1 (over 32 years). Attenuations of the lowest frequency oscillations of more than 4% annually occur in schedules where fertility begins early because of early marriage, and is markedly asymmetrical because of a high degree of fertility control among older women, notably in fertility schedules since 1950 in the United States, Canada, Finland, Hungary, Poland, and Yugoslovia, and in France during the 1930s. High attenuation also occurs in fertility schedules where marriage is early, and little birth control is practiced (the Ukraine in 1926–27, and the Cocos-Keeling Islands), because a large fraction of net fertility occurs before $3\mu_1/4$ and after $5\mu_1/4$.

Higher frequency oscillations are attenuated much more rapidly — at least twice as rapidly as the lowest frequency sinusoidal component. With annual relative decrements of at least 6 to 12%, all oscillations except those of longest period would not exceed $^1/_{20}$ of their original value after the passage of 30 to 50 years, whereas with an annual relative decrement of 2.5 to 5%, low frequency oscillations would maintain $^1/_{20}$ of their initial amplitude relative to the exponential for 60 to 120 years.

Attenuation of oscillatory terms increases with frequency, approaching infinity as frequency does. In four schedules analyzed in detail, attenuation reached 15% annually for oscillations with a period of about six years. Increments in angular frequency of successively more rapid oscillations average $2\pi/\beta$, with smaller intervals surrounding roots associated with $\phi(a)$ in the neighborhood of β — roots having smaller values of x than those of adjacent frequency. As frequency and attenuation approach infinity, increments in the imaginary component become uniform — at $2\pi/\beta$ — and the attenuation of roots at adjacent frequencies approaches uniformity.

The Initial Magnitude of the Components of B(t)

The process of the convergence of a population from an arbitrary initial form to a stable form can be viewed as follows:

(1) The roots of the integral equation (dependent on $\phi(a)$ — the net fertility function — but independent of $N(a)$ — the age distribution) determine the frequencies of oscillations and the rates of increase or decay of the components of $B(t)$.

(2) The interaction of $N(a)$ and $\phi(a)$ determines the initial amplitude and phase of each term of $B(t)$.

(3) As time passes, the oscillatory components diminish relative to the real exponential until they become negligible.

(4) No more than ω years (ω is the greatest age attained) after the births are exponential, the age distribution is stable. We can define the stabilization of the *birth sequence* as occurring at the moment when there are no further deviations from the exponential in excess of an arbitrary small value, say 2%. The *population* may be considered essentially stabilized when the ratio of each annual age group to current annual births is a multiple arbitrarily close to one — say .98 to 1.02 — of the ratio in the stable population.

To this point we have been concerned with the way that characteristics of the net fertility function determine the frequencies and the relative damping of the oscillatory terms in the birth sequence. We have seen that the lowest frequency term, with a period comparable to the mean age of the fertility schedule, is damped at a rate of 2½ to 5% annually relative to the real exponential, that the next two frequencies, with periods of about 20 years and 13 years respectively, are almost always damped at least twice as rapidly as the low frequency term, and that still higher frequencies are damped still more rapidly. The principal question that remains to be answered about this representation of the approach to stability is how large are the various components of $B(t)$ at the outset, since it is their initial size as well as the rate of damping that determines how long it will be before the last relative deviation from the exponential becomes less than 2%. We shall see that deviations from an exponential birth sequence arise because of differences between the age distribution of the initial population under age β and a stable age distribution over this range, and that the largest possible relative amplitude of oscillatory terms — at least of all but the lowest frequency term — results from an initial age distribution consisting wholly of a population element at age 0. With this initial age distribution and the fertility function that has (among those examined) the slowest damping of the low frequency term, about 165 years would be required to reach the last deviation of 2% from the exponential birth sequence, and therefore well over 200 years would be required to satisfy our definition of a stable population with these initial conditions. Of course, such an initial population is wholly hypothetical. At the opposite extreme, an initial population that exactly matched the stable at ages up to β would have a purely exponential birth sequence from the outset and the population would become stable after any groups over age β of unusual size (i.e., deviating substantially from the stable) had reached age ω.

We turn now to an examination of the factors that determine the size at $t = 0$ of the real exponential term and the various oscillatory terms in $B(t)$.

$Q_i(a)$ FOR DIFFERENT FREQUENCIES

At an earlier stage we developed expressions for the coefficients Q_i of the various terms in the birth sequence as a function of the initial age distribution and of the coefficient that would be generated by a unit population element at each age (see Equations (3.19), (3.32), and (3.33)). In the expression $Q_i = \int_0^\beta N(a)Q_i(a)da$, $N(a)$ is nothing other than the age distribution itself up to age β; and $Q_i(a)$ is wholly determined by $\phi(a)$. The next question is how $Q_i(a)$ varies with age. Equation (3.22) shows the factors that determine $Q_0(a)$.

$$(3.22) \qquad Q_0(a) = \frac{e^{r_0 a} \int_a^\beta e^{-r_0 z}\phi(z)dz}{\bar{A}p(a)}.$$

It should be noted again that at $a = 0$ the value of the integral in Equation (3.22) is one because r_0 is a root of the integral equation, that the exponential outside of the integral sign in the numerator is one, and so is $p(a)$; hence $Q_0(0)$ is simply $1/\bar{A}$. For a between 0 and α the value of the integral remains at 1 and $Q_0(a)$ increases or decreases according to the relative change in $e^{r_0 a}$ on the one hand and $p(a)$ on the other. If the sign of the exponent is changed and the exponential term is moved to the denominator, Equation (3.22) can be rewritten as:

$$(3.44) \qquad Q_0(a) = \frac{b}{\bar{A}} \cdot \frac{1}{c(a)} \cdot \int_a^\beta e^{-r_0 z}\phi(z)dz,$$

where $c(a)$ is the proportion at age a in the stable age distribution. As a advances from α to β the value of the integral falls from 1 to 0 monotonically, if r_0 is nonnegative. If r_0 is 0, that is, if the net reproduction rate is 1, the integral is simply the cumulated fertility schedule from β back to age a. Figure 3.6 shows $Q(a)$ for the real exponential term ($Q_0(a)$), for the lowest frequency oscillatory term ($Q_1(a)$) and for the sixth oscillatory term ($Q_6(a)$) based on the net fertility of Sweden 1946–50. (We shall later use this fertility schedule and various initial

92

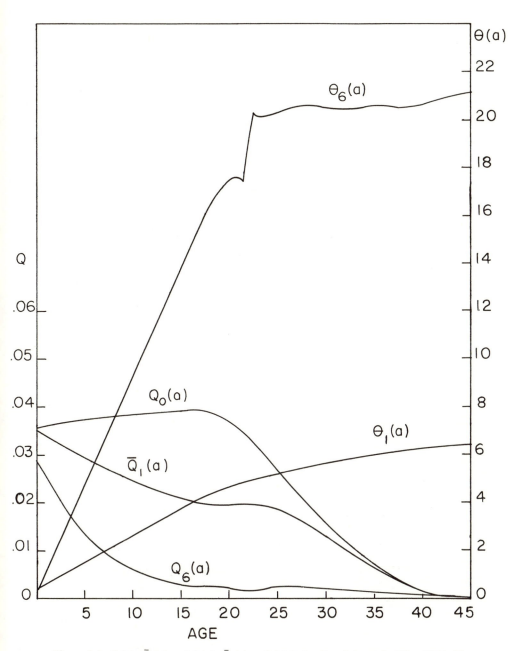

Figure 3.6. $Q_0(a)$, $\bar{Q}_1(a)$ and $\theta_1(a)$, $\bar{Q}_6(a)$ and $\theta_6(a)$, for Swedish net fertility, 1946–50.

age distributions to illustrate some of the aspects of convergence.) To represent the coefficient of one of the oscillatory terms, two numbers are required. One possibility is to give a coefficient for $e^{x_i t} \cdot \cos y_i t$ and another for the term $e^{x_i t} \cdot \sin y_i t$. However, it is usually more illuminating to use the absolute value of $Q_i(a)$ and the initial phase angle of the cosine wave that would be generated by a population element at age a: $\theta_i(a)$. The absolute value of Q and the phase angle are shown for the lowest frequency component and the sixth frequency in Figure 3.6. Note that $2\bar{Q}_i(0) = 2/(G_i^2 + H_i^2)^{1/2}$ and note also that $M_i(a)$ and $N_i(a)$ defined in Equation (3.24) are equal to 1 and 0 respectively for values of $a \leq \alpha$. Therefore $\bar{Q}_i(a)$ is given by Equation (3.45) for values of a between 0 and α.

$$(3.45) \qquad \bar{Q}_i(a) = \frac{\bar{Q}_i(0)e^{x_i a}}{p(a)}; \ 0 \leq a \leq \alpha.$$

Since x_i is generally less than -0.10 for frequencies above the third, and less than -0.15 for frequencies above a cycle every six or seven years, it follows that for all but the lowest frequency roots $\bar{Q}_i(a)$ declines very steeply from 0 to α. The form of $\bar{Q}_i(a)$ as a advances from α to β depends on a rather complicated interaction. Note in Equation (3.25) that the attenuating affect of $e^{x_i a}$ continues to operate, offset only slightly by the presence of $p(a)$ in the denominator. It is the contribution of the $(M_i^2(a) + N_i^2(a))^{1/2}$ that is complicated. $M_i(a)$ can be viewed as the cumulative area from β back to age a under $e^{-x_i z} \cdot \phi(z)$ when multiplied by $\cos y_i z$, and $N_i(a)$ can be viewed as the cumulation backwards of the same function multiplied by $\sin y_i z$. When the cumulation extends back to age α, M_i becomes 1 and N_i becomes 0, but these totals of 1 and 0 respectively are created by the cancellation of positive and negative loops that result from the multiplication by the cosine and sine functions respectively (Figure 3.7). When x_i has large negative values, as it does with higher frequencies, the total positive and total negative areas are quite substantial and the balance from a to β at intermediate ages above α for either function can lead to a value of $M_i^2(a) + N_i^2(a)$ well above 1, the value when a is equal to α. These facts explain in a general way why $\bar{Q}_6(a)$ varies irregularly above age 17 and why $\bar{Q}_1(a)$ has a slight increase from 18 to 22 or 23. For this fertility schedule, however, with frequencies above the lowest, $2\bar{Q}(a)$ for ages within the childbearing span does not exceed one third of $Q(0)$.

The phase of the oscillatory component at a given frequency gen-

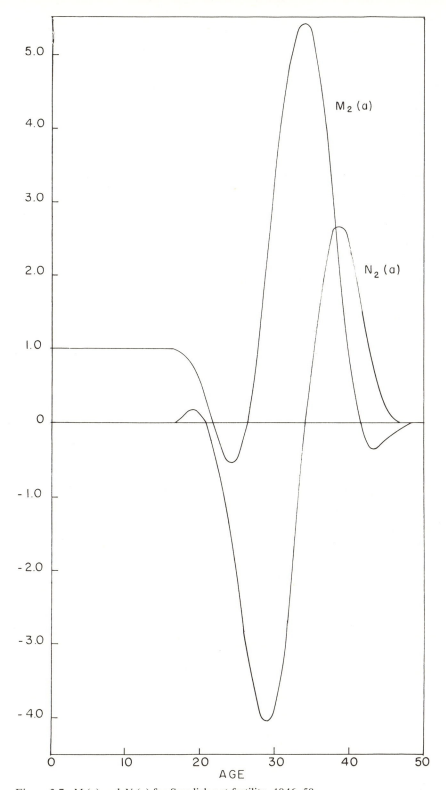

Figure 3.7. $M_2(a)$ and $N_2(a)$ for Swedish net fertility, 1946–50.

$$(M_2(a) = \int_a^\beta e^{-x_2 z} \cos y_2 z \phi(z) dz; \ N_2(a) = \int_a^\beta e^{-x_2 z} \sin y_2 z \phi(z) dz).$$

erated by a population element advances by y_i radians with each additional year of age from 0 to α, as is evident in Equation (3.26). This conforms to common sense: A population element at age 5 will reach the childbearing ages 5 years earlier than one at age 0, and should generate an oscillatory component 5 years in advance. This simple relationship does not hold for population elements that are within the childbearing years at $t = 0$. An element at age 24 and one at age 25 would each have births at about the same rate starting at $t = 0$ and the difference in phase in the oscillatory component generated is not readily visualized. It is not surprising that the increase in phase with age is generally less within the childbearing span than at ages below α.

The significance of $\theta_i(a)$ in determining the overall magnitude of a component of the birth sequence at a particular frequency lies in the fact that population elements at two different ages fully reinforce each other in forming the initial component at a given frequency only if the difference in θ_i is an even multiple of π; two equal values of $Q_i(a)$ where the value of θ_i's differ by an odd multiple of π would precisely cancel.

In order to appreciate the usual relationships among the initial magnitudes of components at various frequencies, it is necessary to have an idea of the usual values of $2\bar{Q}_i(0)$ at various frequencies or of $2/(G_i^2 + H_i^2)^{1/2}$. $(G_1^2 + H_1^2)^{1/2}$ is typically of the same order of magnitude as the mean age of the fertility schedule. The absolute value of $2Q_1(0)$ is thus typically about twice $Q_0(0)$. In the 47 fertility schedules for which low frequency roots were calculated, the highest ratio of $2\bar{Q}_1(0)$ to $Q_0(0)$ was 2.8 (Yugoslavian fertility of 1960) and the lowest value was 1.5 (fertility of the Cocos-Keeling Islands). For higher frequency roots the absolute value of $2Q_i(0)$ varies according to peculiarities of the individual fertility schedule, but the typical value is in the range from $2/35$ to $2/50$ compared to a $Q_0(0)$ of $1/\bar{A}$, where $\bar{A}$ is about 28. By an extension of an argument presented earlier, it can be seen that as y_i approaches infinity, G_i approaches β and H_i approaches 0. Thus, as frequency increases, $2\bar{Q}_i(0)$ approaches $2/\beta$.

Since $\bar{Q}_i(a)$ contains the factor $e^{x_i a}$, $\bar{Q}_i(a)$ declines with age with increasing steepness at higher and higher frequencies of the oscillatory terms, because of the tendency for $-x_i$ to increase with frequency. In fact, as y_i approaches infinity, the value of $\bar{Q}_i(a)$ for an age removed from 0, by no matter how little, approaches 0. For oscillatory terms of frequency of one cycle every 5 or 6 years or higher, the value of $2\bar{Q}_i(a)$ for ages above about 15 years is no more than 10 or 15% of $Q_0(a)$.

Thus not only are high frequency oscillatory terms rapidly damped, but also their initial magnitude is small, unless generated by a population element near age 0 in the initial population. The sequence of births generated by a population element in the early or middle childbearing ages at $t = 0$ varies smoothly with time and is thus not rich in high frequency components. However, when we visualize the birth sequence generated by a population element at or near age 0, we see that births will be 0 until the element in question reaches age α. The principal effect of the high frequency components of $B(t)$ when generated by a population element, is to cancel out the real exponential and the low frequency terms for the first few years and to ensure that the sum of the components adds up to 0 until the initial population element enters the childbearing years.

The steep decline with age of $\bar{Q}_i(a)$ for frequencies above the lowest means that with the exception of the lowest frequency, the oscillatory term generated by a population element at age 0 is larger relative to the real exponential than when generated by an element at any other age. Population elements at different ages produce real exponential birth sequences that are perfectly additive but produce contributions to any oscillatory term that are in general different in phase and therefore not perfectly additive or that are mutually canceling. There is, therefore, special interest in an initial population consisting solely of an element at age 0. In Figure 3.8 there are comparisons of the births generated by such a population element when subjected to the net fertility schedules (normalized so that the net reproduction rate is 1) having the fastest and the slowest damping of the low frequency oscillations. $Q_0 e^{r_0 t} + 2\bar{Q}_1 e^{x_1 t} \cdot \cos(y_1 t + \theta_1)$ is shown for comparison. Notice that the very slowly damped low frequency oscillations produced by the net fertility of Sweden, 1891–1900, are still visible as t approaches 200 years and that a variation of more than 2% from the real exponential (in this instance a horizontal line) occurs at about 165 years. In contrast, the schedule that damps the low frequency oscillations most rapidly (that of Yugoslavia in 1960) last produces a deviation in excess of 2% in the 93rd year. Note also that in both projections, after 40 or 50 years the sum of the real exponential and the low frequency oscillatory term are essentially indistinguishable from the projected births even with an age composition that maximizes the initial magnitude of high frequency components.

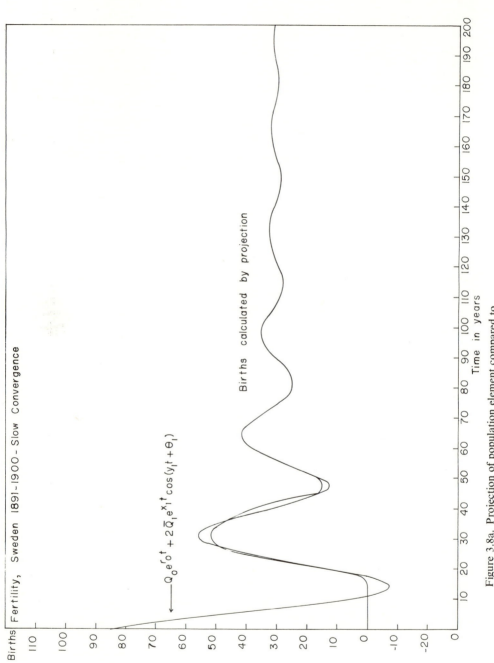

Figure 3.8a. Projection of population element compared to

$$Q_0 e^r 0^t + 2\bar{Q}_1 e^{x_1 t} \cos(y_1 t + \theta_1)$$

Swedish fertility, 1891–1900, mortality "West" females, $e^0 = 70$ years, normalized so that NRR = 1

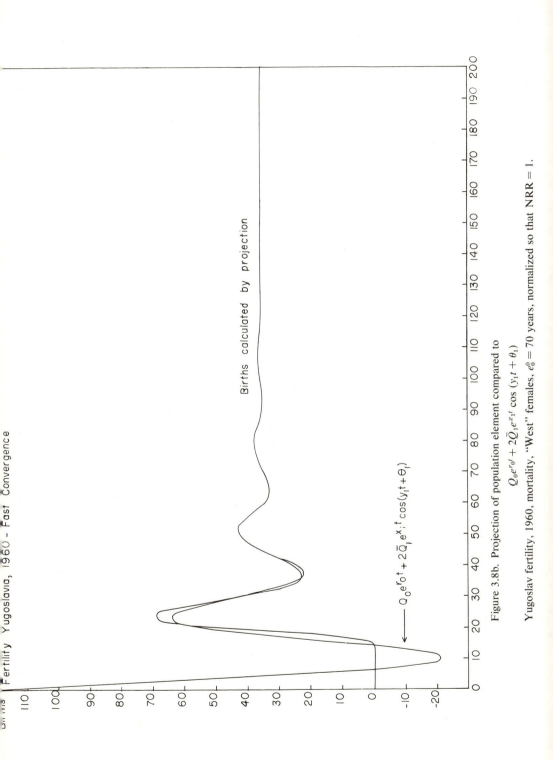

Figure 3.8b. Projection of population element compared to

$$Q_0 e^{r_0 t} + 2\bar{Q}_1 e^{x_1 t} \cos(y_1 t + \theta_1)$$

Yugoslav fertility, 1960, mortality, "West" females, $e_0^0 = 70$ years, normalized so that NRR = 1.

Examples of Stabilization with Various Initial Production

We shall now consider the magnitude of Q_0 and $2\bar{Q}_1$ when four alternative initial age distributions are subjected to the same net fertility function (Sweden, 1946–50). The four populations are: (A) The average female age distribution in Sweden, 1946–50. (B) A population differing from the stable by a 50% reduction in the number of children under age two — simulating the effect of a disastrous disturbance in the preceding two years. (C) A population differing from the stable by a depletion of the cohorts under age five — a depletion equal to what would have been caused by one of the largest short-period reductions of fertility on record, namely the curtailment of fertility in Germany during World War I. (D) A population that would have been produced by a steady decline of fertility of 2% annually at all ages during the pre-

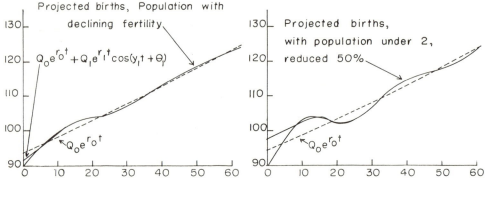

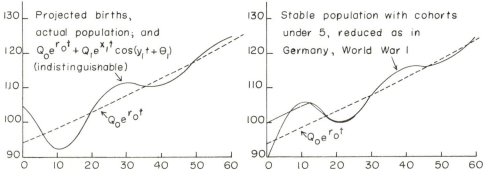

Figure 3.9. Projected births, four initial populations, subject to net fertility of Swedish women, 1946–50, and

$$Q_0 e^{r_0 t}, \quad Q_0 e^{r_0 t} + 2\bar{Q}_1 e^{x_1 t}(\cos y_1 t + \theta_1).$$

ceding 90 to 100 years, culminating in the net fertility of 1946–50. Its age distribution is $Rc(a)(e^{.01a-.01a^2/\mu_1})$, where $c(a)$ is the stable age distribution, and R a factor of proportionality (Coale and Zelnik [4], pp. 82–89, also below, pp. 120–121).

These four populations were projected for 200 years, subject to the given net fertility functions. Figure 3.9 shows the projected births for each population, together with $Q_0 e^{r_0 t} + 2\bar{Q}_1 e^{x_1 t}(\cos y_1 t + \theta_1)$. Table 3.1 lists some of the parameters of the projected birth sequence. Note (in Figure 3.9) that after 25 or 30 years, in every instance, the projected births are indistinguishable from the sum of the first two components (exponential and low frequency oscillatory) of $B(t)$. In determining the data shown in Figure 3.9 and Table 3.1 it was necessary to calculate Q_0, $\bar{Q}_1$, and θ_1 from Equations (3.19), (3.22), (3.32), and (3.33), and to carry out projections for each population. The results show that the actual population and the stable population depleted under 5 as by German World War I fertility have the largest and most persistent deviations from the exponential birth sequence, although in no instance is more than 45 years required for the births to stabilize, in the sense of remaining within 2% of the exponential. In Figure 3.10, the four age distributions are plotted, each in conjunction with the stable. The reasons for the variations in the convergence of the resultant birth sequences are not self-evident. It is not immediately obvious why, for example, the deviations generated by the actual population are so much larger than by the population with a history of steadily declining fertility.

Table 3.1. Parameters explaining aspects of the stabilization of $B(t)$ for four age distributions, subject to net fertility of Sweden, 1946–50 ($r_0 = .00453$, $r_0 - x_1 = .03943$)

Population	$2Q_1/Q_0$	Maximum % deviation from exponential births after $t = 10$	Last deviation of at least 2%
A. Average female population, 1946–50	0.118	7.5% at $t = 12$	$t = 44$ years
B. Stable population, children under 2 reduced by 50%	0.065	3.6% at $t = 12$	$t = 28$ years
C. Stable population, children under 5 reduced as by German fertility reduction during World War I.	0.106	6.1% at $t = 10$	$t = 40$ years
D. Population resulting from long term reduction in fertility at 2% annually	0.030	1.6% at $t = 14$	$t = 4$ years

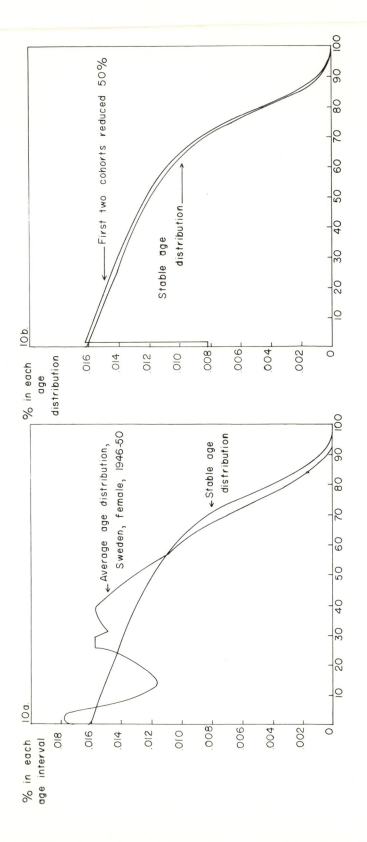

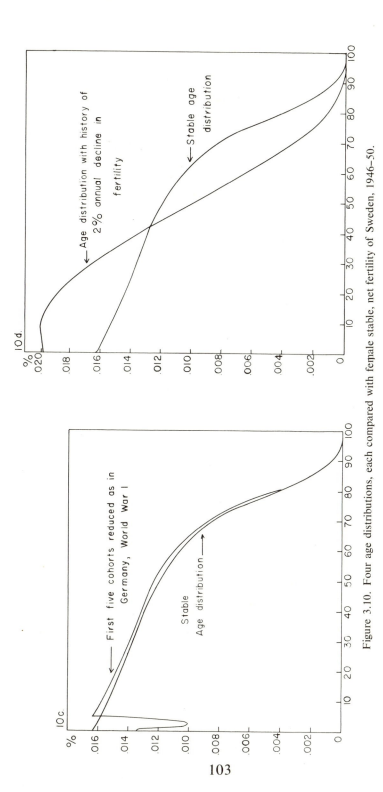

Figure 3.10. Four age distributions, each compared with female stable, net fertility of Sweden, 1946–50.

103

VISUALIZING THE NATURE OF THE APPROACH TO STABILITY

To calculate the birth sequence by population projection methods is not extraordinarily laborious; but, as was noted early in this paper, such a calculation does not make clear what features of the initial circumstances lead to small deviations from the exponential birth sequence and to rapid convergence, and what features to large deviations and slow convergence. On the basis of previous discussion, we know:

(1) Only the lowest frequency oscillation can create deviations from the exponential beyond 30 or 40 years because of the rapid damping of high frequencies.

(2) The low frequency oscillation is damped relative to the exponential at a pace determined by general characteristics (skewness, and concentration between $3\mu_1/4$ and $5\mu_1/4$ of $\phi(a)$), and the rate of relative damping is readily calculated from regression equations. Also, r_0 is easily calculated from the NRR and μ_1.

(3) If the initial age distribution is a population element (at any age from 0 to α, at least) Q_0, $\bar{Q}_1$, and θ can be calculated, since very close regression estimates of G_1 and H_1 are possible, and only r_0, x_1, μ_1, G_1, and H_1, are required. Thus, for an initial population element, we can visualize the birth sequence that the element generates from the time that it reaches age α until it reaches 2α plus four or five years, when second generation births would enter to an important degree; from this time on we can splice in the sum of the first two components of $B(t)$ — the exponential plus the damped low frequency oscillations — since by this time other components are negligible.

These observations are not sufficient, however, to enable us to visualize the process of stabilization for an initial population other than an element concentrated at (or at least near) a single age. A very useful point in such a visualization is recognition of this fact: There must be an initial population that would generate exactly the same exponential birth sequence as any given initial population — without any deviations or fluctuations. This population has a stable age distribution from age 0 to β and a total size to age β $((Q_0/b)\int_0^\beta c(a)da,$ where $c(a)$ is the proportion at age a in the stable population) such that the magnitude of its exponential birth sequence is the same as that of the given population. If this population is subtracted from the given initial age distribution up to age β, the remainder generates exactly the same deviations as the whole initial population — but a zero exponential sequence.

Two procedures can be followed in visualizing the process of stabilization, the choice of procedure depending on the nature of the initial age distribution.

VISUALIZING THE APPROACH TO AN EXPONENTIAL BIRTH SEQUENCE, WHEN THE INITIAL AGE DISTRIBUTION APPROXIMATES THE STABLE EXCEPT FOR "LUMPED" DEVIATIONS

When the differences between the initial age distribution (under age β) and a stable population are concentrated in one or two short age segments (no more than five or six years in width), these deviations from the stable generate a sequence of births closely equivalent to those that would be generated by deviations of the same total size as, but concentrated at the mean age of, the actual deviations. The exponential and low frequency components generated by these equivalent "population elements" are virtually identical to those generated by the actual deviations, because over a short span of years $Q_1(a)$ (as well as $Q_0(a)$) is additive, since over a short span differences in $\theta_1(a)$ are negligible. At high frequencies, a deviation spread over a few years would produce a $\bar{Q}_i$ consequentially different from (less than) the $\bar{Q}_i$ of an element at the mean age of the deviation. However, we propose visualizing the high frequency components solely by picturing the projection of the first generation births to the initial population. Note that the first generation births to a population element concentrated at an exact age precisely trace out the net fertility function itself, while first generation births to a less concentrated initial group trace out the function only approximately. To visualize convergence when the deviations in the initial population to age β from a stable population are concentrated in one or two short age spans, the following steps can be used:

(1) Calculate the exponential sequence that would occur to the stable population in the absence of the deviations $((Q_0)_s e^{r_0 t})$.

(2) Visualize the births that would occur to each of the deviations as each moves through the childbearing ages.

(3) Calculate $N_1 \cdot Q_0(\bar{a}_1)$, and $N_2 \cdot Q_0(\bar{a}_2)$ (N_1 and N_2 are the number of persons in the two deviations from the stable age distribution). As the effect of the "disturbances" vanishes, the birth sequence will approach

$$[(Q_0)_s + N_1 Q_0(a_1) + N_2 Q_0(a_2)]e^{r_0 t}$$

—the deviations will add to (or subtract from, if negative) the long-run exponential sequence.

105

(4) Calculate the values of $N_1\bar{Q}_1(\bar{a}_1)$, $N_2\bar{Q}_1(\bar{a}_2)$ and $\theta_1(\bar{a}_1)$ and $\theta_1(\bar{a}_2)$. The magnitude and initial phase angle ($\bar{Q}_1$ and θ_1) of the damped low frequency cosine wave that results from the two elements together is the *vector* sum of $\bar{Q}_1(\bar{a}_1)$, $\theta_1(\bar{a}_1)$ and $\bar{Q}_1(\bar{a}_2)$, $\theta_1(\bar{a}_2)$. Thus, if $\bar{a}_1$ is age 1 and $\bar{a}_2$ is 15 when the period of the low frequency oscillation is 28 years, $\theta_1(\bar{a}_1)$ and $\theta_1(\bar{a}_2)$ differ by π, and the resultant magnitude of the low frequency term is $|\bar{Q}_1(\bar{a}_1) - \bar{Q}_1(\bar{a}_2)|$; the two deviations would reinforce each other in producing a low frequency term only if opposite in sign.[5]

The formulae for the vector sum are:

$$(3.46) \qquad \theta_1 = \arctan \frac{\bar{Q}_1(\bar{a}_1) \sin \theta_1(\bar{a}_1) + \bar{Q}_1(\bar{a}_2) \sin \theta_1(\bar{a}_2)}{\bar{Q}_1(\bar{a}_1) \cos \theta_1(\bar{a}_1) + \bar{Q}_1(\bar{a}_2) \cos \theta_1(\bar{a}_2)}$$

and

$$(3.47) \quad \bar{Q}_1 = \bar{Q}_1(\bar{a}_1) \cos (\theta(\bar{a}_1) - \theta_1) + \bar{Q}_1(\bar{a}_2) \cos (\theta_1(\bar{a}_2) - \theta_1).$$

(5) The birth sequence starts along the exponential (step (1) above) that would be followed in the absence of deviations; then follows a path of digression from this exponential that consists of the projected first generation births to the "disturbances" from the stable (step (2)); then settles — at no later than $t = 25$ or 30 years — on the sum of an exponential sequence $Q_0 e^{r_0 t}$, where Q_0 is modified by the net effect of the disturbances on the long run births (step (3)), *plus* a damped low frequency oscillatory component of the form $2\bar{Q}_1 e^{x_1 t} \cos y_1(t + \theta_1)$ that is the resultant of the disturbances (step (4)). The interval when the projection determines the form of the sequence is the period before rapid damping removes the contribution of high frequency components; the low frequency damped oscillations continue until negligible relative to the exponential component.

An example of a "lumped" deviation is provided by a population whose approach to stability was calculated earlier: a stable population (Swedish net fertility, 1946–50) that had a 50% deficit in the number of persons under age 2. We shall now analyze this population to illustrate the steps just enumerated.

(1) The exponential that would have occurred to the undisturbed population is $S \cdot b e^{r_0 t}$, where S is the number of persons in the undisturbed stable, or the number of persons in the actual population over 2 plus twice the number under 2.

(2) The "disturbance" from the stable is a population equal to *minus*

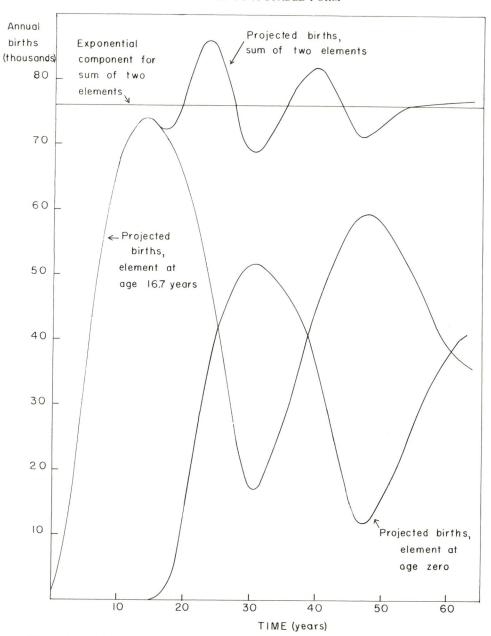

Figure 3.11. The projection of births from a population element (one million persons) at age 0, an element (1.4363 million persons) at age 16.7, and of the two elements combined. Fertility of Swedish females, 1891–1900, mortality "West" females, $e_0^0 = 70$, net fertility adjusted so that $r_0 = 0$.

$S/2 \int_0^2 c(a)da$, or approximately to *minus* $S \cdot c(1)$, where $c(1)$ is the proportion in the stable population in the one-year age group *centered* on age 1. Beginning at $t = \alpha - 1$, this negative element would generate a sequence of negative first generation births equal to $-S \cdot c(1) \cdot \phi(t-1)/p(1)$, or to $-Sbe^{-r_0}\phi(t-1)$. At $t = 26$, this would be $-Sb(.99547)(.0678) = -Sb(.0675)$. ($r_0 = .00453$, and $\phi(25) = .0678$.)

(3) The negative deviation from the stable population would generate an exponential term $-S \cdot c(1) \cdot Q_0(1)e^{r_0 t}$. But $Q_0(1) = b/\bar{A} \cdot c(1)$, so the exponential term from the deviation is $-S(b/\bar{A})e^{r_0 t}$. The ultimate exponential sequence, including the contribution from the population over 2, is (see (1) above):

$$Sb\left(1 - \frac{1}{\bar{A}}\right)e^{r_0 t}.$$

Since μ_1 for this schedule is 28.46 years, $\bar{A}$ is 28.28, and the effect of the deficit under age 2 is to diminish the long range births by 3.53%.[6]

(4) The deficit under age 2 would generate a low frequency oscillatory term $2\bar{Q}_1 e^{-.0349 t} \cos(.2159t + \theta_1)$, where $\bar{Q}_1 = -S \cdot c(1) \cdot \bar{Q}_1(1)$. But

$$\bar{Q}_1(1) = \frac{1}{(G_1^2 + H_1^2)^{1/2}} \frac{e^{x_1}}{p(1)} \quad \text{or} \quad \frac{.9657}{p(1)30.8} = \frac{.0314}{p(1)},$$

and

$$\theta_1 = \theta_1(1) = \arctan\left(\frac{H_1}{G_1}\right) + y_1.$$

$\theta_1 = .44 + .22 = .66$ radians, or about 3 years in a cycle length of $29.1(2\pi/y_1)$. In other words, the low frequency oscillatory component would reach a negative peak at about $(29.1 - 3)$ years, or at about $t = 26$, when it would have a value of $-.0624(e^{-(26)(.0349)})(S[c(1)/p(1)])$ $= -.0251Sb$.

(5) The exponential component contributed by the deficit at age 26 is $-Sb(.0353)e^{(.00453)(26)} = -Sb(.0398)$. The net effect of the reduced exponential and the low frequency term at $t = 26$ is thus a change of $-.0649Sb$. This differs only slightly from the value obtained by projection at the peak age (25) of the net fertility function ($-.0675Sb$), so that a "splicing" of the projected first generation births and the sum of the exponential and the low frequency damped oscillatory term can take place at $t = 26$, or, more exactly, between $t = 26$ and $t = 30$.

(6) Thus births can be approximated during the process of convergence as following the exponential that would have prevailed without

the deficit from the stable under age 2, from $t = 0$ until about $t = \alpha - 1$. This initial part is given by:

$$B(t) = Sbe^{r_0 t} = Sbe^{.00453t}.$$

There follows a period, from $t = \alpha - 1$ (about 15 years) until $t = 26$ to 30, when the birth sequence is approximated by $+Sbe^{r_0 t} - Sbe^{-r_0}\phi(t - 1)$, or

$$B(t) = Sb(e^{.00453t} - .99457\phi(t - 1)).$$

At a point between $t = 26$ and $t = 30$, the birth sequence consists essentially of the reduced exponential component plus damped low frequency oscillations. Then subsequent births can be taken as equal to:

$$Sb\left(1 - \frac{1}{A}\right) e^{r_0 t} - (Q_1(1))Sc(1)e^{x_1 t} \cos (y_1 t + \theta_1(1))$$

$$= Sb(.9647)e^{.00453t} - Sb(.0621)e^{-.0349t} \cos (.2159t + .66).$$

VISUALIZING THE APPROACH TO AN EXPONENTIAL BIRTH SEQUENCE WHEN THE INITIAL POPULATION DIFFERS FROM THE STABLE (UNDER AGE β) OVER BROAD AGE INTERVALS (MORE THAN 5 OR 6 YEARS)

When differences between the initial age distribution (under age β) and the stable distribution (under age β) are spread over broad age intervals, the deviations from the stable can no longer be considered equivalent to population elements. Under these circumstances, a different procedure for picturing the approach to an exponential sequence can be followed. It includes the following steps:

(1) Determine the size of the stable population that would generate exactly the same real exponential birth sequence as the given population. Suppose $N(a)$ is the number at each age a in the given population, and $P \cdot c(a)$ is the appropriate stable. Find the residual $N'(a) = N(a) - P \cdot c(a)$, and represent $N'(a)$ from 0 to β graphically.

The calculation of the size of a stable population that would produce the same exponential sequence as any given population is not difficult. It amounts to finding what size a stable population should have to produce the same Q_0 as does $N(a)$. This means that P must be chosen such that:

(3.48) $$P \int_0^\beta c(a)Q_0(a)da = \int_0^\beta N(a)Q_0(a)da,$$

109

where $c(a)$ is the proportion at age a in the stable population. In other words, we seek a stable population whose weighted sum to age β (with $Q_0(a)$ as the weight) is the same as that of the actual population. The weighting function varies as the reciprocal of $c(a)$ from 0 to α, and then falls more or less linearly to zero from about age 20 to about age 45. Its effect can usually be adequately approximated by a weight of one from 0 to 20, .75 from 20 to 30, .20 from 30 to 40, and .05 from 40 to 45. Thus P can be determined approximately as follows:

(3.49)

$$
P = \frac{\int_0^{20} N(a)da + .75 \int_{20}^{30} N(a)da + .2 \int_{30}^{40} N(a)da + .05 \int_{40}^{45} N(a)da}{\int_0^{20} c(a)da + .75 \int_{20}^{30} c(a)da + .2 \int_{30}^{40} c(a)da + .05 \int_{40}^{45} c(a)da}.
$$

(2) Determine the first generation births that would occur to $N'(a)$ as it experiences (from $t = 0$ to $t = \beta$) the net fertility rates $\phi(a)$. These births can be calculated from the relation

$$
B_1(t) = \int_0^{\beta} \frac{N'(a - t)}{p(a - t)} \phi(a)da.
$$

One can visualize the approximate form of this birth sequence by picturing $N'(a)/p(a)$ moving out along the age axis as time passes, and estimating the approximate net number of births generated each year by the part of $N'(a)/p(a)$ then within the fertile years. $N'(a)$ must contain both positive and negative areas (otherwise it would generate a nonzero exponential sequence) so some of the births that would occur in the first generation to $N'(a)$ would be positive and some negative.

(3) Examine the graph of the projected first generation births for a broad maximum or minimum, preceded (or followed) by a sequence of births of the opposite sign.

(4) The approximate phase of the low frequency oscillations, and an upper limit of the magnitude as of a specific time (which information is sufficient to fix the subsequent course of this component) is obtained by assuming that the maximum deviation (positive or negative) in the projected births can be identified as a peak of the low frequency oscillations.

(5) The synthesis of these steps is similar to the one suggested when deviations from the stable age distribution are viewed as equivalent to population "elements": The exponential component is identified by determining the size of the equivalent stable population; deviations

about the exponential are estimated for the first few years by the approximate projection of first generation births occurring to $N'(a)$; the magnitude and phase of low frequency oscillations are estimated as those of a damped cosine function with a peak that coincides with the maximum deviation (separated from $t = 0$) in the projected first generation births. This estimated oscillation is then spliced to the projected first generation births at a peak value of the latter.

This procedure is illustrated by the birth sequence generated with constant net fertility by the population resulting from a long history of declining fertility prior to the establishment of the unchanging regime. This age distribution is shown in Figure 3.10d; note how widely it differs from the stable. However, Figure 3.12 shows the much smaller difference up to age 50 between this population and the stable population of a size that would produce the same exponential birth sequence. In Figure 3.13 are seen the ingredients for determining the first generation births that would occur to $N'(a)$. In the first panel the large negative portion of $N'(a)/p(a)$ beyond age 22 would produce more negative births than the small positive segment between 15 and 22, so $B_1(t)$ begins with a negative intercept. By $t = 10$, the positive portions of $N'(a - 10)/p(a - 10)$ from 15 to 33 produce more births than the negative portions in the relatively low fertility ages above 33. $B_1(t)$ reaches a positive maximum of moderate amplitude just short of $t = 15$. Figure 3.14 shows $B_1(t)$ with a damped low frequency oscillatory term "spliced" so as to coincide with this maximum. The resultant composite is indistinguishable from the births projected by standard techniques by single years of time and age, less the exponential component, $Q_0 e^{r_0 t}$.

In Figure 3.15 there appears the average age distribution of Swedish females, 1946–50 (up to age 50) with the stable population that would produce the same exponential birth sequence. A comparison of Figures 3.15 and 3.12 makes evident the larger relative magnitude of $N'(a)$ in the actual Swedish age distribution than in the age distribution with a history of declining fertility. It is also evident that the first generation births that could be projected from $N'(a)$ in this instance would start at a larger positive value than the initial negative births associated with the other age distribution, and rise to a very much larger negative peak in 13 or 14 years. Again, one can splice together the deviations from $Q_0 e^{r_0 t}$ by switching from $B_1(t)$ to damped low frequency oscillations at the maximum of $B_1(t)$. In short, inspection of $N'(a)$ makes it possible to visualize the nature and approximate

111

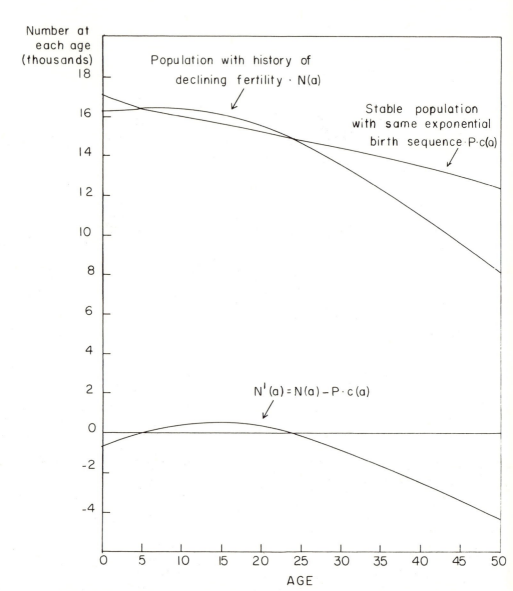

Figure 3.12. Age distribution (0 to 50 years) of a population with the current fertility and mortality of Swedish females, 1946–50, and a history of declining fertility at 2% annually, compared to stable population yielding same exponential birth sequence.

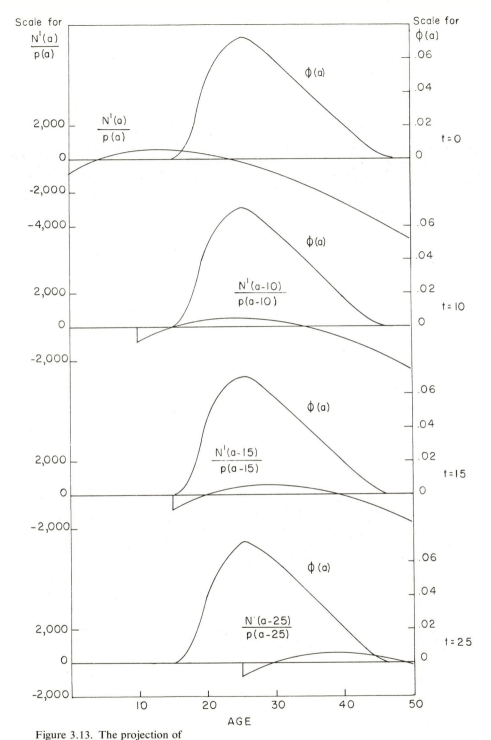

Figure 3.13. The projection of

$$B_1(t) = \int_0^\beta (N'(a-t)/p(a-t))\phi(a)da$$

for population with history of declining fertility.

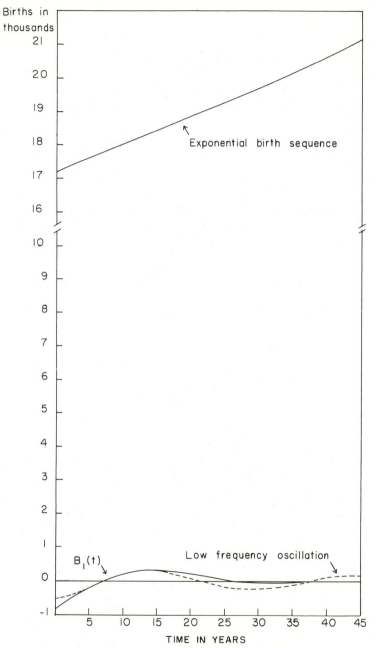

Figure 3.14. First generation births to $N'(a)$; exponential component, and low frequency oscillatory component for population with history of declining fertility.

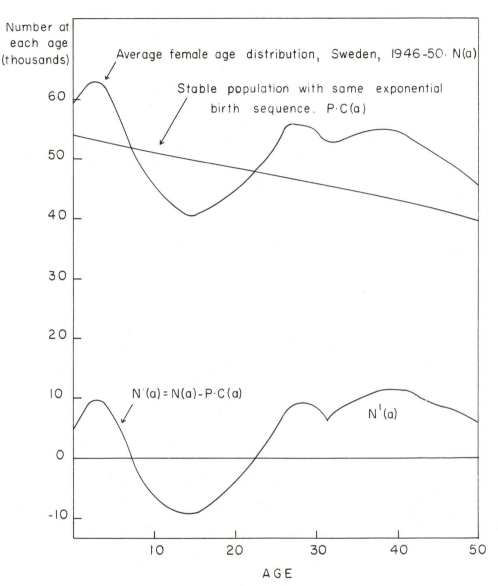

Figure 3.15. Age distribution (0 to 50 years) of the average female population of Sweden, 1946–50, compared to stable population yielding same exponential birth sequence.

magnitude of deviations in the birth sequence from the exponential component – to visualize the process of stabilization.

NOTES

[1] See Lotka [8].

[2] Lopez [6], p. 15. A difficult feature of Lotka's proof is the question of whether the exponential terms, when added together, will always approach the sequence of births generated by the arbitrary initial age distribution. This question (of whether the sequence of exponential functions converges), not satisfactorily treated by Lotka, has been resolved by Lopez ([6], Chapter I) when the fertility and mortality functions are continuous and have positive values only over a finite age span.

[3] When $\phi(a)$ is considered constant in each single-year interval, the integrals in Equations (3.6a) and (3.6b) are approximated by:

$$\sum_{\alpha-.5}^{\beta-.5} \phi(a) \int_{a-.5}^{a+.5} e^{-xu} \cos yu \, du = 1,$$

$$\sum_{\alpha-.5}^{\beta-.5} \phi(a) \int_{a-.5}^{a+.5} e^{-xu} \sin yu \, du = 0,$$

$$\int e^{-xu} \cos yu \, du = \frac{e^{-xu}(-x \cos yu + y \sin yu)}{x^2 + y^2},$$

and

$$\int e^{-xu} \sin yu \, du = \frac{e^{-xu}(-x \sin yu - y \cos yu)}{x^2 + y^2}.$$

[4] When $\int_0^\beta \phi'(a)da = e^{.01972}\mu_1$, substitution in Equation (3.41) leads to $r_0' = .020$.

[5] The canceling effect of the oscillations produced by elements separated by π/y_1 years is illustrated in Figure 3.11. Births are projected for an initial population consisting of 1,000,000 females, at age 0; another consisting of 1,436,000 females at age 16.7 (π/y_1); and for the sum of these two. Fertility is that of Sweden, 1891–1900, mortality "West" females, $e_0^0 = 70$ years, with net fertility adjusted so that $r_0 = 0$. The element at age 16.7 equals that at age 0 times $e^{-16.7x_1}$. Therefore, $Q_1 = 0$ – there are no low frequency oscillations. This illustrates a general point: It is always possible to add to a population an element (of selected size and age) so that all oscillations of a given frequency (here specifically the lowest) are canceled.

[6] $\bar{A} \doteq \mu_1 - 1.4 \log R_0$.

REFERENCES

[1] Bourgeois-Pichat, J. *The Concept of a Stable Population. Application to the Study of Populations with Incomplete Demographic Statistics.* New York, United Nations, 1968.

[2] Coale, A. J., "A New Method of Calculating Lotka's r," *Population Studies,* Vol. 11, No. 1, July, 1957, pp. 92–99.

[3] Coale, A. J., and Demeny, P., *Regional Model Life Tables and Stable Populations,* Princeton, Princeton University Press, 1966.

[4] Coale, A. J., and Zelnik, M., *New Estimates of Fertility and Mortality in the United States,* Princeton, Princeton University Press, 1963.

[5] Fisher, R. A., *The Genetical Theory of Natural Selection,* New York, Dover Publications, 1958, 2nd Revised Edition (1st Edition, 1929), 291 pp.

[6] Lopez, A., *Some Problems in Stable Population Theory,* Princeton, Office of Population Research, 1961.

[7] Lotka, A. J., "The Progeny of a Population Element," *The American Journal of Hygiene,* Vol. 8, No. 6, November, 1928, pp. 875–901.

[8] Lotka, A. J., "A Contribution to the Theory of Self-Renewing Aggregates, with Special Reference to Industrial Replacement," *Annals of Mathematical Statistics,* Vol. 10, No. 1, March, 1939, pp. 1–25.

Population with Fertility That Changes
at a Constant Rate

THE stable population is a device that displays the implications for age composition, birth rates, death rates, and rates of increase, of specified schedules of fertility and mortality, on the assumption that the schedules prevail long enough for other influences to be erased. In the last chapter the evolution of the population during the disappearance of these other influences was analyzed. In actual fact the stable population is never achieved, and its characteristics are closely approached in actual populations only because of a tendency for certain kinds of demographic change to have limited or self-canceling effects on age composition. A question of some theoretical as well as practical interest is the effect of *changes* in fertility and mortality on growth and age composition. We have noted earlier that the effect of any specified sequence of schedules — and hence of any particular change one wants to examine — can be calculated by standard methods of population projection, and that if the specified sequence is long enough, it becomes the sole determinant of age composition and growth. However, the possibility of calculation (or even its application) does not explain what features of change in fertility and mortality are responsible for particular features of age composition; and it would be valuable to have analytical expressions relating birth rates, death rates, rates of increase, and various parameters of age composition to changing schedules of fertility and mortality, just as the stable population provides such expressions when schedules are fixed.

The Birth Sequence and Age Composition of a Population
with Fertility That Changes at a Constant Rate, "Forever"

Approximate formulae have been presented for a particular instance of changing schedules (Coale and Zelnik [1]). In this chapter, this special case will be further explored. The particular circumstances that can be analyzed in a manner roughly analogous to stable population theory are the sequence of births and the number of persons at each age that evolve when fertility continuously declines (or continuously rises) while mortality remains fixed. It is possible, as will be shown below, to derive a simple equation that provides a close approximation (and a more complicated equation that provides a *very* close approximation) to the sequence of births generated when fertility persistently changes at a constant rate, and to determine the birth rate, death rate,

117

and rate of increase of the population. The characteristics of the population generated under these circumstances can be related to characteristics of stable populations to show just how a history of changing fertility (as compared to a history of constant fertility at the current level) affects the age composition, and hence the birth rate, the death rate, and the rate of increase of a population.

Demographic analysis of this sort is relevant to (among others) the French and American populations from 1800 to the 1930s, when both experienced prolonged declines of fertility, and to some extent to the populations of most highly industrialized countries during an extended part of their histories.

A decrease of fertility to replacement at low mortality levels is the only alternative, in the long run, to an increase in mortality. Rapid reduction to, or below, replacement is a goal strongly advocated by some groups today—advocated as a goal for almost all populations. The demography of a population in which fertility has just reached replacement after a sustained decline thus has some special topical interest.

An Approximate Analytical Expression for the Sequence of Births When Mortality Is Constant and Fertility Is Subject to a Constant Annual Change

In any closed population of one sex there is a simple-appearing relation between the births at a given moment and births in the past:

$$(4.1) \qquad B(t) = \int_\alpha^\beta B(t - a)m(a,t)p(a,t)da.$$

When α and β are the upper and lower limits of the childbearing span, $m(a,t)$ is the proportion of women at age a and time t giving birth to a female child, and $p(a,t)$ is the proportion of women surviving from births occurring t years ago to age a at time t. Equation (4.1) can be expressed in a different form as

$$(4.2) \qquad B(t) = R(t) \int_\alpha^\beta B(t - a)f(a,t)da,$$

where $R(t)$ is the "net reproduction rate" at time t, and $f(a,t)$ is $m(a,t)p(a,t)$ divided by $\int_0^\beta m(a,t)p(a,t)da$. Thus births at t are equal to the net reproduction rate at time t (defined in a peculiar way) and the weighted average of births occurring α to β years ago. Note that $f(a,t)$ has the characteristics of a frequency distribution. $R(t)$ is a "net reproduction rate" defined by the age-specific maternity rates at time t, combined with the survival to age t of cohorts born a years ago. Thus at each age the past mortality over a different time span enters the definition of this "net reproduction rate." The case that we shall explore is one wherein $p(a,t)$ is fixed, and can be written as merely $p(a)$, and $m(a,t) = m(a,0)e^{kt}$ —fertility is fixed in age structure, but changing in level at a constant annual rate. Our goal is to find out what we can about the birth sequence, and also the age composition, birth and death rates, that result when

$$(4.3) \qquad B(t) = R(0)e^{kt} \int_{\alpha}^{\beta} B(t-a)f(a)da.$$

If we can find an analytical expression for the birth sequence that satisfies Equation (4.3) we can be sure that it is indeed the birth sequence that would be approached as a constant rate of fertility change continued for a long time, because of the proven tendency for the effect of initial conditions to vanish with the passage of time.

We shall offer two approximate solutions to Equation (4.3). The first is a good approximation to the true solution, an approximation derived by making a contrary-to-fact assumption about the age structure of fertility, or to put the same assumption in a different way, about the distribution in the past of the time of birth of the women who experience maternity in a given year. The second approximation is a modification of the first, and consists of an adjustment for the distorting effects of the contrary-to-fact assumption.

Our basic approach is to simplify Equation (4.3) by replacing the weighted average of births α to β years before time t (i.e., $\int_{\alpha}^{\beta} B(t - a)f(a)da$) by the births at a single point in the interval $B(t - \beta)$ to $B(t - \alpha)$. According to the mean value theorem of integral calculus, if $B(t)$ is continuous, there must be a value, $T(t)$, between α and β, such that $\int_{\alpha}^{\beta} B(t - a)f(a)da = B(t - T(t))$. It follows that

$$(4.4) \qquad B(t) = R(0)e^{kt}B(t - T(t)),$$

where $T(t)$ is a number (that may be constantly changing) that lies between α and β.

Our first approximation is obtained by making the contrary-to-fact assumption that $T(t)$ is a fixed number. To simplify the subsequent analysis, the time origin is set at the moment when the net reproduction is unity: i.e., $R(0) = 1.0$. We now assume that $T(t)$ remains fixed at the value of the mean length of generation approached as the net reproduction rate approaches unity. We shall use, in short, a fixed value of $T(t)$, T_0, where

(4.5)
$$T_0 = \frac{\int_\alpha^\beta ap(a)m(a)da}{\int_\alpha^\beta p(a)m(a)da}.$$

Thus, the version of Equation (4.4) that we are trying to solve is

(4.6)
$$B(t) = R(0)e^{kt}B(t - T_0).$$

If we let $Y(t) = \log B(t)$, Equation (4.6) can be rewritten as

(4.7)
$$Y(t) - Y(t - T_0) = \log R(0) + kt.$$

Equation (4.7) is a simple difference equation that is readily solved; for example, by assuming that $Y(t) = b_1 t + b_2 t^2$. Substituting this form of $Y(t)$ in Equation (4.7) and solving for the undetermined coefficients b_1 and b_2 leads to the solution

(4.8)
$$B(t) = B(0)e^{(k/2)t+(k/2T_0)t^2}.$$

(Note that by choosing the origin at the time when the net reproduction rate is unity, we ensure that $\log R(0)$ is zero.)

This approximate solution implies an age distribution having a fixed relationship to the stable age distribution that is associated with the net fertility of any given moment. The number of persons at age a in a population with this birth sequence would be

(4.9) $\quad N(a,t) = B(t - a)p(a)$

$$= B(0)e^{(k/2)t+(k/2T_0)t^2}e^{-(k/2)a+(k/2T_0)a^2}e^{-(kt/T_0)a}p(a)$$

or

(4.10)
$$N(a,t) \doteq B(t)e^{-(k/2)a+(k/2T_0)a^2}e^{-r(t)a}p(a).$$

The approximate nature of Equation (4.10) arises from the fact that $r(t)$ ($r(t)$ means the rate of increase in the stable population defined by the fertility and mortality at time t) is not exactly equal to kt/T_0. It may be recalled from stable population analysis that $r(t) = (\log R(t))/T(t)$. Thus kt/T_0 differs from $r(t)$ to the extent that T_0 and $T(t)$ are different. The proportionate age distribution at time t is given by

(4.11) $\quad c(a,t) = \dfrac{N(a,t)}{N(t)} = b(t)e^{-(k/2)a+(k/2T_0)a^2}e^{-r(t)a}p(a).$

But the stable age distribution based on the fertility and mortality at time t is

(4.12) $$c_s(a,t) = b_s(t)e^{-r(t)a}p(a).$$

Hence, Equation (4.11) can be rewritten as

(4.13) $$c(a,t) = \frac{b(t)}{b_s(t)} \, e^{-(k/2)a+(k/2T_0)a^2}c_s(a).$$

Thus, according to this approximate formula, the age distribution of a population with a history of changing fertility is equal to a constant (the ratio of the birth rates) times the stable age distribution modified by a second order exponential term. Equation (4.13) is derived, of course, from the approximate solution for the birth sequence given in Equation (4.8). As an empirical test of how good this approximate solution is, we have projected a population for many years with fertility falling each year by one percent. The initial population had an age distribution consisting of a stable population modified according to Equation (4.13). It was deliberately chosen with very high fertility (gross reproduction rate 4.07) and low mortality (e_0^0 70 years). The age structure of fertility was arbitrarily selected as that of the Swedish population from 1891 to 1900 (with the level of fertility approximately doubled). T_0 is 32.1 years. The population was projected for 200 years. The natural logarithm of the births for each subsequent year divided by the births in the initial year is shown in Figure 4.1 on the basis of two different calculations: first, based on a precise projection that was carried out by single years of age and single years of time, and second, based on Equation (4.8). The fit is quite close, although there is a gradual divergence that reaches a maximum of about 6% after more than a century. The example shows clearly enough that, at least for this fertility schedule, the approximation is quite serviceable. We now turn to an examination of an improvement in the approximation, an examination that leads to a virtually perfect second approximation, which in turn shows what factors cause divergence of the first approximate solution from the accurately calculated birth sequence.

The basic source of the failure of the approximation to fit the actual birth sequence perfectly is that it began with Equation (4.6) in which the value of $T(t)$ in Equation (4.4) is held fixed at T_0 rather than being allowed to vary. As a first step in improving the approximation, consider Equation (4.4) for the special case where k is zero, implying, of course, fixed fertility. Then the proper relationship between births in

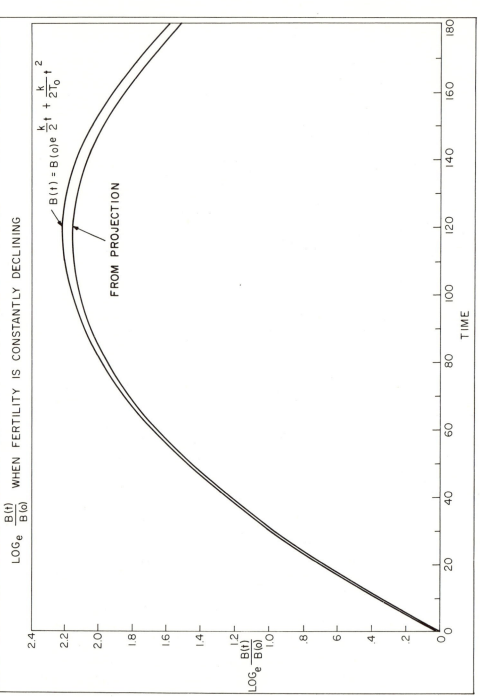

Figure 4.1. Natural logarithm of the ratio of births at time t to births at time 0 when fertility is constantly declining by 1% annually; exact value from projection and approximate value from Equation (4.8).

one generation and births at a fixed point a generation earlier is

(4.14) $$B(t) = RB(t - T).$$

If Equation (4.14) is solved in a manner analogous to the solution of Equation (4.6) the solution is found to be

(4.15) $$B(t) = B(0)e^{[(\log R)/T]t},$$

which is precisely the correct solution for the birth sequence in a stable population, provided T is the mean length of generation in the stable population, since, as is well known, in a stable population the rate of increase $r = (\log R)/T$. However, the mean length of generation differs in stable populations with different levels of fertility even when the stable populations share the same age structure of fertility and the same mortality schedule. In fact, as shown by Lotka,

(4.16) $$T = T_0 - \frac{\sigma}{2} r + \cdots$$

where T_0 is the mean age of childbearing in the net fertility schedule and σ^2 is the variance of the net fertility schedule. Since $\sigma^2/2T_0$ is in the order of .6 to .9 in most recorded fertility schedules, T differs from T_0 by a proportion that is approximately $-.7r$. Thus, if the intrinsic rate of increase is 3%, the mean length of generation is slightly more than 2% less than the mean age of the net fertility schedule. In other words, if we look again at Equations (4.3) and (4.4), it is apparent that the value of $T(t)$ that produces the same result as the weighted average of the births during the preceding generation varies with the level of fertility. The higher the level of fertility, the lower the value of $T(t)$, even though $f(a)$ in Equation (4.3) remains unchanged. We shall now construct a second approximation by modifying the basis of the first approximation (Equation (4.6)) in a way that allows for a value of $T(t)$ that varies with the level of fertility rather than retaining the incorrect assumption that $T(t)$ is fixed at T_0. We shall actually incorporate two adjustments. One is to assume that we can use as a value of $T(t)$ the mean length of generation in the stable population defined by the fixed mortality schedule and the fertility schedule at time t. The second adjustment will make allowance for the fact that the second order exponential indicated by the approximate solution in Equation (4.8) introduces a systematic difference between the weighted average of the births α to β years ago, and the births T years ago (where T is the mean length of generation in a stable population)—a systematic difference

123

between this relationship in the stable population on the one hand, and in the population with a second order exponential birth sequence on the other.

We are searching for a solution to an equation of the form shown in Equation (4.4). However, if we try to allow the interval between the births at different times that are related by the equation to vary, it is not possible to convert the equation into a difference equation and apply standard difference equation techniques for a solution. What we shall do instead is indicated in Equation (4.17).

$$(4.17) \qquad B(t) = R(0)e^{kt}B(t - T_0)\frac{B^*(t - T(t))}{B^*(t - T_0)}.$$

If the B^* values in Equation (4.17) were identical with values without the $*$, Equation (4.17) would reduce simply to Equation (4.4). The $*$ indicates values taken from the approximate solution given in Equation (4.8). To improve the original approximation, we shall assume that the relationship of births at $t - T(t)$ to births at $t - T_0$ is the same in the exact solution as in the approximate solution. The next step is to determine the value of $B^*(t - T(t))/B^*(t - T_0)$. Since $T(t)$ differs only slightly from T_0, we can assume that

$$(4.18) \qquad \log_e\left(\frac{B^*(t - T(t))}{B^*(t - T_0)}\right) = (T_0 - T(t))\left(\frac{d \log B^*(t)}{dt}\right)_{t=t-T_0};$$

but $T_0 - T(t)$ is one-half $\sigma^2 r$, or approximately $\sigma^2 kt/2T_0$ and

$$(4.19) \qquad \left[\frac{d \log B^*(t)}{dt}\right]_{t=t-T_0} = \frac{k}{2} + \frac{kt}{T_0} - k = -\frac{k}{2} + \frac{kt}{T_0}.$$

Hence

$$(4.20) \qquad \log\left(\frac{B^*(t - T(t))}{B^*(t - T_0)}\right) = -\frac{\sigma^2 k^2}{4T_0}t + \frac{\sigma^2 k^2}{2T_0^2}t^2;$$

and

$$(4.21) \qquad \frac{B^*(t - T(t))}{B^*(t - T_0)} = e^{-(\sigma^2 k^2/4T_0)t + (\sigma^2 k^2/2T_0^2)t^2}.$$

If we modify Equation (4.6) as indicated in Equation (4.17) by using the value of $B^*(t - T(t))/B^*(t - T_0)$ indicated in Equation (4.21), there remains another minor adjustment still to be allowed for. As indicated in Equation (4.14), the relationship between the births at a given time and the births T years earlier in a stable population depends on the level of fertility; but the birth sequence that we are trying to find resembles $B^*(t)$ (the function given in Equation (4.8)), a second order exponential, rather than the first order exponential birth sequence of the stable population. When $B^*(t)$ is substituted in the integral in Equation (4.1), it fails to satisfy it exactly. Making the substitution, we find, after simplification,

$$(4.22) \quad B^*(t) = B^*(t) \int_\alpha^\beta e^{-(k/2)a+(k/2T_0)a^2} e^{-(kt/T_0)a} p(a)m(a,t)da.$$

The modifications that we are proposing above yield a solution in which T_0 is, in effect, replaced by $T(t)$, in which case we can see that the integral equation would be satisfied provided that

$$(4.23) \quad \int_\alpha^\beta e^{-(k/2)a+(k/2T(t))a^2} e^{-r(t)a} p(a)m(a,t)da = 1.0.$$

The new term $r(t)$ appears because $r(t)$ is equal to $\log R(t)/T(t)$, and $\log R(t) = kt$. The terms after the second order exponential in a in Equation (4.23) represent a nonnegative continuous function with finite values in the range from α to β that has the aggregate value of 1.0, according to the fundamental equation of stable population analysis,

namely $\int_0^\beta e^{-ra}p(a)m(a)da = 1.0$. Thus our solution will fail to satisfy

the integral equation to the extent that the integral in Equation (4.23) differs from 1.0 with a nonzero value of k (it clearly equals 1.0 if k is equal to zero).

To see the effect of a nonzero value of k on the integral in Equation (4.23), we define $Z(t)$ as

$$(4.24) \quad Z(t) = \int_\alpha^\beta e^{-(k/2)a+(k/2T(t))a^2} e^{-r(t)a} p(a)m(a,t)da$$

and find the value of $(dZ(t)/dk)$ when $k = 0$.

$$(4.25) \quad \left(\frac{dZ(t)}{dk}\right)_{k=0} = \int_\alpha^\beta \left(-\frac{a}{2} + \frac{a^2}{2T(t)}\right) e^{-r(t)a} p(a)m(a,t)da$$

or

$$(4.26) \quad \left(\frac{dZ(t)}{dk}\right)_{k=0} = -\frac{\bar{A}}{2} + \frac{\gamma_2 + \bar{A}^2}{2T(t)},$$

where $\bar{A}$ is the mean age of fertility in the stable population and γ_2 is the variance in age of net fertility in the stable population. If we accept the approximation that the mean length of generation is about equal to

125

the mean age of fertility, we find

(4.27)
$$\left(\frac{dZ(t)}{dk}\right)_{k=0} \doteq \frac{\gamma_2}{2T(t)} = \frac{\sigma^2}{2T_0}.$$

Thus, for small values of k the value of the integral $Z(t)$ is

(4.28)
$$Z(t) \doteq 1.0 + \frac{k\sigma^2}{2T_0} \doteq e^{\frac{k\sigma^2}{2T_0}}.$$

The difference between $Z(t)$ and 1.0 can be visualized in these terms: the value of $\int_\alpha^\beta B(t-a)f(a)da = B(t-T(t))$ exactly, when $B(t) = B(0)e^{r(t)t}$. However, when $B(t)$ is a second order exponential of the form $B(t) = B(0)e^{(r(0)+(k/2))t+(k/2T)t^2}$, $B(t-a)$ is concave upward or downward (depending on the sign of k) over the range $a = \alpha$ to β, and $\int_\alpha^\beta B(t-a)f(a)da$ is greater or less than $B(t-T(t))$—greater if k is positive, and less if k is negative. The needed adjustment to make $B(t-T(t))$ equal to $\int_\alpha^\beta B(t-a)f(a)da$ is multiplication by $e^{(k/2)(\sigma^2/T)}$.

Incorporating the expression in Equation (4.21) in the appropriate place in Equation (4.17), multiplying by the factor very close to 1.0 indicated in Equation (4.28), we finally reach

(4.29) $\quad B(t) = R(0)B(t-T_0)e^{kt-(\sigma^2k^2/4T_0)t+(\sigma^2k^2/2T_0^2)t^2+(\sigma^2k/2T_0)}$

or, if $Y(t) = \log B(t)$,

(4.30)
$$Y(t) - Y(t-T_0) = a_0 + a_1 t + a_2 t^2,$$

where $a_0 = (\sigma^2k/2T_0)$, $a_1 = k(1-(\sigma^2k/4T_0))$, and $a_2 = \sigma^2k^2/2T_0^2$. The solution of this difference equation leads to the following expression for $B(t)$:

(4.31) $\quad B(t)$

$$= B(0)e^{[k/2+(\sigma^2k/2T_0)(1/T_0-k/12)]t+(k/2T_0)(1+\sigma^2k/4T_0)t^2+(\sigma^2k^2/6T_0^3)t^3}.$$

Thus, allowance for a changing value of T, and for the effect on the relationship between births in consecutive generations of a higher order exponential birth sequence converts a second order exponential function of t, depending only on the annual rate of change of fertility and on the mean age of the net fertility function, into a third order exponential that depends on the variance of the net fertility function as well. When numerical values are substituted in Equation (4.31), the fit with projected fertility is extraordinary. The maximum difference between projected births and births calculated by Equation (4.31) is .6% over a 200 year span, a difference that cannot be shown on the scale of Figure 4.1. The numerical differences in the parameters found in Equation (4.8) and those found in Equation (4.31) are small, as might be expected. In Equation (4.8), the coefficient of t is -5.0×10^{-3} and the coefficient of t^2 is -1.557×10^{-4}. In Equation (4.31), the coefficient of t is -5.21×10^{-3}; the coefficient of t^2 is -1.552×10^{-4}; the coefficient of t^3 is 2.14×10^{-8}.

Given the values of σ^2 and T_0 found in actual human fertility schedules, the adjustments incorporated in Equation (4.31) become important only for relatively rapid changes in fertility and large values of t; and in reality, a combination of a large value of k and a large value of t is not possible; that is, it would not be possible to maintain a large proportionate rate of increase or decrease in fertility for a long period of time without fertility either approaching zero or surpassing biologically or socially possible levels. In fact then, the approximate solution provided by Equation (4.8) is perfectly adequate to indicate the nature of the age composition in a population with changing fertility, the nature of the birth sequence, and the like. To avoid carrying the cumbersome expressions developed from Equations (4.14) to (4.31), we shall, in the remainder of our analysis, accept the approximation expressed in Equation (4.8).

Characteristics of the Birth Sequence and of the Population Resulting from Continuously Changing Fertility

As is evident in Figure 4.1, if fertility declines continuously from a high level, the birth sequence rises at a diminishing rate, reaches a maximum, and begins to fall at an accelerating pace. Were we to plot a birth sequence resulting from continuously rising fertility from low levels, we would find a curve that fell ever less rapidly till it reached a minimum, and then began to rise at an accelerating pace. We shall now consider the rate of increase of births under these circumstances. If we accept the approximate solution given in Equation (4.8), it is readily seen that the rate of increase of births in a population with changing fertility is

$$(4.32) \qquad \frac{d \log B(t)}{dt} \doteq \frac{k}{2} + \frac{kt}{T_0} \doteq r(t) + \frac{k}{2},$$

the intrinsic rate of increase plus one-half the annual rate of change of fertility. The rate of increase of the population may be found as follows:

127

$$(4.33) \quad P(t) = \int_0^\omega B(t-a)p(a)da$$

$$= B(0)e^{(k/2)t+(k/2T_0)t^2} \int_0^\omega e^{-(k/2)a+(k/2T_0)a^2} e^{-kta/T_0}p(a)da.$$

Hence

$$(4.34) \quad \frac{dP(t)}{dt} = \left(\frac{k}{2} + \frac{kt}{T_0}\right)P(t)$$

$$+ B(t)\int_0^\omega -\frac{ka}{T_0} e^{-(k/2)a+(B/2T_0)a^2} e^{-(kt/T_0)a}p(a)da$$

or

$$(4.35) \qquad\qquad \frac{dPt}{dt} = P(t)\left[\frac{k}{2} + \frac{kt}{T_0} - \frac{k}{T_0}\bar{a}(t)\right].$$

Hence

$$(4.36) \qquad \frac{d \log P(t)}{dt} = \frac{k}{2} + \frac{k}{T_0}(t - \bar{a}(t)) \doteq \frac{k}{2} + r(t - \bar{a}(t)).$$

The rate of increase of the population is equal to the rate of increase of births at the time that the cohort whose age is now the average age of the population was born.

The births reach a maximum (if fertility is continuously declining) when the rate of increase in births is zero. From Equation (4.32) we can see that this occurs when the intrinsic rate of increase of the population is $-k/2$, or at a time equal to $-T_0/2$ (recalling that our origin has been maintained at the moment when the net reproduction rate becomes 1.0). In other words, the births reach a maximum half a generation before the population is at replacement. It is interesting to note that the sequence of white births in the United States reached a maximum in the early 1920s, just about half a generation before the net reproduction rate fell to 1.0. The population reaches a maximum $\bar{a}(t)$ years later than the births do. In the projection with fertility falling at one percent a year represented in Figure 4.1 the mean age of the net fertility function is 32.1 years, so the maximum of births is reached more than 16 years before the net reproduction rate reaches unity. At the time that the projected population reaches a maximum, the mean age of the population is about $37\frac{1}{2}$ years, so the population continues to increase for about 21 years after the intrinsic rate of increase is zero.

128

An expression for the age distribution of the population with changing fertility relative to the stable population has already been given, and is repeated here for convenience:

$$(4.13) \qquad c(a,t) = (b(t)/b_s(t))e^{-(k/2)a+(k/2T_0)a^2}c_s(a).$$

The easiest way to visualize the relationship between a stable age distribution and the distribution of the population with changing fertility is first to imagine two populations that have the same number of births at time t, one of which has always experienced the current fertility and mortality schedules, and the other of which has experienced a history of constantly changing fertility. One, of course, would be the stable population, and the other the population whose age distribution we are now examining. The number of persons at each age in the stable population would be $N_s(a,t) = B(t)e^{-r(t)a}p(a)$; the number of persons at each age in the population with a history of constantly changing fertility would be $N_k(a,t) = N_s(a,t)e^{-(k/2)a+(k/2T)a^2}$. The second order exponential multiplying $N_s(a,t)$ is shown in Figure 4.2 for various values of k.

The salient characteristics of the second order exponential relating $N_k(a,t)$ to $N_s(a,t)$ are: The number of persons at age zero and at an age equal to the mean length of generation are the same in the two populations. When fertility has been declining, the number of persons at ages between zero and the age equal to the mean length of generation is slightly greater than in the stable population. The ratio of N_k to N_s reaches a maximum of $e^{-kT/8}$ at an age equal to one-half the mean length of generation. At ages above the mean length of generation, the ratio of N_k to N_s falls rapidly below 1.0.

In sum, the effect of a history of declining fertility on the numbers at each age (relative to a stable population) is to produce slightly greater numbers (assuming the current number of births to be equal) from ages zero to T and sharply diminishing numbers above age T. The effect of a slight increase in numbers relative to the stable at ages from zero to T and increasing diminution above age T on the *proportionate* age distribution depends upon the age structure of the stable population itself. A proportionate distribution is defined as the number at each age divided by the total number. If the total number in the two populations were the same, the proportionate distributions would be related to each other precisely by the functions shown in Figure 4.2; that is, if the total number in each population were the same, the ratio of the proportions in the population with a history of declining fertility to that in the stable

129

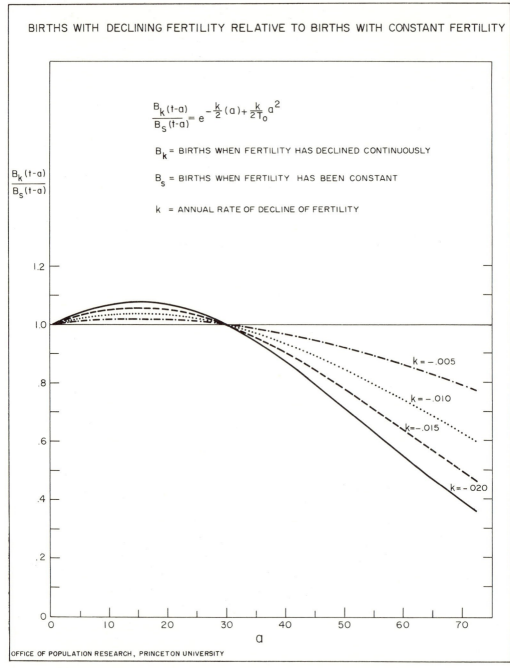

BIRTHS WITH DECLINING FERTILITY RELATIVE TO BIRTHS WITH CONSTANT FERTILITY

$$\frac{B_k(t-a)}{B_S(t-a)} = e^{-\frac{k}{2}(a) + \frac{k}{2T_0}a^2}$$

B_k = BIRTHS WHEN FERTILITY HAS DECLINED CONTINUOUSLY

B_S = BIRTHS WHEN FERTILITY HAS BEEN CONSTANT

k = ANNUAL RATE OF DECLINE OF FERTILITY

$\dfrac{B_k(t-a)}{B_S(t-a)}$

$k = -.005$

$k = -.010$

$k = -.015$

$k = -.020$

OFFICE OF POPULATION RESEARCH, PRINCETON UNIVERSITY

Figure 4.2. Births *a* years ago in a population with a history of declining fertility relative to births in a population with constant fertility when births at given moment are equal in two populations, for various rates of decline.

would be $e^{-(k/2)a+(k/2T)a^2}$. However, the number of persons in the two populations would be the same only if the small proportionate increases below age T somehow offset the large proportionate decreases above age T. Such a balance might occur in a stable population that declines very steeply with age. In fact, such a balance occurs in a stable population where the mean age is about 57% of the mean length of generation. Thus if the mean length of generation is 30 years, a stable population with a mean age of a little over 17 years would have about the same number of persons as a population with the same births and a history of constantly declining (or constantly rising) fertility. (With a life expectancy of 70 years, a stable population with a mean age of 17 years would have a gross reproduction rate of about 5, and a rate of increase of about 5.3% per year. It is doubtless more plausible in such an instance to analyze the age distribution of a population with a history of rising rather than declining fertility.) The effect of multiplying by the function shown in Figure 4.2 on stable populations that diminish at a more moderate rate with age is to decrease the total number. Hence the ratio of $c_k(a)/c_s(a)$ is usually a function of the sort shown in Figure 4.2 multiplied by a constant greater than one. In fact, as is shown in Equation (4.13), the multiplier is the ratio of the birth rate in the population with changing fertility to the birth rate in the stable. Since we have been assuming that the number of births in the two populations is the same, the ratio of the birth rates is simply the reciprocal of the ratio of the population sizes.

In a given stable population, as the above consideration suggests, the ratio of b_k/b_s will be less for a given value of k, the greater is the mean length of generation—the greater the age at which the function shown in Figure 4.2 crosses unity. Conversely, in a population with a given mean length of generation, the ratio of b_k/b_s will be greater the greater are the proportions in the stable population at the older ages. The ratio b_k/b_s depends upon the extent to which the function shown in Figure 4.2 diminishes the stable population. The younger the stable population, the less it is diminished; the greater the age at which the function crosses unity, the less the stable population is diminished. These considerations suggest the hypothesis that the ratio of b_k/b_s might be the same in two stable populations if the relationship between the point where the function shown in Figure 4.2 has a value of unity, and the average age of the population is the same—in other words, in stable populations with the same ratio of $\bar{a}_s/T$. We have calculated b_k/b_s for 36 stable populations ($e_0^0 = 20$, 30, 50, 60, and 70 years, growth rates

−0.01, 0.00, 0.01, 0.02, 0.03, and 0.04) for values of k ranging from −.005 to −.030 with values of T at 28 and 30 years. The calculations involved a numerical evaluation of the integral in Equation (4.38). Figure 4.3 shows the values of b_k/b_s for different values of $\bar{a}_s/T$. Some of the points closely clustered in Figure 4.3 are derived from stable populations with very different growth rates and mortality schedules; for example, the stable population with $e_0^0 = 30$ and $r = -0.01$ has a mean age only slightly different from the stable population with $e_0^0 = 70$ and $r = 0.01$. The stable populations that we utilized were drawn from the "West" family of model stable populations. By fitting curves to the values of b_k/b_s calculated for these populations, we arrived at the following empirical relationship between b_k/b_s and k for a given value of $\bar{a}_s/T$:

(4.37) $\quad \dfrac{b_k}{b_s}$

$$= 1.0 + \left[3.807 - 1.039 \frac{\bar{a}_s}{T} - 9.839 \left(\frac{\bar{a}_s}{T}\right)^2\right] k + \left(66.0 - 149.0 \frac{\bar{a}_s}{T}\right) k^2.$$

Equation (4.37) provides estimates of b_k/b_s within about 1% of the true value over the stated range of k except at very large values of $\bar{a}_s/T$. Its accuracy is within the same margin for positive values of k up to 0.03.

Equation (4.37) is based on a geometric argument suggesting that b_k/b_s should be a function of $\bar{a}_s/T$ and k. It is also possible to express b_k (as well as b_s) in terms of integrals that can be evaluated as accurately as one pleases by numerical methods, and finally to express b_k/b_s in terms of the moments of the stable age distribution. If we note that the total population at time t, $N(t)$, is $\int_0^\omega N(a,t)da$ and that $N(a,t)$ is as given in Equation (4.10), it follows that

(4.38) $$b_k = \frac{1}{\displaystyle\int_0^\omega e^{-(k/2)a + (k/2T)a^2} e^{-ra} p(a)da}.$$

We shall now approximate b_k by expanding the expression in Equation (4.38) in a MacLaurin series, and accept the first two terms as a usable approximation. According to this expansion,

(4.39) $\quad b_k = (b_k)_{k=0} + \left(\dfrac{db_k}{dk}\right)_{k=0} \cdot k + \left(\dfrac{d^2b_k}{dk^2}\right)_{k=0} \cdot \dfrac{k^2}{2} + \cdots .$

But

132

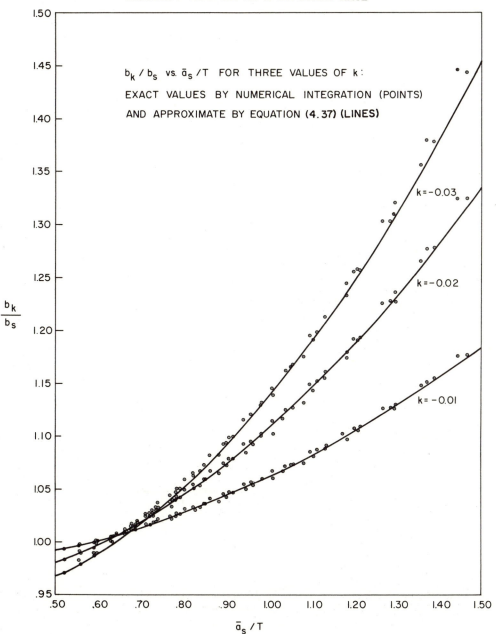

Figure 4.3. The birth rate in populations with a history of declining fertility relative to the birth rate in a population with a history of constant fertility, for various values of the ratio of the mean age of the stable population to the mean length of generation, and various rates of decline in fertility.

133

(4.40) $\quad \left(\dfrac{db_k}{dk}\right)_{k=0} = (-b_k^2)_{k=0} \displaystyle\int_0^\omega \left(-\dfrac{k}{2} + \dfrac{a^2}{2T}\right) e^{-ra} p(a)\,da$

or

(4.41) $\quad\quad\quad\quad\quad\quad \left(\dfrac{db_k}{dk}\right)_{k=0} = \dfrac{b_s}{2}\left(A_1 - \dfrac{A_2}{T}\right),$

where

$$A_n = b_k \int_0^\omega a^n e^{-(k/2)a+(k/2T)a^2} e^{-ra} p(a)\,da \quad \text{and} \quad A_n = b_s \int_0^\omega a^n e^{-ra} p(a)\,da$$

when $k = 0$. Note that

(4.42) $\quad \left(\dfrac{dA_n}{dk}\right)_{k=0} = \left(\dfrac{db_k}{dk}\right)_{k=0} \cdot \dfrac{A_n}{b_s} + b_s \displaystyle\int_0^\omega \left(-\dfrac{a^{n+1}}{2} + \dfrac{a^{n+2}}{2T}\right) e^{-ra} p(a)\,da$

or

(4.43) $\quad \left(\dfrac{dA_n}{dk}\right)_{k=0} = \dfrac{1}{2}\,(A_1 A_n - A_{n+1}) + \dfrac{1}{2T}\,(A_{n+2} - A_2 A_n).$

Thus

(4.44) $\quad\quad\quad\quad \left(\dfrac{d^2 b_k}{dk^2}\right)_{k=0} = \dfrac{b_s}{2}\left(\dfrac{dA_1}{dk} - \dfrac{1}{T}\dfrac{dA_2}{dk}\right)_{k=0}$

or, after substitution and rearrangement,

(4.45) $\quad \left(\dfrac{d^2 b_k}{dk^2}\right)_{k=0} = \dfrac{b_s}{4}\left[A_1^2 - A_2 - \dfrac{1}{T}\left(2(A_1 A_3 - A_3) + \dfrac{A_4 - A_2^2}{T}\right)\right].$

Hence

(4.46)

$$b_k = b_s \left\{1 + \left(A_1 - \dfrac{A_2}{T}\right)k + \left[A_1^2 - A_2 - \dfrac{1}{T}\left(2(A_1 A_3 - A_3) + \dfrac{A_4 - A_2^2}{T}\right)\right]\dfrac{k^2}{8}\right\}.$$

In trial calculations, Equation (4.46) yielded estimates of b_k a little less exact than those produced by Equation (4.37). Equation (4.37) shows the dependence of b_k/b_s on two parameters ($\bar{a}_s/T$ and k) whereas Equation (4.46) relates the same ratio to k, the first four moments of the stable age distribution, and T. In principle, Equation (4.46) should indicate how b_k/b_s depends on the structure of the stable age distribution, but it is hard to visualize the influence of the properties of the age distribution in this somewhat complicated expression. Equation (4.37) provides at least as good an approximation because of the existence of systematic relationships among the moments of stable age distributions. Equation (4.37) arises from intuitively appealing geometric relations; the relations in Equation (4.46), on the other hand, would apply to the age structure of any growing aggregate, whether in a human population or not, characterized by constantly changing fertility (although it might be necessary to incorporate higher moments in some aggregates to obtain a close approximation).

We are now in a position to explain, in succinct terms, how the birth rate, the death rate, and the rate of increase of a population with a history of changing fertility are related to the corresponding parameters of a stable population. Figure 4.3 shows the relation of b_k/b_s to k and $\bar{a}_s/T$, a relationship expressed analytically in Equation (4.37). The larger $\bar{a}_s$ is relative to T, the larger is the birth rate with declining fertility relative to the birth rate in the stable population. When $\bar{a}_s/T$ is a little less than 60%, the slightly greater proportions in the population with declining fertility below T just offset the smaller proportion above age T, and the population with changing fertility has the same birth rate as the stable. However, such equality could occur only in a population with an extremely low average age, a population not likely in fact to occur. From Equation (4.36) it is possible to derive a direct relationship between the rate of increase of the population with declining fertility and the stable population. This relationship is

$$(4.47) \qquad r_k = r_s + \left(\frac{1}{2} - \frac{\bar{a}_k}{T}\right) k.$$

If k is negative, it is evident that the rate of increase in the population with a history of changing fertility is greater than the intrinsic rate of increase, provided the mean age of the population is greater than one-half the mean length of generation. It is hard to imagine a population with a history of declining fertility where $\bar{a}_k$ is less than one-half of T, since very high fertility—a gross reproduction rate of five or more— is required to produce a low $\bar{a}_s$, and $\bar{a}_k$ is generally less than $\bar{a}_s$. It is certainly difficult to visualize arriving at such a gross reproduction rate after a long history of steadily declining fertility. However, it is possible to imagine a population with steadily *increasing* fertility in which r_k would be less than r_s, contrary to the relationship at moderate levels of fertility.

The death rate in a population with constantly changing fertility can be expressed as the difference between b_k and r_k. In populations with very high fertility it is imaginable that d_k would be no greater than d_s, but within the range of fertilities commonly observed the death

135

rate in the population with declining fertility is lower than the death rate in a stable population based on the same mortality and fertility schedules. The tendency towards a lower death rate is easily visualized by considering the typical relationship of the age distributions in the two populations. The population with a history of declining fertility has substantially lower proportions at the older ages, and slightly to moderately higher proportions under age T. This relative age structure is favorable to lower population death rates, especially in populations where the mortality schedule has moderate to low rates. In such low mortality schedules, death rates at the older ages are especially prominent, and the fact that the population with a history of declining fertility has higher proportions in early childhood offsets only to a very slight degree the reduction in the overall death rate caused by the low proportions above age 60. In a very high mortality life table, the relative advantage in producing a lower death rate enjoyed by the population with a history of declining fertility is much less. Table 4.1 shows birth rates, death rates, and rates of increase for stable populations, and for populations with a history of declining fertility at an annual rate of 2% for various levels of fertility and mortality.

Table 4.1 Birth rates, death rates, and rates of increase in stable populations at various levels of fertility and mortality, and in populations with the same fertility and mortality, but a history of a prolonged decline in fertility at 2% annually

	r_s	−.0100	0.000	0.0100	0.0200	0.0300	0.0400
$e_0^0 = 30$	r_k	−.0003	0.0074	0.0154	0.0237	0.0322	0.0400
	b_s	0.0245	0.0333	0.0437	0.0552	0.0676	0.0808
	b_k	0.0287	0.0372	0.0468	0.0574	0.0687	0.0807
	d_s	0.0345	0.0333	0.0337	0.0352	0.0376	0.0408
	d_k	0.0290	0.0298	0.0314	0.0337	0.0366	0.0399
	GRR	1.60	2.11	2.77	3.62	4.71	6.11
$e_0^0 = 50$	r_k	0.0024	0.0098	0.0174	0.0253	0.0335	0.0420
	b_s	0.0139	0.0200	0.0275	0.0361	0.0457	0.0560
	b_k	0.0178	0.0239	0.0309	0.0389	0.0476	0.0569
	d_s	0.0239	0.0200	0.0175	0.0161	0.0157	0.0160
	d_k	0.0154	0.0141	0.0135	0.0136	0.0141	0.0149
	GRR	1.04	1.32	1.80	2.36	3.08	4.01
$e_0^0 = 70$	r_k	0.0045	0.0116	0.0189	0.0266	0.0346	0.0428
	b_s	0.0095	0.0143	0.0203	0.0276	0.0358	0.0448
	b_k	0.0131	0.0181	0.0240	0.0307	0.0382	0.0463
	d_s	0.0195	0.0143	0.0103	0.0076	0.0058	0.0048
	d_k	0.0086	0.0065	0.0051	0.0041	0.0037	0.0034
	GRR	.80	1.06	1.40	1.84	2.41	3.14

The Birth Sequence and the Age Distribution in the Early Years
After the Initiation of a Fertility Decline and in the Years
After a Decline Has Ended

In the earlier sections of this chapter expressions are derived for the birth sequence, the age composition, and other parameters of a population experiencing a continuous decline of fertility over a very long time. We shall see in this section that it is possible to find analytic expressions for the birth sequence that occurs as a population moves from fertility that is constant to fertility that is steadily declining and also for the birth sequence that occurs as a long continuing constant annual decline of fertility stops, fertility levels off, and becomes constant at a lower level.

To determine the birth sequence — and the age distribution — in the early years after a fertility decline has been initiated (at $t = 0$), we can begin with the known sequence that would have occurred if fertility had been declining for a long time, plus the known relation of the age distribution of the population with such a history to the age distribution of the population now of interest — a population stable prior to $t = 0$. The birth sequence generated in the stable population that subsequently experiences continuously declining fertility after $t = 0$ can be determined by the following steps:

(1) Determine the birth sequence $B_k(t)$ that would be generated with constantly declining fertility by a population with a prior history of continuously declining fertility, employing Equation (4.8) (or for greater precision, Equation (4.31)).

(2) Consider a population whose number at each age (the highest age being β, the upper limit of childbearing) is defined as the number of persons in a population with a history of declining fertility *minus* the number in a stable population with the same number of births at $t = 0$. Call this population D, and its age distribution $D(a)$. ($D(a)$ is negative at some ages.) Note that if $N_k(a,0)$ is the number of persons at age a at time zero in the population with a history of declining fertility

(4.48) $$D(a) = N_k(a,0)[e^{(k/2)a-(k/2T)a^2}-1].$$

(3) Suppose the births experienced by population D and its progeny are $B_D(t)$, and that $Q(t)$ is $B_D(t)/B_k(t)$. Then the births that will occur to the population of interest (the stable population ex-

137

periencing declining fertility after $t = 0$) will be $B_k(t) \cdot (1 - Q(t))$. Thus to find the birth sequence that occurs in the early years of fertility decline, we need to determine the relation of the births generated by population D to $B_k(t)$.

In analyzing the birth sequence generated by the population D, we begin with a plausible hypothesis that will be accepted after being confirmed by a numerical example: namely, that $Q(t)$ (the ratio $B_D(t)/B_k(t)$) is scarcely affected by the subsequent course of fertility; in particular, if births occurring to $N_k(a)$ are compared to those occurring to $N_s(a)$ under a regime of constant fertility and under a regime of declining fertility, the relation between the two birth sequences will be the same. To restate the hypothesis more precisely: Suppose two initial populations with a difference of the form $D(a)$ are subjected to a sequence of constantly changing fertility, and consider the sequence of ratios of births in one population to births in the other; then suppose instead that the two were subjected to constant fertility at $t = 0$ and subsequently, and consider this second sequence of ratios of births in one population to births in the other. The two sequences of ratios will be essentially the same. This hypothesis is strongly supported when tested by an empirical example: a set of four population projections over a 200 year period, projections made by single years of age and time. The four projections were two in which fertility (constant in age pattern) fell by one percent annually. and two in which fertility was held fixed. In all four, mortality was constant. There were two initial populations: a stable population embodying the fertility and mortality held fixed in two of the projections, and a population with the same number of births as the stable, but with the age distribution at $t = 0$ that results from a history of constantly declining fertility. Thus the projected populations were $N_s(a)$ and $N_k(a)$, and the difference between them was $D(a)$. Figure 4.4 shows the ratio (births occurring to the population with a history of declining fertility, births occurring to the stable population) in both projections. The birth sequences in the two sets of projections are, of course, quite different. With declining fertility the number of births reaches a maximum less than nine times the number at $t = 0$; with fertility held at its high initial level, on the other hand, the number of births is multiplied by more than 5,000 during the 200 years of the projection. Yet, for the first 60 years or so the two sets of ratios are indistinguishable even on a rather large scale diagram. In the later years of the projections, the very small amplitude fluctuations begin to differ slightly in amplitude and increasingly in phase. One sequence is an example of the convergence of a birth sequence to stability discussed at some length in Chapter 3. What is notable is the very close similarity to convergence to stability of the other sequence of ratios, in which a birth sequence converges on the form produced by a history of constantly declining fertility. When the age structure of fertility is the same, as it is in these calculations, convergence to a stable sequence and convergence to a sequence dictated by changing fertility are remarkably alike.

The slight differences that appear in the two sets of ratios after 80 or 90 years can be explained in terms of the analysis introduced in Chapter 3. The fertility pattern employed in all four projections was that of Sweden in 1891 to 1900, and the mortality the "West" female

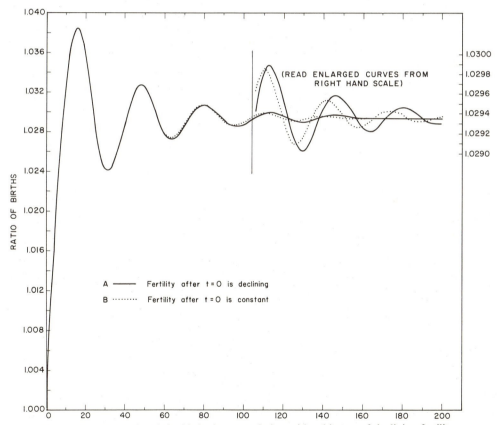

Figure 4.4. The ratio of the births in a population with a history of declining fertility (prior to $t = 0$) to the births in a population with a history of constant fertility: A—when fertility is constant after $t = 0$; B—when fertility constantly declines after $t = 0$.

139

model life table with e_0^0 at 70 years. If we substitute the parameters calculated for this net fertility function in the equations given in Chapter 3 that determine the period of the low frequency oscillatory term and its relative damping, we find an estimated period of about 31.3 years for the stable population at the high fertility assumed for $t = 0$. This estimated figure increases to 33.5 years when the net reproduction rate falls to zero (at $t = 133.5$ years) and lengthens further as fertility continues to fall. Thus the difference in cycle length increases from zero to 2.4 years in this 133 year period; the average difference in cycle length is about 1.2 years and in 4.1 cycles the difference in the point at which the two cross the equilibrium value should be about 5 years, as indeed it is. For this fertility schedule relative damping calculated as in Chapter 3 is slightly less at high values of r than at low, consistent with the slightly larger amplitude of the ratios with falling fertility in Figure 4.4.

We now return to the births generated by the difference between the stable population and the population with a history of declining fertility — to the progeny of $D(a)$ relative to the births produced by the population with a history of declining fertility, or $Q(t)$. $D(a)$ is shown in Figure 4.5. The two populations, which, when differed, constitute $D(a)$, have the same number of births at $t = 0$, and therefore $D(a)$ necessarily has zero births at $t = 0$. Births are zero because the negative numbers in $D(a)$ from age T to β are offset by positive numbers of women in the childbearing ages below T.

In the long run, $D(a)$ adds to the size of the birth stream in the population with a history of declining fertility, because starting at $t = 0$ the negative segment of $D(a)$ begins to pass beyond age β, and the positive segment from zero to T begins to produce additional births that would not occur in the absence of $D(a)$. These additional progeny will in turn have children of their own. The maximum value of $D(a)$ occurs at an age equal to $T/2$ where the population with a history of declining fertility exceeds the stable by a factor of $e^{-kT/8}$. The long run increment to the birth sequence produced by $D(a)$ will be less than this maximum, since when the cohort aged $T/2$ is at the central ages of childbearing, other cohorts in the childbearing span will be smaller. The mean value of the ratio of the declining fertility population to the stable from age zero to T is $-kT/12$; the long run increment in births in the projections illustrated in Figure 4.4 is $-kT/10.5$. A good estimate of the ultimate greater flow of births that would result from a history of declining fertility is the latter figure ($e^{-kT/10.5}$).

For the first few years the number of births occurring to a population with constant fertility prior to $t = 0$ and constantly falling fertility thereafter is perfectly evident. When fertility begins its decline, the number of women of childbearing age is not affected at first, and the number of births is simply reduced below $B(0)e^{r(0)t}$ by a factor e^{kt}. In other words, until the progeny produced by falling fertility enter the ages at which they bear children, the birth sequence is $B(0)e^{(r(0)+k)t}$ We also know that ultimately the birth sequence in this population comes to a course exactly parallel to the births in a population with a long history of declining fertility, and that births in the formerly stable population will then equal births in the other multiplied by a factor of approximately $e^{kT/10.5}$. The only problem in arriving at an exact understanding of the birth sequence as a population enters declining fertility is the transition from the readily calculated first α years (α being the youngest age of childbearing) to the longer-run form of $B(0)e^{kT/10.5 + (k/2)t + (k/2T)t^2}$

An accurate representation of the transition from the first α years to the second order exponential birth sequence can be obtained by viewing the transition as part of the projection of the initial difference be-

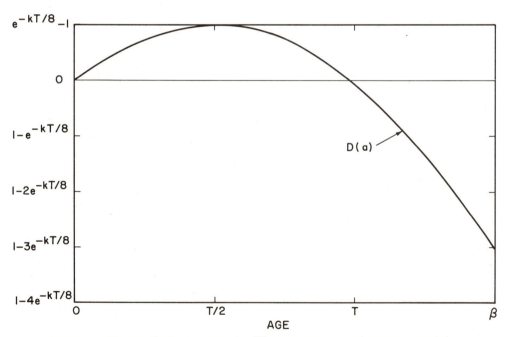

Figure 4.5. The age distribution $D(a)$: the difference, up to age β, between a population with a history of declining fertility and a population with a history of constant fertility.

tween the stable population and the population with a history of declining fertility, and by taking account of the very close resemblance
of this projection to the convergence of the progeny of $D(a)$ to stability.
The ratio of the births occurring during the first α years in the population with a history of declining fertility to the births in the population
that was initially stable is $e^{-(k/2)t+(k/2T)t^2}$. This ratio reaches a maximum
deviation from unity of $e^{-kT/8}$ just $T/2$ years after the decline begins.
This deviation is greater than the long run difference (which is a factor
of $e^{kT/10.5}$) between the two birth sequences. (Figure 4.6 shows the
ratio of the births in the formerly stable population to those in the
continuously declining fertility population for the first 30 years, together with the factor $e^{-(k/2)t+(k/2T)t^2}$.) The age structure of $D(a)$ is
broad and smooth, so the fluctuations after $t = T/2$ consist almost
entirely of the lowest frequency term in the representation of the
progeny of $D(a)$ as the sum of a number of damped oscillatory components. Consequently, a precise representation of the birth sequence is

(4.49)

$$B(t) = B(0)e^{(r(0)+k)t} \qquad\qquad\qquad\qquad\qquad\qquad t \leq T/2$$

$$B(t) = B(0)e^{kT/10.5+(r(0)+k/2)t+(k/2T)t^2}[1 + e^{kT(1/8-1/10.5)}e^{x_1 t}\cos y_1(t - T/2)]$$

$$t > T/2$$

where x_1 and y_1 are the real and imaginary parts of the first complex
root of

$$\int_0^\beta e^{-ra}p(a)m(a)da = 1.0.$$

Equation (4.49) does not lend itself to a simple representation of the
age distribution at time t because of the damped oscillatory component.
A less accurate but still serviceable approximation can be found by
neglecting the oscillatory component expressed in the latter part of
Equation (4.49) after its first intersection with zero. (In most fertility
schedules there is either no childbearing or childbearing at extremely
low rates at ages less than $T/2$.) Such an approximation is obtained by
assuming that the birth sequence remains on the path $B(0)e^{(r(0)+k)t}$
until this path intersects with $B(0)e^{kT/10.5+(r(0)+k/2)t+(k/2T)t^2}$. A serviceable
rule of thumb is that the birth sequence remains on the path $B(0)e^{(r(0)+k)t}$
from $t = 0$ until $t = 0.75T$, since $e^{.75kT} = e^{(k/2)(.75T)+(k/2T)(.75T)^2+kT/10.67}$.
The error introduced in this approximation by neglecting the fluctua-
tions subsequent to the first half cycle is less than one-half percent.

142

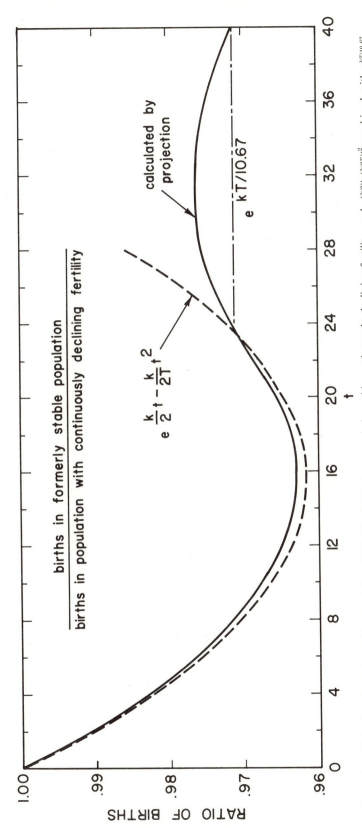

Figure 4.6. Births in a formerly stable population divided by births in a population with continuously declining fertility, and $e^{(k/2)t-(k/2T)t^2}$ combined with $e^{kT/10.67}$, for $t > 3T/4$.

The resultant approximation for the birth sequence in the years near $t = 0$ when the fertility decline begins at that point is

$$B(t) = B(0)e^{r(0)t} \qquad\qquad t < 0$$

(4.50) $$B(t) = B(0)e^{(r(0)+k)t} \qquad\qquad 0 < t < 3T/4$$

$$B(t) = B(0)e^{.09375kT+(r(0)+(k/2))t+(k/2T)t^2}$$

From Equation (4.50) we can obtain an expression for the age distribution of a population that has recently initiated a continuous decline in fertility, relative to the age distribution of a stable population based on the fertility at time t. The basis for such formulae is a calculation of an expression for $B(t - a)$. We must distinguish two cases:

Case I: $t < .75T$.

If $a < t$,

(4.51) $$B(t - a) = B(t)e^{-(r(0)+k)a}$$

but

(4.52) $$r(0) \doteq r(t) - \frac{kt}{T}$$

or

(4.53) $$B(t - a) = B(t)e^{-r(t)a - k(1-t/T)a} \qquad\qquad a < t.$$

If $a > t$,

(4.54) $$B(t - a) = B(0)e^{r(0)(t-a)} = B(t)e^{-r(0)t - kt + r(0)t - r(0)a}$$

or

(4.55) $$B(t - a) = B(t)e^{-r(t)a - k(1-a/T)t} \qquad\qquad a > t.$$

Case II: $t > .75T$.

Let $m = t - .75T$. If $a < m$,

(4.56) $$B(t - a) = B(t)e^{-r(t)a - (k/2)a + (k/2T)a^2} \qquad\qquad a < m.$$

If a lies between m and t,

(4.57) $$B(t - a) = B(0)e^{(r(0)+k)(t-a)}$$

or

(4.58) $$B(t - a) = B(t)e^{-.09375kT - (r(0)+k/2)t - (k/2T)t^2 + (r(0)+k)t - (r(0)+k)a}.$$

But

144

(4.59)
$$r(0) + k = r(t) + k\left(1 - \frac{t}{T}\right).$$

Hence

(4.60) $\quad B(t - a) = B(t)e^{-r(t)a - .09375kT + (k/2)t - (k/2T)t^2 - k(1-t/T)a}.$

If $a > t$

(4.61) $\qquad B(t - a) = B(0)e^{r(0)(t-a)}$

or

(4.62) $\qquad B(t - a) = B(t)e^{-r(t)a - .09375kT - (k/2)t - (k/2T)t^2 + kta/T}.$

For convenience we shall reassemble the results for Case I ($t < .75T$) and Case II ($t > .75T$).

(4.63)
$$
\left.
\begin{array}{ll}
B(t - a) = B(t)e^{-r(t)a - k(1-t/T)a} & a < t \\
B(t - a) = B(t)e^{-r(t)a - k(1-a/T)t} & a > t
\end{array}
\right\} t < 3T/4
$$

and, with $m = t - 3T/4$,

(4.64)

$$
\left.
\begin{array}{ll}
B(t - a) = B(t)e^{-r(t)a - (k/2)a + (k/2T)a^2} & a < m \\
B(t - a) = B(t)e^{-r(t)a - .09375kT + (k/2)t - (k/2T)t^2 - k(1-t/T)a} & m < a < t \\
B(t - a) = B(t)e^{-r(t)a - .09375kT - (k/2)t - (k/2T)t^2 + kta/T} & a > t
\end{array}
\right\} t > 3T/4
$$

Since the births in a stable population with the fertility of time t would be $B(t-a) = B(t)e^{-r(t)a}$, the ratio of the birth sequence in the population in question to a stable population is apparent. Mortality is assumed constant throughout, and therefore the age distribution in the population in question relative to the age distribution of a stable population can be ascertained by first multiplying the number in each age interval in a stable population of arbitrary size by the ratio of $B(t - a)$ in the given population to $B(t - a)$ in the stable for the central age in each interval. The resultant figures are the number of persons in a population having the same current number of births as the stable population, but with the age distribution that is sought. The desired proportionate age distribution is obtained by dividing the number in each age interval by the total number. Figure 4.7 shows the projected age distribution of a population with fertility declining at one percent annually calculated by projection and by Equation (4.64) 50 years after the decline begins. Figure 4.8 shows the age distributions, relative

145

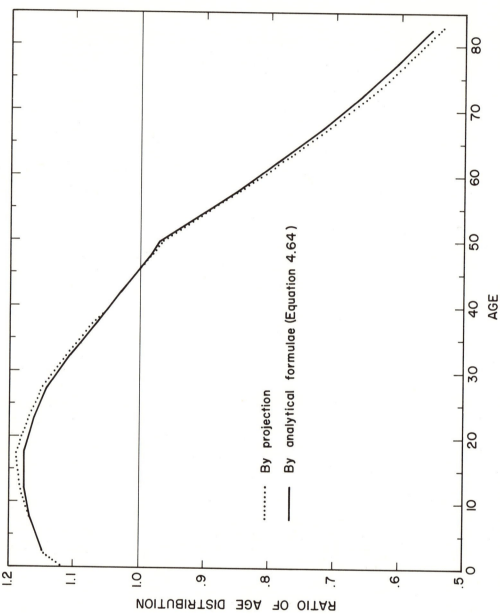

Figure 4.7. Projected age distribution 50 years after fertility begins to decline by 1% annually, and age distribution according

to the stable, of populations where fertility has been declining by one percent annually for 10, 20, 30, and 60 years, and "forever."

The calculation of the birth sequence and age distribution that occur in the years after the constant decline in fertility has stopped begins with a set of equations parallel to those given in Equation (4.50).

$$B(t) = B(0)e^{(r+k/2)t+(k/2T)t^2} \qquad\qquad t < 0$$

(4.65)
$$B(t) = B(0)e^{(r-k/2)t+(k/2T)t^2} \qquad\qquad 0 < t < 3T/4$$

$$B(t) = B(0)e^{-.09375kT+r(t)} \qquad\qquad t > 3T/4.$$

The steps leading to these equations are fully analogous to the steps leading up to Equation (4.50).[1] Again one obtains expressions for $B(t-a)$ that are different when t is less than $0.75T$ and when t is

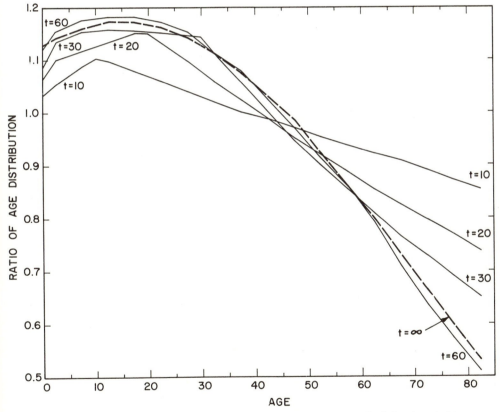

Figure 4.8. $c_k(a,t)/c_s(a,t)$ where $k = -0.01$, and fertility has been declining for 10, 20, 30, and 60 years, and "forever."

147

greater than $0.75T$. (Note that $t = 0$ when fertility stops declining.) In the first case we find

$$B(t = a) = B(t)e^{-ra+k(1/2-t/T)a+(k/2T)a^2} \qquad a < t$$

(4.66)

$$B(t - a) = B(t)e^{-ra+k(1-a/T)t-(k/2)a+(k/2T)a^2} \qquad a > t,$$

and in the second case, letting $m = t - 3T/4$

(4.67)

$$B(t - a) = B(t)e^{-ra} \qquad a < m$$

$$B(t - a) = B(t)e^{-ra+.09375kT-(k/2)t+(k/2T)t^2+k(1/2-t/T)a+(k/2T)a^2} \qquad m < a < t$$

$$B(t - a) = B(t)e^{-ra+.09375kT+(k/2)t+(k/2T)t^2-k(1/2+t/T)a+(k/2T)a^2} \qquad a > t.$$

Figure 4.9 shows the age distributions (relative to the stable) of populations in which fertility was declining by one percent annually until

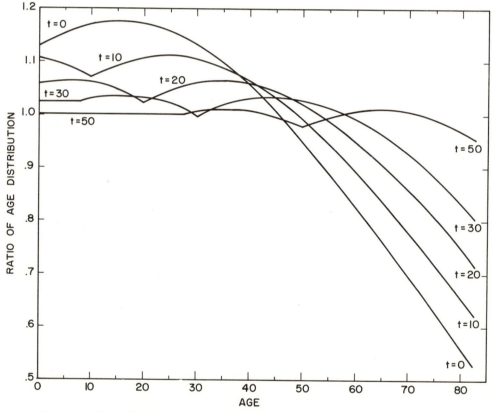

Figure 4.9. Proportion in each age group relative to the stable population in a population where fertility was declining until $t = 0$, for $t = 10$, 20, 30, and 50 years.

$t = 0$, and has been constant for 10, 20, 30, and 50 years. Figure 4.9 shows the evolution of the age distribution to a stable form, and Figure 4.8 the evolution of the age distribution to the form that occurs when fertility has been declining "forever."

Growth After Fertility Has Fallen to the Level That Just Ensures Replacement

An important aspect of the convergence of a population to stability when fertility has fallen to replacement during a sustained decline is the substantial remaining growth potential. How much would the population grow if fertility fell steadily until a net reproduction rate of unity were attained and then remained constant? This question is readily answered by comparing the population with a history of declining fertility to the stationary population with the same number of births the declining fertility population has when it reaches a net reproduction rate of one. The future sequence of births from this point generated with no further changes in fertility by the population with a history of declining fertility is given in Equation (4.65) with r set equal to zero. The ultimate annual number of births exceeds those in the year at which net reproduction rate reaches one by a factor of about $e^{-.09375kT}$. The ultimate population would have the age structure of the stationary population and the number of annual births just given. But the stationary population with a given annual number of births is related in size to the population with a history of declining fertility and a given annual number of births as the ratio of b_k/b_s. Hence the remaining growth in the population at the time its fertility reaches replacement multiplies it by $(b_k/b_s)e^{-.09375kT}$. If e_0^0 is 70 years, and the mean length of generation is 28, the population would increase by $17\frac{1}{2}\%$ after reaching replacement if the rate of decrease of fertility were 1% annually, by $32\frac{1}{2}\%$ if the rate of decrease were 2%, and by 45.4% if the rate of decrease of fertility were 3% annually.

This last point—the greater growth potential of a population with a history of declining fertility than of a stable population with the same fertility and mortality—returns us to one of the early uses of stable population analysis. Lotka, in his classic article "On the True Rate of Natural Increase," showed that the stable population had a rate of natural increase of only 5.47 per thousand, although the actual population had a rate of natural increase of 10.99 per thousand (white female population of the United States, 1920). The primary reason for the difference was that the actual population was one with a history of

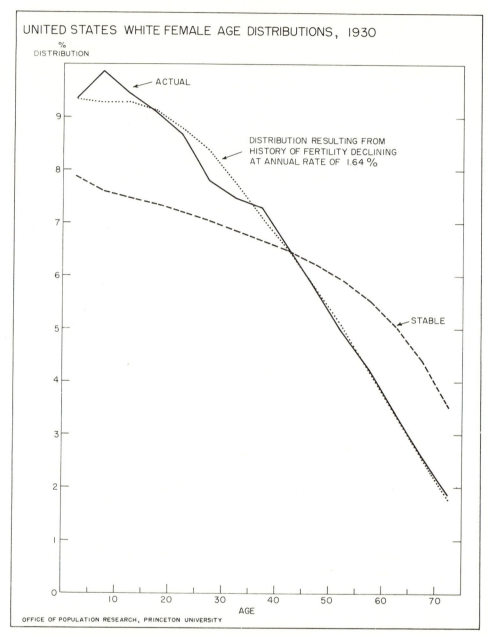

UNITED STATES WHITE FEMALE AGE DISTRIBUTIONS, 1930

% DISTRIBUTION

ACTUAL

DISTRIBUTION RESULTING FROM HISTORY OF FERTILITY DECLINING AT ANNUAL RATE OF 1.64 %

STABLE

AGE

OFFICE OF POPULATION RESEARCH, PRINCETON UNIVERSITY

Figure 4.10. Age distributions for the United States white female population, 1930: actual, stable, and distribution resulting from a history of fertility declining at average rate observed in United States 1910–30.

150

declining fertility. Figure 4.10 shows the stable population in 1930, the estimated actual population, and a population with a history of constantly declining fertility at the average rate of decline, 1910–30. We can now explain the approximate extent of the difference between the intrinsic and actual rates by noting the existence and average pace of a long downtrend in fertility.

NOTES

[1] The transition from zero change in fertility to an annual change of k given Equation (4.50) and from k to zero in Equation (4.65) is readily generalized to a transition from an annual change of k_1 to one of k_2; the equations are

$$B(t) = B(0)e^{(r(0) + k_1/2)t + (k_1/2T)t^2} \qquad\qquad t < 0$$

$$B(t) = B(0)e^{(r(0) - k_1/2 + k_2)t + (k_1/2T)t^2} \qquad\qquad 0 < t < 3T/4$$

$$B(t) = B(0)e^{.09375(k_2 - k_1)T + (r_0 + k_2/2)t + (k_2/2T)t^2} \qquad\qquad t > 3T/4.$$

The development of equations for $B(t - a)$ and for the age composition relative to the stable population is straightforward.

REFERENCE

[1] Coale, A. J., and Zelnick, M., *New Estimates of Fertility and Population in the United States: A Study of Annual White Births from 1855 to 1960 and of Completeness of Enumeration in the Censuses from 1880 to 1960*, Princeton, Princeton University Press, 1963.

Birth Sequences and Age Distributions with Changing Mortality

IN THIS chapter the age distribution effects of mortality change will be examined by a case study of one form of change — the effects of entering a period of constantly declining mortality after a long history of unchanging mortality. It will be necessary to impose somewhat unrealistic specifications on the nature of the change in mortality, but the general circumstances (major sustained changes in mortality newly initiated) are shared by many populations in low income countries, and the effects on the age distribution are thus of some importance. Much of the argument is closely analogous to that employed in treating one of the sequences of changing fertility examined in Chapter 4 — specifically, the age distribution created when, after a long history of constant fertility, a population experiences steadily changing fertility. As in Chapter 4, restrictive assumptions are required: We shall assume that the fertility schedule is fixed, and that mortality change follows a specified monotonic time pattern. In Chapter 4 a fixed age pattern of fertility was postulated, but an exactly analogous postulate for changing mortality would not be acceptable for two reasons: (1) the age pattern of mortality is characteristically very different in high level and low level mortality schedules respectively, and (2) the age pattern of mortality change itself has a major effect on the age distribution.

The postulates that will be employed with regard to the age structure and time pattern of mortality change are as follows:

(1) As mortality changes, a fixed age structure is assumed in the difference in age-specific death rates from any moment to any other. Thus if $\mu(a,t_1)$ and $\mu(a,t_2)$ are age-specific mortality schedules at two moments when mortality is changing, $\mu(a,t_1) - \mu(a,t_2) = M\Delta\mu(a)$, where M is a constant and $\Delta\mu(a)$ is a non-altering characteristic age schedule of mortality change.

(2) The age pattern of change in mortality rates can be approximated by a steeply declining section from age 0 to about age 5, a section that can be considered level from age 5 to 45, and a section that rises linearly with age above 45.

(3) The time pattern of the mortality change initiated at $t = 0$ is one of linear change at each age. Thus $\mu(a,t) = \mu(a,0) - t\Delta\mu(a)$.

The first of these postulates is a fair approximation to the recorded experience of many actual populations during substantial changes in mortality. In the families of model life tables, each conforming closely to a collection of recorded schedules at widely different levels of mortality, the difference in age-specific rates forms a very nearly fixed pattern at expectations of life at birth from about 20 to 50 years. At higher life expectancies (60 to 77.5 years) the age pattern changes: Declines in childhood become smaller (perforce, since mortality cannot be negative), and declines at upper ages become more prominent. As a consequence the formulae proposed in this chapter are better fitted to explain the effects of mortality change at high to moderate than at low mortality levels. Figure 5.1 shows the difference between the age-specific death rates in the "West" female model life tables at $e_0^0 = 20$ and 50 years, and Table 5.1 shows that difference together with 13.9 times the difference in rates at $e_0^0 = 35$ and 37.5 years. Note the close similarity in age pattern in the table.

The second postulate (asserting that $\mu(a)$ consists of three sections with certain characteristics) is a fair characterization of the age structure of most accurately recorded major changes in mortality with these qualifications: First, changes in mortality from 5 to 45 are not in fact the same at every age, but rather rise gradually as in Figure 5.1; and second, the rising portion of $\mu(a)$ above age 45 is not precisely linear, may not begin at age 45, and is nonexistent in the mortality experience of males in some modern advanced countries.

Table 5.1. Difference in age-specific mortality rates,
'West' female model life tables

Age x	$\Delta\mu(x)$, $e_0^0 = 20$ and 50	$13.9\Delta\mu(x)$, $e_0^0 = 35$ and 37.5
0.5	.351	.346
1.5	.106	.110
2.5	.054	.054
3.5	.038	.037
4.5	.030	.030
7.5	.011	.011
12.5	.008	.009
17.5	.011	.011
22.5	.013	.014
27.5	.015	.016
32.5	.017	.018
37.5	.018	.019
42.5	.019	.020
47.5	.019	.020
52.5	.024	.025
57.5	.030	.031
62.5	.044	.045
67.5	.055	.056
72.5	.075	.075
77.5	.096	.095

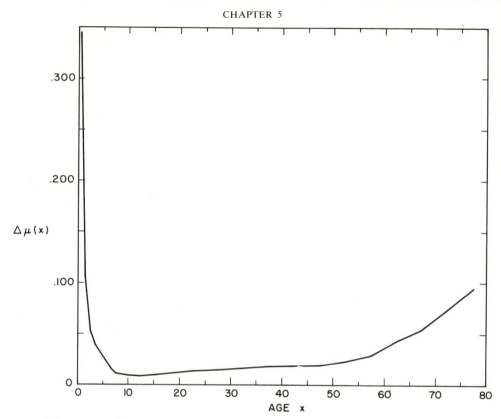

Figure 5.1. Difference in age-specific mortality rates, "West" model life tables, females: rates in table where $e_0^0 = 20$ minus rates where $e_0^0 = 50$.

The third postulate — that the time pattern of mortality change is linear — is doubtless rarely followed by the experience of actual populations. However, actual changes sometimes fluctuate around a linear trend, and this postulate (as well as the not-strictly-correct assumption that $\Delta\mu(a)$ is flat from 5 to 45) makes it possible to express the effects of changing mortality in analytical form.

The strategy that will be followed in showing the effects of changing mortality on age distribution is first to subtract from $\Delta\mu(a)$ (the annual change in age-specific mortality) the approximately level portion from 5 to 45 ($\Delta\mu_{min}$). The remaining function, which will be labeled $r(a)$, thus consists of a steeply declining portion falling from a maximum at age 0 to zero at age 5, is zero from 5 to 45, and rises linearly from zero at 45 to another maximum at the highest age considered. It will be seen that annual change with the form of $r(a)$ (with the flat portion $\Delta\mu_{min}$ subtracted from $\Delta\mu(a)$) has exactly the same effect on the age distribution as $\Delta\mu(a)$ itself. The effects of the two nonzero portions of $r(a)$ will be considered separately.

The horizontal part of $\Delta\mu(a)$ does not influence the effect of $\Delta\mu(a)$ on age composition because a change in mortality that takes the form of equal increments (positive or negative) at all ages in age-specific mortality has no age distributional consequences at all. This fact is proven by the following argument: The proportion surviving from age a to $a + d$ is $e^{-\int_a^{a+d}\mu(x)dx}$. If $\mu_2(x)$ is equal to $\mu_1(x) - s$ at all ages, the probability of surviving from a to $a + d$ is multiplied by e^{sd} — by the same amount at all ages. In particular, the probability of surviving by one year is multiplied by e^s at all ages. Hence, if the mortality regime $\mu_2(x)$ replaces the regime $\mu_1(x)$, there will be e^s more persons at all ages in the following year than there would have been if the old regime had continued. There will also be e^s more births, because the number of persons at all parental ages is increased by this factor. In short, the population will have increased by precisely the same factor at every age compared to what it would have been with no change in mortality; consequently there are more people, but the age composition is exactly as it would have been. If a single constant increment in mortality at all ages has no effect on age composition, a series of changes of this sort also has no effect.

The Effect on Age Composition of Declining Mortality Under Age Five

In this section it will be assumed (provisionally) that the component of mortality in excess of the minimum (or $r(a)$) under age five is the only change in mortality that occurs. The first step is to establish the equivalence (in a way soon to be defined) between a constant annual $r(a)$ under age five and multiplication of fertility each year by e^k.

The equivalence between declining mortality under age five as defined by a linear time change with the age pattern $r(a)$ and rising fertility involving multiplication each year by a factor e^k is this: If the magnitudes of k and $r(a)$ are properly chosen, it is possible for a population with a history of declining mortality to have exactly the same age distribution above age five as a population with a history of rising fertility. We shall discuss two populations. Both share the same unchanging mortality schedule above age five, and both experience the same time sequence of children arriving at age five. Clearly the number of persons at each age above five in the two populations is the same. We shall now see that these conditions are fulfilled if population (1) is

155

a population with continuously rising fertility and unchanging mortality under age five and population (2) a population with unchanging fertility and continuously declining mortality under age five.

Let $l(5,t)$ be the proportion surviving from birth to age five according to the cross-sectional life table at time t, and $p(5,t)$ be the proportion surviving to five in the cohort reaching five at time t. In general, $l(5,t) = e^{-\int_0^5 \mu(a,t)da}$ and $p(5,t) = e^{-\int_0^5 \mu(a,t-5+a)da}$. In population (1) $l_1(5,t) = p_1(5,t)$, but in population (2) mortality is constantly declining, and $l_2(5,t) > p_2(5,t)$. Suppose at each age under five $\mu(a,t+1) = \mu_2(a,t) - r(a)$, and more generally $\mu_2(a,t+n) = \mu_2(a,t) - nr(a)$; it follows that

(5.1) $$l_2(5,t+n) = l_2(5,t)e^{\,n\int_0^5 r(a)da};$$

also

(5.2) $$p_2(5,t) = l_2(5,t)e^{\int_0^5(5-a)r(a)da} = l_2(5,t)e^{(5-\bar{a}_r)\int_0^5 r(a)dr}$$

where $\bar{a}_r$ is the mean age of $r(a)$ from zero to five.

Let the gross reproduction rate in the two populations be $G_1(t)$ and $G_2(t)$ respectively. $G_1(t+n) = G_1(t)e^{nk}$, while $G_2(t)$ is constant. Let $f(a)$ be $m(a,t)\big/\int_0^\beta m(a,t)da$; we assume the age structure of fertility in the two populations is the same, or that $f_1(a) = f_2(a) = f(a)$. Our aim is to determine under what circumstances

(5.3) $$B_1(t-5)p_1(5,t) = B_2(t-5)p_2(5,t).$$

But for any population,

(5.4) $$B(t-5) = G(t-5)\int_\alpha^\beta N(a,t-5)f(a)da.$$

Hence, for the number arriving at age five in the two populations to be the same (since $f(a)$ and $N(a,t)$ for $a > 5$ in the two is the same),

(5.5) $$G_1(t-5)p_1(5,t) = G_2(t-5)p_2(5,t).$$

We shall assume that the current life table in the two populations is the same, or that $l_1(a,t) = l_2(a,t)$. Then Equation (5.5) can be rewritten as

(5.6) $$G_1(t)e^{-5k}l(5,t) = G_2(t)l(5,t)e^{-(5-\bar{a}_r)\int_0^5 r(a)da}.$$

Equation (5.6) is satisfied if

(5.7) $$\int_0^5 r(a)da = k$$

and

156

(5.8) $$G_2(t) = G_1(t)e^{-k\bar{a}}r.$$

Thus, the two populations have the same number arriving at age five annually, provided the cumulative value of $r(a)$ to age five is k, or that the annual increase in the proportion surviving to age five in population (2) is e^k, and provided current fertility in population (2) is lower than in population (1) as specified in Equation (5.8).

To be precise, it is not the annual increase in the proportion surviving to age five in population (2) that should equal e^k, but the increase in the proportion surviving to age five in excess of the increase that would occur if the annual change in mortality at every age under age five were the same as in the "plateau" of mortality change from 5 to 45. A good approximation to the relevant annual increase in survival to age five is l_5'/l_5 divided by $_5p_{25}'/_5p_{25}$, where the prime indicates a value from a mortality schedule one year later. This formulation assumes that the change in the proportion surviving from 25 to 30 can be taken as representative of the mortality change in the "plateau." In the sense that we have been discussing (namely, the annual change in the number arriving at age five) the change from one mortality schedule to another is equivalent to multiplying fertility by e^{kt}. Table 5.2 shows the values of kt inherent in changes in life expectancy by two-and-a-half year increments from 20 to 77.5 in the "West" model life tables for females. From this table it can be inferred that the change in age distribution caused by an increase in life expectancy from 20 to 22.5 years ($kt = .071$) is about as great as in going from 32.5 to 37.5 years ($kt = .072$), or in changing from a life expectancy of 45 to 52.5 years ($kt = .072$).

In sum, if mortality had long been declining along the somewhat peculiar time path that would be equivalent to a constant change in

Table 5.2. Values of kt, βt, and β/k in "West" female model life tables

Change in e_0^0	kt	$\beta t \times 10^3$	β/k	Change in e_0^0	kt	$\beta t \times 10^3$	β/k
20.0 to 22.5	0.0708	0.299	0.0042	50.0 to 52.5	0.0241	0.070	0.0029
22.5 to 25.0	0.0611	0.258	0.0042	52.5 to 55.0	0.0199	0.069	0.0035
25.0 to 27.5	0.0535	0.227	0.0042	55.0 to 57.5	0.0184	0.071	0.0039
27.5 to 30.0	0.0473	0.200	0.0042	57.5 to 60.0	0.0170	0.073	0.0043
30.0 to 32.5	0.0424	0.179	0.0042	60.0 to 62.5	0.0158	0.074	0.0047
32.5 to 35.0	0.0379	0.161	0.0043	62.5 to 65.0	0.0147	0.073	0.0050
35.0 to 37.5	0.0345	0.145	0.0042	65.0 to 67.5	0.0137	0.075	0.0054
37.5 to 40.0	0.0315	0.133	0.0042	67.5 to 70.0	0.0120	0.079	0.0065
40.0 to 42.5	0.0289	0.121	0.0042	70.0 to 72.5	0.0092	0.114	0.0124
42.5 to 45.0	0.0266	0.111	0.0042	72.5 to 75.0	0.0079	0.133	0.0168
45.0 to 47.5	0.0246	0.103	0.0042	75.0 to 77.5	0.0062	0.156	0.0251
47.5 to 50.0	0.0233	0.095	0.0041				

fertility, the age distribution above five would (if we continue to ignore the effect of above minimum improvements in mortality at old age) resemble that of a population with a history of rising fertility at the appropriate rate, provided further that the population with rising fertility now had slightly higher fertility than the population with declining mortality. Under age five, the population with a history of declining mortality would have slightly different numbers. The number of births would be less in the same proportion that its fertility is lower. Since $\bar{a}_r$ is 1.27 in the "West" model life tables, with a value of k of 0.01, the difference in the number of births in the two populations is only 1.27%, and the difference in number under age five is no more than about half this proportion.[1]

The relation of the age distribution of P_2 (the population with continuously declining mortality) to the current stable population is so closely linked to the relation of P_1 (a population with continuously rising fertility) to the current stable that to obtain the former relation we shall modify the latter, which has already been developed in Chapter 4. Note that in speaking of P_2 we are continuing our provisional neglect of the effects of the above minimum changes in age-specific mortality that occur at older ages. Recall that P_1 and P_2 are alike above age five, but that P_1 has higher current fertility by a factor of $e^{k\bar{a}_r}$. This fact has two implications:

(1) Above age five P_2 bears a relation to a stable population that is the same as P_1's relation to a stable; but P_2's relation is to a stable based on a fertility higher than the current by a factor of $e^{k\bar{a}_r}$. Hence, to find the ratio of P_2 at age a to a stable based on current fertility, the ratio of P_1 to a stable population with higher fertility than the current must be determined. This determination requires multiplying the ratio of P_1 to the current stable at age a by $e^{-\Delta ra}$, where $\Delta r = k\bar{a}_r/T$.

(2) Below age five P_2 has lower proportions than P_1: a proportion at age zero equal to that in P_1 times $e^{-k\bar{a}_r}$, and a proportion under age five equal to that in P_1 times about $e^{-k\bar{a}_r/2}$.

If allowance is made for these two adjustments, the equations developed in Chapter 4 for calculating the age distribution during the early years of constantly changing fertility can be adapted for approximate calculation of the effect of continuously declining mortality. However, there remains a necessary allowance for the age distribution effects of decreases in excess of the minimum in age-specific mortality at ages above 45. We turn now to the allowance for these effects.

The Effect on the Age Distribution of a Population with Declining Mortality of Above Minimum Changes in $\mu(a)$ at Older Ages

Changes in mortality above age 45 can be treated separately because there is no "feedback" on the stream of births of mortality changes occurring past the childbearing span. The projected birth sequence would be the same if, on the one hand, all the women died at the last age of childbearing, or if on the other, there were no mortality at all past that age. Thus we are at liberty to assume that when mortality is declining, the age structure under 45 is determined by factors discussed above, and the changes in mortality above 45 will have a direct effect on age composition only of older persons. The sole effect below age 45 will be through increases or decreases in the size of the total population, changes that alter in a uniform way the proportion that each young age group forms of the whole population.

The annual decrease in $\mu(a)$ above age 45 is assumed to take the form $\Delta\mu(a) = (a - 45)\beta + \Delta\hat{\mu}$, where $\Delta\hat{\mu}$ is the "plateau" from 5 to 45. Thus $r(a) = (a - 45)\beta$. For economy of exposition, let $y = a - 45$, so that $r(y) = \beta y$. Since $\Delta\hat{\mu}$ has no effect on age composition we shall for simplicity ignore it, and deal only with annual change in mortality in excess of $\Delta\hat{\mu}$. Suppose that the mortality decline begins at $t = 0$; then

(5.9)
$$\mu(y, t - x) = \mu(y, t) + \beta y x \qquad x < t$$
$$\mu(y, t - x) = \mu(y, t) + \beta y t \qquad x > t$$

and, of course,

(5.10)
$$\mu(y - x, t - x) = \mu(y - x, t) + (y - x)\beta x \qquad x < t$$
$$\mu(y - x, t - x) = \mu(y - x, t) + (y - x)\beta t \qquad x > t.$$

Let $s(y, t)$ be the proportion surviving from age 45 to $45 + y$ in a cohort reaching age $45 + y$ at time t, and let $l(y, t)$ be the proportion surviving from 45 to age $45 + y$ in the life table current at time t. Note that $l(y, t) = e^{-\int_0^y \mu(y-x, t)dx}$, and that $s(y, t) = e^{-\int_0^y \mu(y-x, t-x)dx}$.

The age distribution in a population with a history of declining mortality will differ from the stable as a result of mortality changes at the older ages because of differences between $l(y, t)$ and $s(y, t)$. If the two were the same, the distribution of persons above age 45 would agree with the stable, except for modifications caused by the existence of the

159

$r(a)$ values under age five discussed above. However, if mortality has been falling, persons now at a particular age above 45 are fewer in number than they would be if the current mortality conditions had prevailed in the past, since they will have experienced higher mortality in the last few years than characterizes the current life table. Our goal in this section, then, is to determine the extent to which the proportion in the cohort falls short of the proportion that would survive in the current life table. We shall consider two cases, one where y is less than or equal to t, and the other where y is greater than t.

Case I: $y \leq t$.

$$(5.11) \qquad s(y,t) = e^{-\int_0^y [\mu(y-x,t)+\beta x(y-x)]dx},$$

or

$$(5.12) \qquad s(y,t) = l(y,t)e^{-\beta(y^3/2-y^3/3)} = l(y,t)e^{-\beta(y^3/6)}.$$

Case II: $y > t$.

$$(5.13) \qquad s(y,t) = e^{-\int_0^t \mu(y-x,t-x)dx - \int_t^y \mu(y-x,o)dx}.$$

Therefore,

$$(5.14) \qquad s(y,t) = l(y,t)e^{-\int_0^t \beta(y-x)xdx - \int_t^y \beta(y-x)tdx},$$

or

$$(5.15) \qquad s(y,t) = l(y,t)e^{-\beta(yt^2/2-t^3/3+y^2t-yt^2-yt/2+t^3/2)}$$

or finally

$$(5.16) \qquad s(y,t) = l(y,t)e^{-\beta[yt(y/2-t/2)+t^3/6]}.$$

By applying Equations (5.12) and (5.16) it is possible to make allowance for the difference between the age distribution at the older ages in a population with a history of declining mortality from the stable population, if the value of β is known. We have calculated the value of βt for each pair of the "West" female model life tables from a life expectancy of 20 years to one of 77.5 in increments of two and a half years. Table 5.2 shows these values, together with the previously calculated values of kt, and finally shows the ratio of β/k. Notice that this ratio is approximately constant as expectation of life increases from 20 to 50 years. At this point there is a discontinuity and a changeover to a steadily rising value of β relative to k. The discontinuity is the complicated result of the mechanics of the calculation of model life tables and would not show up in the experience of actual populations; but the rising value of β/k at higher life expectancies is a genuine historical property of changing mortality among women. As mortality rates are reduced to very low levels, further reductions under age five become difficult to achieve as the effects of infectious diseases are essentially eliminated and mortality rates beyond the first month of life reach very low levels. At this time in the course of reducing mortality, the rates at older ages are still substantial and leave room for improvement. In general, there are substantial differences in the experience of different populations in the value of β, and this fact means that in the absence of accurately recorded age-specific mortality rates, it is not possible to make trustworthy estimates of the effects of declining mortality on the portion of the age distribution above age 45.

The Age Distribution of a Population with a History of Declining Mortality Relative to the Stable Age Distribution

We are now in a position to present a method for calculating the approximate age distribution of a population with a history of continuously declining mortality during the preceding t years. The required data are the current fertility and mortality schedules (which determine the current stable population), the number of years that mortality has been declining (t), the value of k (the annual proportionate increase in fertility to which the annual increase in survival at young ages is equivalent), and the value of β (the slope of the line approximating the rate at which the annual change in age-specific mortality rates increases above age 50). The value of k can be estimated as follows: Calculate the natural log of $l_5 \cdot l_{25}/l_0 \cdot l_{30}$ for the current mortality schedule, and for a mortality schedule x years ago. The difference between the two logarithms divided by x is an estimate of k. Similarly, β can be estimated by taking the difference between the age-specific death rate from 65 to 70 and from 50 to 55 in the life table x years ago and in a current life table. The difference between these differences divided by $15x$ is an estimate of β.

The age distribution of the population with a history of declining mortality characterized by specified values of k, β, and t is then obtained by estimating the age distribution of a population with a history of rising fertility at an annual rate k, employing Equation (4.63) or (4.64) from the previous chapter. From Equations (4.63) and (4.64) we obtain, if $t \leq 3T/4$

(5.17)
$$R(a,t) = (b_k/b_s)e^{-k(1-t/T)a} \qquad a < t$$
$$R(a,t) = (b_k/b_s)e^{-k(1-a/T)t} \qquad a > t$$

161

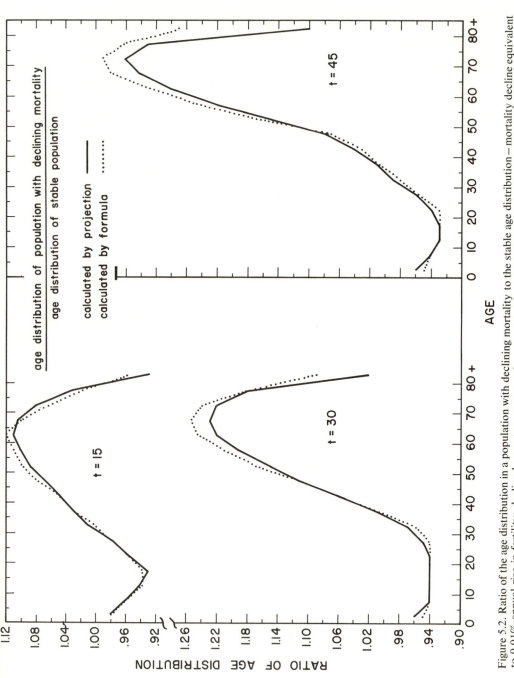

Figure 5.2. Ratio of the age distribution in a population with declining mortality to the stable age distribution — mortality decline equivalent to 0.01% annual rise in fertility; decline began t years age, where $t = 15$, 30, and 45. Age distribution calculated by projection, and by Equations (5.17) and (5.18).

(where $R(a,t)$ is the ratio of the proportion at age a in a population with a history of changing fertility at an annual rate of k for t years to the proportion at age a in a stable population), and, if $t > 3T/4$ and $m = t - 3T/4$

$$R(a,t) = (b_k/b_s)e^{-(k/2)a+(k/2T)a^2} \qquad\qquad a < m$$

$$(5.18) \quad R(a,t) = (b_k/b_s)e^{-.09375kT+(k/2)t-(k/2T)t^2-k(1-t/T)a} \qquad m < a < t$$

$$R(a,t) = (b_k/b_s)e^{-.09375kT-(k/2)t-(k/2T)t^2+kta/T} \qquad a > t.$$

Our starting point is thus $R(a,t)$ from Equation (5.17) or (5.18) (depending on whether t is greater or less than $3T/4$); the next step is to allow for the fact that the population with a history of declining mortality has an age distribution above age five related to that of a rising fertility population with slightly higher fertility. We calculate $W(a,t) = R(a,t)e^{-(1.27ka)/T}$, and next we calculate $W_1(a,t)$ for five year age groups, as follows:

$$W_1(2.5,t) = W(2.5,t)^{-0.633k}$$

$$(5.19) \quad W_1(a,t) = W(a,t) \qquad\qquad a = 7.5, 12.5 \cdots 42.5$$

$$W_1(a,t) = W(a,t)s(y,t)/l(y,t) \qquad a = 47.5, 52.5 \cdots 60,$$

where $y = a - 45$, and $s(y,t)/l(y,t)$ is taken from Equation (5.12) or (5.16), depending on whether $y > t$ or $y < t$. $W_1(a,t)$ is a set of multipliers that may be applied to the stable age distribution to give the number of persons in each age group in a population with a history of declining mortality. The proportionate distribution by five year age intervals of this population is:

$$(5.20) \qquad\qquad c_{dm}(a) = \frac{W_1(a)c_s(a)}{\Sigma(W_1(a)c_s(a))}.$$

We have calculated the age distribution of a population with a history of declining mortality by projecting the "West" female model stable population e_0^0 of 20 years, and an intrinsic rate of increase of zero, for 60 years, holding fertility constant, and utilizing a fertility schedule with a mean age of 29 years. The life tables employed at each stage in the projection were selected so that the decline in mortality was equivalent to a one percent annual increase in fertility. The ratio of the resultant projected populations to the stable population with the fertility and mortality of the moment is shown in Figure 5.2 after 15,

163

30, and 45 years. At each point the age distribution calculated by the procedure just outlined is shown for comparison.

NOTE

[1] In an earlier short development of this argument, the author failed to see the difference in fertility between the two populations. See A. J. Coale, "Estimates of Various Demographic Measures Through the Quasi-Stable Age Distribution," in *Emerging Techniques in Population Research,* New York, Milbank Memorial Fund, 1963, pp. 175–195.

The Birth Sequence and the Age Distribution That Occur When Fertility Is Subject to Repetitive Fluctuations

IN THIS chapter we continue the examination of the birth sequences and age distributions that result from certain time sequences of change in fertility and mortality. In Chapters 4 and 5 the sequences analyzed were monotonic trends in fertility or mortality; here our attention turns to the effects of repetitious fluctuations in fertility. Most of the chapter will be devoted to the simplest form of repetitive variation—a pure sine wave. We shall find that a sinusoidal fluctuation in fertility produces fluctuations in births (around an exponential trend) that may be different in magnitude and phase from the fertility fluctuations, and may contain "harmonics" as well as the same frequency as the fertility variations themselves. Whether the birth cycles are amplified or attenuated relative to the fertility cycles, whether in phase, leading, or lagging, and whether or not distorted by the presence of harmonics, depends on the frequency and amplitude of the fluctuations in fertility, and on the age structure of the net fertility function.

The fundamental relation governing the birth sequence already given in earlier chapters is repeated here:

$$(6.1) \qquad B(t) = \int_0^\beta B(t-a)p(a,t)m(a,t)da.$$

In Equation (6.1) $p(a,t)m(a,t)$ can be written as $\phi(a,t)$; also, if $\int_0^\beta \phi(a,t)da = R(t)$, and $f(a,t) = \phi(a,t)/R(t)$,

$$(6.2) \qquad B(t) = R(t) \int_0^\beta B(t-a)f(a,t)da.$$

Cyclical Variations in $\phi(a,t)$, Cyclical Fluctuations in Births About an Exponential Trend, and a Cyclically Repeating Age Composition

Suppose $\phi(a,t)$ follows a recurrent cycle T years in length, so that $\phi(a,t+T) = \phi(a,t)$ for all values of t. One way of stating the independence of birth sequences of the remote past is as follows: If two populations have the same net fertility sequence and the same fertility history, one birth sequence is a constant multiple of the other. But if $\phi(a,t)$ is cyclical, the fertility sequence and history viewed at time t and at $t + T$ are the same; hence

165

$$(6.3) \qquad \frac{B(t+T)}{B(t)} = k.$$

The value of k is the same for *any* points T years apart; therefore

$$\frac{B(t+2T)}{B(t)} = k^2, \text{ etc.}$$

Suppose $H(t) = B(t)/e^{rt}$, where $e^{rT} = k$. Since $B(t+T)/B(t) = k = e^{rT}$ and $H(t)e^{rt} = B(t)$, it follows that $H(t+T) = H(t)$. Hence when $\phi(a,t)$ is a cyclical function, $B(t)$ can in turn be expressed as the product of a cyclical function (with the same cycle length as $\phi(a,t)$) and an exponential with a constant coefficient (r) of t.

If the cyclical fluctuations in $\phi(a,t)$ are of a form such that $m(a,t)$ and $p(a,t)$ have the same value at points separated by a cycle, that is, if $m(a,t+T) = m(a,t)$ and $p(a,t+T) = p(a,t)$, then the age distribution at t and $t+T$ is always the same, because two populations with the same histories of fertility and mortality have the same age composition.

We shall now assume that cyclical fluctuations in fertility take the form of a constant age pattern of net fertility that rises and falls from year to year in the same proportion at all ages, or that $\phi(a,t) = \phi(a) \cdot G(t)$ where $G(t)$ is a periodic function with cycle length T. We have just shown that under these circumstances, $B(t) = e^{rt} \cdot H(t)$, where $H(t)$ is also a periodic function of cycle length T. Any periodic function $f(t)$ can be expressed in a Fourier series (Courant [1]):

$$(6.4) \qquad f(t) = a_0 + \sum_{n=1}^{\infty} \left(a_n \cos \frac{2\pi nt}{T} + b_n \sin \frac{2\pi nt}{T} \right),$$

and our purpose is to show how the components (i.e., the coefficients of the sine and cosine terms at various frequencies, including the fundamental frequency $1/T$, and the harmonics n/T) of the periodic factor in the birth sequence can be calculated from the components of $G(t)$.

We shall write the periodic net fertility function as $\phi(a,t) = \phi(a)(1 + g(t))$, and the birth sequence as $B(t) = Be^{rt}(1 + h(t))$. Thus the constant term in the Fourier series (a_0 in Equation (6.4)) is eliminated from $g(t)$ and $h(t)$, which are periodic functions with an aggregate value of zero over each cycle. If these expressions for $B(t)$ and $\phi(a,t)$ are inserted in Equation (6.1) (noting that $\phi(a,t) = p(a,t)m(a,t)$), we find

$$(6.5) \quad Be^{rt}(1 + h(t)) = \int_0^{\beta} Be^{r(t-a)}\phi(a) \cdot (1 + g(t))(1 + h(t-a))da,$$

hence

166

$$(6.6) \quad 1 + h(t) = \int_0^\beta e^{-ra}\phi(a)da(1 + g(t))$$

$$+ \int_0^\beta e^{-ra}\phi(a)h(t - a)da(1 + g(t)),$$

or

$$(6.7) \quad 1 + h(t) = y(1 + g(t)) + z(t)(1 + g(t)) = y(1 + g(t)) + z(t) + x(t),$$

where $y = \int_0^\beta e^{-ra}\phi(a)da$, and $z(t) = \int_0^\beta e^{-ra}\phi(a)h(t - a)da$ and $x(t) = g(t) \cdot z(t)$. Before considering unrestricted forms of the periodic function, $g(t)$, expressing fluctuations in fertility, we shall assume that $g(t)$ is a simple sinusoidal variation, and examine the effect of variations in the period (T) or the frequency $(f$, which equals $1/T)$ of fertility fluctuations on the nature of the consequent fluctuating component of the birth sequence. We shall rewrite $2\pi ft$ (or $2\pi t/T$) as wt, let $g(t) = g \cos wt$, and $h(t) = \sum_{n=1}^\infty (a_n \cos nwt + b_n \sin nwt)$. To simplify the analysis somewhat, we shall make use of the identity $a \cos x + b \sin x = \frac{1}{2}(a - ib)e^{ix} + \frac{1}{2}(a + ib)e^{-ix}$, where $i = (-1)^{1/2}$. Then $g(t)$ can be written as $g/2(e^{iwt} + e^{-iwt})$, the component of $h(t)$ at frequency nf as $h_n(t) = h_n'e^{inwt} + h_n^*e^{-inwt}$ (where h_n' and h_n^* are complex conjugates), $z_n(t)$ as $z_n'e^{inwt} + z_n^*e^{-inwt}$, and $x_n(t)$ as $x_n'e^{inwt} + x_n^*e^{-inwt}$.

Equation (6.7) can now be expanded by writing a separate equation for those terms containing the same exponent of e, giving the following set:

$$1 = y + x_0$$

$$(6.8) \quad h_1'e^{iwt} = y(g/2)e^{iwt} + z_1'e^{iwt} + x_1'e^{iwt}$$

$$h_n'e^{iwt} = z_n'e^{inwt} + x_n'e^{inwt}.$$

The equations in Equation (6.8) beyond the first are matched by a set involving the complex conjugates (h_n^*, z_n^*, and x_n^*) as coefficients of e^{-inwt}. The next step is to eliminate $z_n(t)$ and $x_n(t)$ by expressing them in terms of $h_n(t)$ and $g(t)$. Recall that $z(t)$ is defined as $\int_0^\beta e^{-ra}\phi(a)h(t - a)da$, so that

$$(6.9) \quad z_n(t) = \int_0^\beta e^{-ra}\phi(a)(h_n'e^{inw(t-a)} + h_n^*e^{-inw(t-a)})da,$$

or

167

$$(6.10) \quad z_n(t) = h_n' e^{inwt} \int_0^\beta e^{-inwa} e^{-ra} \phi(a) da$$

$$+ h_n^* e^{-inwt} \int_0^\beta e^{inwa} e^{-ra} \phi(a) da,$$

or

$$(6.11) \quad z_n(t) = h_n'(c_n - is_n) e^{inwt} + h_n^*(c_n + is_n) e^{-inwt},$$

where

$$c_n = \int_0^\beta e^{-ra} \phi(a) \cos (nwa) da,$$

and

$$s_n = \int_0^\beta e^{-ra} \phi(a) \sin (nwa) da.$$

Hence

$$(6.12) \quad \begin{aligned} z_n' &= h_n'(c_n - is_n); \\ z_n^* &= h_n^*(c_n + is_n). \end{aligned}$$

Earlier, $x(t)$ was defined as $g(t) \cdot z(t)$. Thus

$$(6.13) \quad x(t) = \sum_{n=1}^\infty (z_n' e^{inwt} + z_n^* e^{-inwt}) \cdot ((g/2)e^{iwt} + (g/2)e^{-iwt}),$$

or

$$(6.14) \quad x(t) = \sum_{n=1}^\infty \left(\frac{g z_n'}{2} e^{i(n+1)wt} + \frac{g z_n^*}{2} e^{-i(n+1)wt} + \frac{g z_n'}{2} e^{i(n-1)wt} \right.$$

$$\left. + \frac{g z_n^*}{2} e^{-i(n-1)wt} \right).$$

Thus

$$(6.15) \quad x_n(t) = g/2(z_{n-1}' e^{inwt} + z_{n-1}^* e^{-inwt}) + g/2(z_{n+1}' e^{inwt} + z_{n+1}^* e^{-inwt})$$

or

$$(6.16) \quad x_n' = g/2(z_{n-1}' + z_{n+1}') = g/2(h_{n-1}')(c_{n-1} - is_{n-1})$$

$$+ g/2(h_{n+1}')(c_{n+1} - is_{n+1}),$$

and x_n^* is the complex conjugate. Note in Equation (6.14) that when $n = 1$, $x(t)$ contains $(g z_n'/2 + g z_n^*/2)$ 1.0, since $e^0 = 1.0$. Thus $x_0 = g/2$ $(z_1' + z_1^*)$, or $x_0 = g/2(h_1'(c_1 - is_1) + h_1^*(c_1 + is_1))$. Also $x_1' = h_2'(c_2 - is_2)$, and $x_1^* = h_2^*(c_2 + is_2)$. Substituting in Equation (6.8), and canceling the common exponential term, we find

(6.17) $1 = y + (g/2)(h_1'(c_1 - is_1) + h_1^*(c_1 + is_1));$

$h_1' = y(g/2) + h_1'(c_1 - is_1) + (g/2)h_2'(c_2 - is_2);$

$h_n' = (g/2)(h_{n-1}')(c_{n-1} - is_{n-1}) + h_n'(c_n - is_n)$

$$+ (g/2)(h_{n+1}')(c_{n+1} - is_{n+1}).$$

The corresponding equations in h_n^* are redundant, since in every instance h_n^* is the conjugate of h_n'. Thus we have arrived at a set of linear equations for h_n' that can be solved from calculable quantities, provided: (1) r (in $y = e^{-ra}\phi(a)da$) can be determined; and (2) the sequence of equations in Equation (6.17) can be truncated at the equation for some h_k by virtue of values of h_n ($n > k$) of negligible magnitude. As we shall see, a generous upper limit for truncation is $k = 5$ or 6. The value of r can be calculated if y is known; the value of r determines the c_n's and s_n's since $c_n = \int_0^\beta e^{-ra}\phi(a) \cos nwa \, da$ and $s_n = \int_0^\beta e^{-ra}\phi(a)$ $\sin nwa \, da$. However, y is affected by x_0, which depends on the c's and s's. For small values of g (the relative amplitude of fertility fluctuations) ($g < 0.1$), x_0 is negligible; for large values of g, the values of h_n' can be determined by a quickly convergent process of successive approximation. In the first step, y is assumed equal to one, and a first approximation to r obtained; this value leads to approximate values of the c_n's and s_n's; from these in turn, a value of x_0 can be obtained, leading to a new value of y from which a second approximation to r is obtained, etc.

When the h_n''s have been calculated, we have determined $h(t)$, since

$$h(t) = \sum[(h_n' + h_n^*) \cos nwt + (h_n' - h_n^*)i \sin nwt];$$

the coefficient of each cosine term is twice the real part of h_n', and the coefficient of each sine term is twice the imaginary part of h_n^*.

Fertility Fluctuations of Small Amplitude

An important feature of Equation (6.17) is that the nature of the solutions depends on g (the amplitude of the fertility fluctuations). If g is small, so that terms in the order of g^2 can be neglected, only two equations are left:

(6.18)
$$y = 1.0$$

$$h_1' = g/2 + h_1'(c_1 - is_1).$$

The second of these equations gives

$$h' = \frac{g/2}{1 - c_1 + is_1}$$

or

$$h' = g/2 \left(\frac{1 - c_1 - is_1}{(1 - c_1)^2 + s_1^2} \right).$$

Since twice the real part of h' is the coefficient of cos wt and twice the imaginary part of h^* is the coefficient of sin wt, we are left with

(6.19) $$h(t) = g \frac{(1 - c_1) \cos wt + s_1 \sin wt}{(1 - c_1)^2 + s_1^2}.$$

Also, r is the real root of $y = 1$, thus determining c_1 and s_1 for every frequency f. These solutions (when fluctuations in fertility are small) suggest a simple picture of the relation of changing net fertility to the resultant changing birth sequence. The age schedule of net fertility (or more precisely, the product $e^{-ra}\phi(a)$) can be viewed as analogous to an electrical network, or more appropriately, to an amplifier of signals, or of fluctuations in voltage. Fluctuations in fertility (rather than voltage) form the input to the "amplifier" whose frequency response is determined by the age structure of the net fertility function. The frequency response determines the output from a given input; an output consisting of fluctuations in births about an exponential trend. If the amplitude of the fluctuations in fertility at a given frequency is g_f, the amplitude of fluctuations in the output at that frequency is $[g_f/((1 - c_f)^2 + s_f^2)^{1/2}]$; and the phase angle between the output and the input (between fluctuations in births and in fertility) is arctan $(s_f/(1 - c_f))$. Unfortunately, this simple interpretation is applicable only to special cases. The nonlinearity of the birth equation in cyclical form (Equation (6.7)) implies that harmonics are introduced in the birth sequence when large amplitude fluctuations in fertility occur at a given frequency, and that when a number of different frequencies are present in the fertility variations, fluctuations at certain frequencies interact with others (*modulate* the components at other frequencies is the term used by communications engineers) in the resultant birth fluctuations.

The "nonlinearity" referred to is embodied in the term $z(t) \cdot g(t)$ in Equation (6.7). The product $g(t) \cdot z_n(t)$ generates further terms at frequencies $(n - 1)f$ and $(n + 1)f$, and introduces terms with subscripts $(n - 1)$ and $(n + 1)$ in Equation (6.17). The product $g \cdot z_1$ causes a change in y (and hence in r), and also generates a term at $2f$. The product $g \cdot z_2$ causes a change in h_1', and also generates a term at $3f$; etc.

We shall begin with the simplest case: the relationship of birth fluctuations to fertility fluctuations when the latter are very small amplitude sinusoidal variations at a simple frequency, so that the effect of nonlinearity is unimportant. Amplification and phase shift implied by Equation (6.18) have been calculated for 45 net fertility schedules, involving single-year age-specific fertility rates for a variety of populations combined with the mortality of "West" model life tables with an e_0^0 of 70 years, each net fertility schedule adjusted so that NRR = 1. (The schedules include four from Canada, seven from Sweden, six from Belgium, five from France, four from Portugal, three from Poland, two each from Latvia, Finland, Hungary, Germany, and Yugoslavia, and one each from Norway, the Ukraine, Denmark, the United States, Italy, and Czechoslovakia.) For each fertility schedule, amplification and phase shift have been calculated at frequencies of fertility fluctuations ranging from one fourth of a cycle per century to 100 cycles per century (periods of repetition from 1 to 400 years). The frequency response (to very small amplitude fluctuations) of the net fertility function of the United States in 1960 is shown in Figures 6.1 and 6.2.

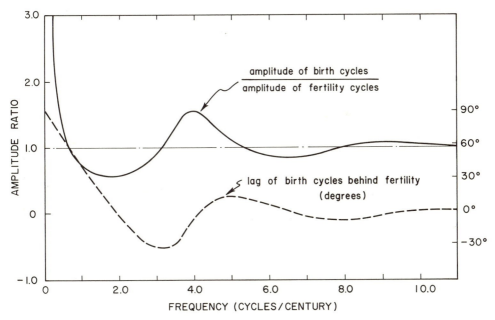

Figure 6.1. Amplification (amplitude of birth cycle/amplitude of fertility cycle) and lag (in degrees) of birth cycles behind fertility cycles as functions of frequency (cycles per century) of fertility variation. Net fertility of U.S. females, 1960, adjusted so that NRR = 1.0.

171

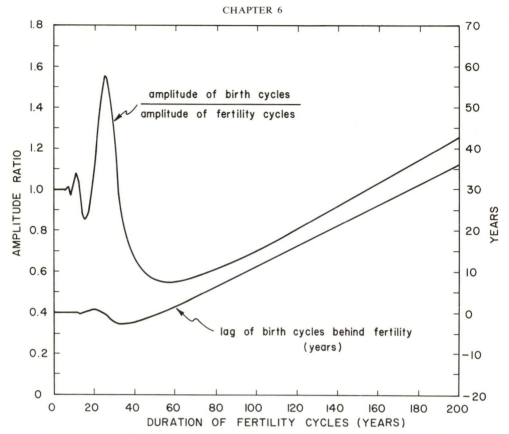

Figure 6.2. Amplification (amplitude of birth cycle/amplitude of fertility cycle) and lag (in years) of birth cycles behind fertility cycles as a function of duration of fertility cycle. Net fertility of U.S. females, 1960, adjusted so that NRR = 1.0.

Figure 6.1 shows the ratio (proportionate variation of births above and below the exponential/proportionate variation of fertility above and below the average) as a function of frequency (number of fertility cycles per century). It also shows the phase difference (in degrees) between the fertility sequence and birth sequence. A positive angle indicates that the birth cycles lag behind the fertility cycles. Figure 6.2 presents essentially the same information, but in this instance, "amplification" is shown as a function of the period of fluctuation (the reciprocal of frequency), and the lag between fertility and birth fluctuations is shown in years, rather than as a fraction of a cycle.

Typical Features of the Relation of Birth Cycles
to Small Amplitude Fertility Cycles

The notable features of this frequency response curve are:

(1) Amplification increases just about linearly with period when the cycle length is above about 80 or 100 years. This linear increase in amplification continues, in fact, indefinitely, as will be shown below. In terms of variation with *frequency*, the effect of the fertility function on fluctuations is partly that of a low-pass amplifier, with amplification at very low frequencies inversely proportional to frequency, approaching infinity as frequency approaches zero.

(2) Amplification has a broad minimum, with "output" only about 55% of "input" when the length of period is about twice the mean age of the net fertility function, or the frequency is about one cycle every two generations.

(3) There is a rather sharp peak of amplification, with a maximum "gain" of about 1.56 at a frequency of about one cycle per generation, or more precisely, with a period closely approximating the median of the net fertility function.

(4) Additional minima and maxima alternate at higher frequencies, with a gain differing less from one at each successive extremum. For cycles more frequent than ten per century (less than ten years in duration), gain never differs from unity by more than 5%.

(5) The phase difference between the fertility and birth fluctuations falls from a lag of birth cycles behind fertility cycles of about 22% of a period (about 80°) for very low frequency fluctuations — one cycle every 500 years — linearly to zero as frequency increases to a cycle every 52 or 53 years; then birth cycles *lead* the fluctuations in fertility by a maximum of about 30° at a frequency of 3.1 cycles per century; subsequently the phase angle alternates between leads and lags, with zero differences in phase generally occurring at a frequency slightly higher than a point of maximum or minimum amplification. The maximum phase differences diminish with frequency, with no difference exceeding 3° at frequencies above 10 cycles per century.

We shall now undertake an explanation of some of these features. The general basis of amplification and phase difference can be seen in Equation (6.18) for $h_1'(h_1' = g/2 + h_1'(c_1 - is_1))$. The last term in this equation is, in fact, z_1'. We know that the real part of z_1' is one-half the coefficient of $\cos wt$ and the imaginary part is minus one-half the coefficient of $\sin wt$ in $z(t)$, which is defined as $z(t) = \int_0^\beta h(t-a)e^{-ra} \times$

173

$\phi(a)da$. Amplification thus depends on the nature of the reinforcement of fertility fluctuation by the fluctuations in births one generation earlier (weighted by $e^{-ra}\phi(a)$). If the peak of the fertility cycle occurs when there is an above average number of mothers, $h(t)$ is enlarged relative to $g(t)$; if fertility peaks coincide with below average numbers of mothers, $h(t)$ is reduced below the amplitude of $g(t)$. Given such favorable or unfavorable phase relations, the amount of amplification or attenuation depends on the amplitude of z_1'. This rough idea can be given precision by employing a method of analysis customarily applied to the steady-state response of electrical circuits to voltage from a source that produces sinusoidal variations at a single frequency. In this technique a sinusoidal varying quantity of magnitude M is viewed as the real component of Me^{iwt}, or as the projection on the real axis of a rotating vector of length M. The addition of two quantities at the same frequency is accomplished by adding the two vectors, with due regard to the magnitude of each and the angle (phase angle) between them. If the two magnitudes are M_1e^{iwt} and $M_2e^{i(wt+\theta)}$, the resultant magnitude is obtained by the ordinary rules of vector addition, such as completing the parallelogram in Figure 6.3.

The resultant quantity is the diagonal of the parallelogram. The use of this form of analysis for the second part of Equation (6.18) leads to

$$(6.20) \qquad\qquad h_1 = g + z_1,$$

where h_1, g, and z_1 are all complex, with the understanding that h_1 represents a sinusoidal variation equal to the real part of h_1e^{iwt}, z_1 a variation equal to real part of z_1e^{iwt}, etc. The relation among h_1, g, and z_1 is that of a vector sum, and since g is given, h_1 and z_1 adjust themselves, so to speak, until the vector sum $h_1 - z_1$ is equal to g.

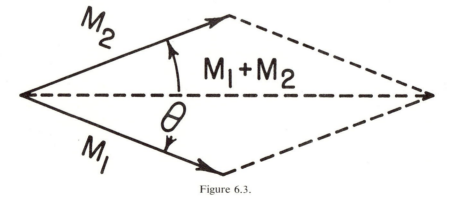

Figure 6.3.

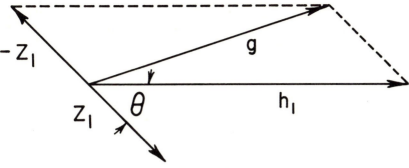

Figure 6.4.

The values of h_1 and z_1 that will produce the requisite vector sum depend on the phase angle between them. If this angle is zero (the two vectors, h_1 and z_1 in phase), then $|h_1| = |g| + |z_1|$; and if the angle is π (the two vectors out of phase), $|h_1| = |g| - |z_1|$. The angle by which z_1 lags h_1 is arctan (s_1/c_1), and the magnitude of z_1 is the magnitude of h_1 times $(c_1^2 + s_1^2)^{1/2}$. To construct h_1 from g exactly, we can draw a vector, provisionally of arbitrary length, in an arbitrary position, say, for convenience, on the real axis, and label it h_1. (See Figure 6.4.) Then draw another vector at an angle with h_1 of $\theta = $ arctan $(-s_1/c_1)$, and of length $h_1 \cdot (c_1^2 + s_1^2)$; this vector is z_1, on the same arbitrary scale as h_1. Draw a vector of length equal to z_1 in the opposite direction; this is $-z_1$. Construct the sum (resultant) of h_1 and $-z_1$; this vector must equal g. The angle between g and h_1, and the relative amplitude of h_1 and g correctly indicate the amplification of birth cycles and the phase difference between fertility and birth fluctuations.

Figure 6.5a shows (at frequencies from one cycle every five centuries to 16 cycles per century) s_f, c_f, and $(c_f^2 + s_f^2)^{1/2}$, calculated for the net fertility schedule of the United States, 1960, after adjustment by a scalar to make $\int_0^\beta \phi(a)da = 1.0$. Note that $(c_f^2 + s_f^2)^{1/2}$ (which is the ratio $|z_1|/|h_1|$) falls from a value of 1.0 at frequencies near zero to less than .05 for frequencies above 11 cycles per century.

The phase angle between h_1 and z_1 can be represented as rising continuously from about zero at frequencies in the neighborhood of zero to π at a frequency of about 1.93 cycles per century, to 2π at about 4.11 cycles per century, etc., reaching 7π at some 17.8 cycles per century, as is evident in Figure 6.5b. When the angle is between 0 and π (or between any even multiple of π and the next odd multiple) h_1 leads z_1, and ranges from exactly in phase with z_1 (phase difference of

175

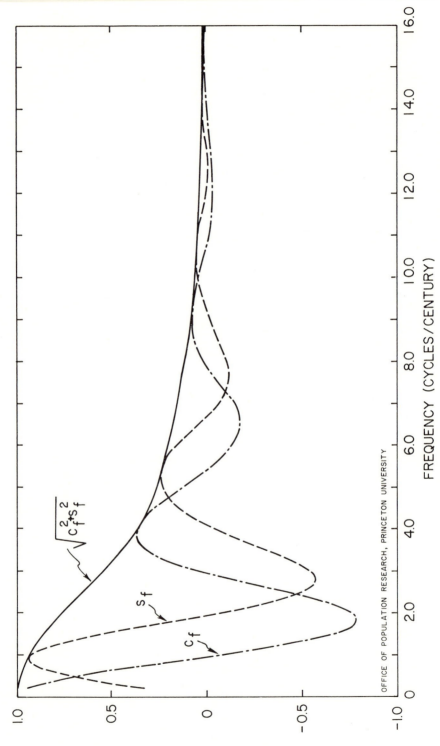

OFFICE OF POPULATION RESEARCH, PRINCETON UNIVERSITY

FREQUENCY (CYCLES/CENTURY)

Figure 6.5a. c_f, s_f, and $(c_f^2 + s_f^2)^{1/2}$ calculated for net fertility of U.S. females, 1960, adjusted so that NRR = 1.0.

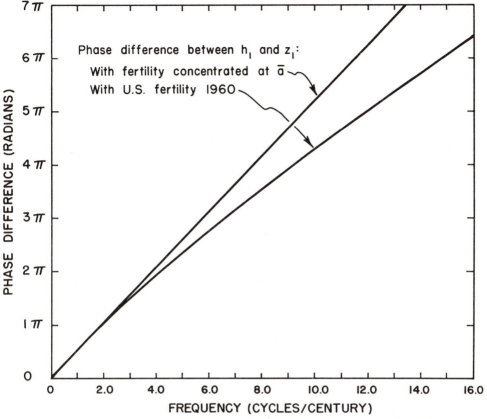

Figure 6.5b. Phase lag (in radians) of $z(t)$ behind $h(t)$ [arctan (s_f/c_f)], net fertility of U.S. females, 1960, adjusted so that NRR = 1.0.

0, or of $N \cdot 2\pi$) to exactly out of phase (difference of π, or $(2N + 1)\pi$). From π to 2π (or $(2N + 1)\pi$ to $(2N + 2)\pi$) the difference ranges from exactly out of phase to exactly in phase, with h_1 lagging z_1.

The Relation of Birth Cycles to Fertility Cycles at Very Low Frequencies

The very large amplification at low frequencies, falling rapidly with frequency, can be explained qualitatively by the large amplitude of z_1 (approaching equality with the amplitude of h_1 at f near zero) plus a phase relationship in which the angle between h_1 and z_1, virtually zero at very low frequencies, rises linearly to π at a frequency of 1.9 cycles per century, or one cycle every 53 years. When the period of variation is very long, the interval between generations becomes a very small

177

fraction of one cycle in fertility, and hence parents and offspring are born in essentially the same phase.

In fact, with small amplitude fluctuations that occur very slowly, we approach circumstances wherein the age distribution at each moment is essentially the stable age distribution associated with the net fertility of the moment; and the rate of increase of births at each moment approximates log $(NRR(t))/\bar{a}$, where $\bar{a}$ is the mean age of net fertility. $NRR(t)$ is $\overline{NRR}(1 + g(t))$, or $\overline{NRR}(1 + g \cos 2\pi ft)$; hence the rate of increase in births, $r(t)$, is $\bar{r} + [\log (1 + g \cos 2\pi ft)/\bar{a}]$. When the rate of increase at time x is $r(x)$,

$$(6.21) \qquad b(t) = b_0 e^{\int_0^t r(x)dx},$$

or

$$(6.22) \qquad b(t) = b_0 e^{\bar{r}t} e^{(1/\bar{a})\int_0^t \log (1+g \cos 2\pi fx)dx}$$

When g is very small, $\log (1 + g \cos 2\pi fx) \doteq g \cos 2\pi fx$; hence

$$(6.23) \qquad b(t) = b_0 e^{\bar{r}t} e^{(g/2\pi\bar{a}f) \sin 2\pi ft}.$$

Expanding the exponential, we find

(6.24)

$$b(t) = b_0 e^{\bar{r}t}(1 + (g/2\pi\bar{a}f) \sin 2\pi ft + \tfrac{1}{2}[(g/2\pi f) \sin 2\pi ft]^2 + \cdots).$$

When g is very small, the terms past the first (which in any event involve only harmonics of f) may be ignored. We are left with a fluctuation in births one fourth of a cycle behind the fertility fluctuations ($\sin 2\pi ft$ lags $\cos 2\pi ft$ by a quarter cycle) with an amplification of $1/2\pi\bar{a}f$—inversely proportional to frequency, or directly proportional to the length of the period.

The above approximation is not a close one except for *very* long cycles (500 years or more) as is evident from the nature of the argument. (When the period is 500 years, amplification calculated from Equation (6.19) is 3.043, $1/2\pi\bar{a}f$ is 3.025.)

The low frequency response of the net fertility function is better approximated by the response of a hypothetical schedule in which all fertility is concentrated at the mean age of the net fertility schedule. With such a schedule, c_f would be $\phi(\bar{a}) \cos 2\pi\bar{a}f$, and s_f would be $\phi(\bar{a}) \sin 2\pi\bar{a}f$. Amplification at f would be $1/((1 - \cos x)^2 + (\sin x)^2)^{1/2}$, where x is $2\pi\bar{a}f$. But since $\cos^2 + \sin^2 = 1$ for any angle, and $\cos x = 1 - 2 \sin^2 (x/2)$, the amplification at f can be written as $1/(2 \sin \pi\bar{a}f)$. The phase angle between h_1 and z_1 is arctan $(-\sin 2\pi\bar{a}f/\cos 2\pi\bar{a}f)$, or simply $-2\pi\bar{a}f$. Hence $-\theta$, the angle between h_1 and z_1, increases linearly with frequency, increasing by 2π each time f increases by $1/\bar{a}$. (See Figure 6.5b.)

Figure 6.6 shows the amplification that would be experienced at frequencies from 0.2 cycles per century to 4.0 cycles per century if fertility were concentrated at $\bar{a}$. At frequencies near zero and in the neighborhood of $1/\bar{a}$, amplification approaches infinity. In fact, the calculated amplification for such a fertility function repeats this cycle from frequencies of $1/\bar{a}$ to $2/\bar{a}$, $2/\bar{a}$ to $3/\bar{a}$, etc. Such a pattern is wholly different from the rapidly diminishing alternate peaks of amplification and attenuation that occur with the U.S. net fertility of 1960 (cf. Figure 6.1). However, at frequencies up to $1/2\bar{a}$ (and slightly beyond) amplification when fertility is concentrated at $\bar{a}$ differs only slightly from that calculated for the actual schedule. We have remarked above on the linear rise in the angle between h_1 and z_1, which is virtually identical with the corresponding phase angle variations for the actual U.S. fertility schedule for frequencies up to $1/2\bar{a}$. In Figure 6.6 there is also sketched another phase angle — that between fertility variations and the consequent birth variations. This difference is readily calculated for the hypothetical schedule where fertility is concentrated at $\bar{a}$. The phase difference is arctan $(s_f/(1 - c_f))$; under the assumption of fertility concentrated at $\bar{a}$, it becomes arctan $(\sin x/(1 - \cos x))$ where x is $2\pi\bar{a}f$. But arctan $(\sin x/(1 - \cos x))$ falls linearly from $\pi/2$ to $-\pi/2$ as x increases from 0 to 2π, or as frequency increases from 0 to $1/\bar{a}$; at $1/\bar{a}$, the phase difference jumps discontinuously to $\pi/2$, and again falls linearly. (It is readily shown that arctan $(\sin x/(1 - \cos x)) = \pi/2 - x/2$. In the unit circle drawn in Figure 6.7, it is clear that angle y is arctan $(\sin x/(1 - \cos x))$; but y intercepts an arc of $\pi - x$; an inscribed angle is measured by one-half the intercepted arc; hence $y = \pi/2 - x/2$.) Note in Figure 6.6 that the phase difference calculated from the U.S. fertility schedule, and a hypothetical schedule with fertility concentrated at $\bar{a}$ are virtually identical for frequencies less than $1/2\bar{a}$, but the large negative differences in phase at frequencies just below $1/\bar{a}$ are not found with the actual fertility schedule; nor is there a discontinuity in phase at the "resonant" point. (The similarity at low frequencies in the frequency response of an actual fertility schedule and one with fertility concentrated at $\bar{a}$, together with their dissimilarity above about $3/4\bar{a}$ explains when the difference equation solution gives a good approximation to the birth sequence: when $g(t)$ contains very little energy above very low frequencies.)

179

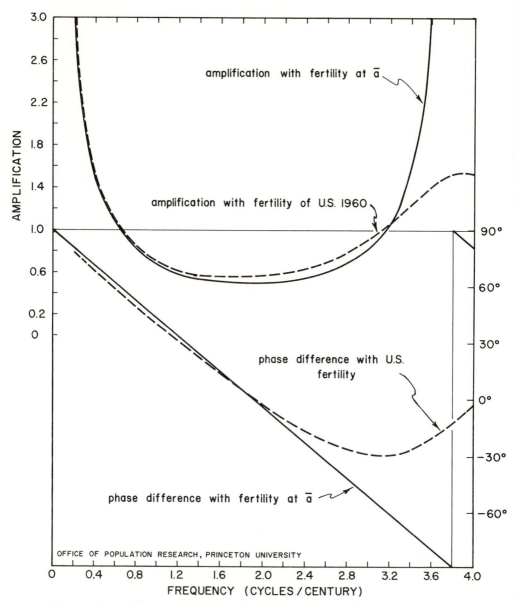

Figure 6.6. Amplification and phase difference between birth fluctuations and fertility fluctuations as functions of frequency (cycles per century); net fertility of U.S. females, 1960, and hypothetical fertility concentrated at $\bar{a}$.

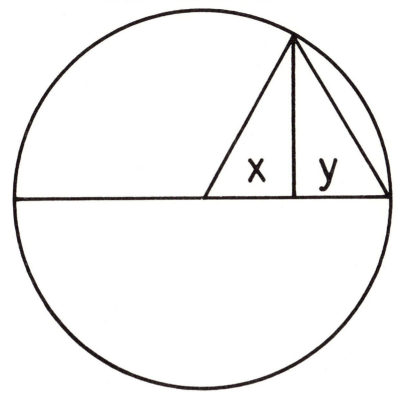

Figure 6.7.

"Resonance" at Frequencies of About One Cycle Per Generation, and "Anti-resonance" at About Half That Frequency

Variations in fertility that occur with a period about equal to the mean age of childbearing create amplified birth cycles for reasons that are obvious: Each maximum of fertility occurs when the number of mothers is also at a maximum because of high fertility one generation earlier. The variation in fertility is reinforced by the variation in age composition. The phase difference between h_1 and z_1 is close to zero, hence $|h_1|$ is approximately $|g| + |z_1|$. If $|z_1|$ were as great as $|h_1|$, amplification would approach infinity, as it would with the hypothetical concentration of fertility at $\bar{a}$. Conversely, when the period of fluctuation in fertility is one cycle every two generations, maximum fertility occurs when the number of mothers is near a minimum, and the variation in fertility is partially offset by the variation in age composition. At this frequency, the phase difference between h_1 and z_1 is very

181

nearly one-half cycle (180′ out of phase), so that $|h_1|$ is approximately $|g| - |z_1|$. If $|z_1|$ were as great as $|h_1|$, birth fluctuations would be half as large at this frequency as fertility fluctuations.

In fact the sequence of varying amplification seen in Figure 6.1 can be interpreted in terms of the variation in $(c_f^2 + s_f^2)^{1/2}$ and of the phase angle between h_1 and z_1. The interpretation is enhanced by a comparison with $(c_f^2 + s_f^2)^{1/2}$ and the phase difference between h_1 and z_1 in a hypothetical fertility schedule concentrated at $\bar{a}$. With the U.S. fertility schedule of 1960, the phase between h_1 and z_1 changes continuously as frequency increases, from a phase difference near zero at a frequency near zero through successive cycles of lagging z_1 until wholly out of phase with h_1, then leading z_1 until in phase with h_1 etc. The result is a series of points of resonance (large amplification when the two are in phase) and anti-resonance (attenuation when out of phase). At low frequencies the phase changes with frequency almost exactly as it would if fertility were concentrated at $\bar{a}$, but as frequency increases above $1/(2\bar{a})$ the rate of change of phase with frequency diminishes slightly, and the increase proceeds at a gradually lessening slope, falling ever farther below the phase increase associated with fertility concentrated at $\bar{a}$. The latter increase remains perfectly linear. Thus the sequence of resonant and anti-resonant frequencies become more widely spaced than in a schedule with all fertility at $\bar{a}$. (See Figure 6.5b.) The most conspicuous difference, however, is in the relation of amplification to frequency. Only at low frequencies is the magnitude of amplification in the two instances (with a real and a hypothetical schedule) approximately the same. The value of $(c_f^2 + s_f^2)^{1/2}$ starts at 1.0 and falls monotonically to a little less than 0.8 at the first point of anti-resonance ($f \doteq 1/2\bar{a}$); and to about 0.38 at the first point of resonance ($f \doteq 1/\bar{a}$) and thence to less than 5% at frequencies above 11 cycles per century. Therefore amplification at anti-resonance is about 1/1.8 instead of 1/2.0, and at resonance is about 1/0.62 instead of approaching infinity. In contrast, $(c_f^2 + s_f^2)^{1/2}$ is 1.0 at all frequencies with the hypothetical concentration of fertility at $\bar{a}$; it does not diminish with frequency at all. (See Figure 6.5a.)

If the highest amplification occurred precisely when h_f and z_f were in phase, s_f would be zero at points of resonance (and also at anti-resonance). The actual points of maximum and minimum amplification occur more nearly at the frequencies where c_f takes on extreme values, which occurs at slightly lower frequencies than the zero points of s_f.

The exact expression for the amplification of small fertility variations is $1/((1 - c_f)^2 + s_f^2)^{1/2}$; since the extrema fall near extreme values of c_f and at frequencies where s_f is near zero, amplification at minimum and maximum points is about $1/(1 - c_f')$, where c_f' is itself an extreme value. The first two extreme values of c_f occur at frequencies such that the peak of the cosine cycle (cos $2\pi fa$) corresponds approximately with the mean of $e^{-ra}\phi(a)$; the extreme values would fall *precisely* at such points if $e^{-ra}\phi(a)$ were symmetrical (and with a single mode at the mean). The lowest frequency that leads to this result is $f = 1/2\bar{a}$; at this frequency there is a negative peak of the cosine at $\bar{a}$, and consequently minimum amplification. The next frequency wherein a peak coincides with $\bar{a}$ is $f = 1/\bar{a}$; here there is a positive peak of the cosine, and maximum amplification. The *amount* of amplification at the extrema depends on the effect on $\int_0^\beta e^{-ra}\phi(a)da$ of multiplying $e^{-ra}\phi(a)$ by cos $2\pi fa$. At the first extremum (the minimum at $1/2\bar{a}$) the negative half cycle extends from about $\bar{a}/2$ to $3\bar{a}/2$, encompassing 97% of the area under the fertility schedule. Hence $|c_f|$ is not drastically less than one ($c_f = .78$), and the gain at this point of anti-resonance is only slightly greater than with hypothetically concentrated fertility (.56 instead of .50). At the second extremum (the maximum at about $1/\bar{a}$), the positive half cycle of cos $(2\pi a/\bar{a})$ extends only from $(3/4)\bar{a}$ to $(5/4)\bar{a}$, encompassing only 74% of the area of the fertility schedule; the other 26% is multiplied by negative values of the cosine in calculating c_f. Hence $|c_f|$ is only 0.36, and amplification has a maximum value of 1.55 instead of approaching infinity. At the subsequent minimum (a frequency of about $1.7/\bar{a}$), there is a negative half cycle of cos $2\pi fa$ that extends from 19.3 to 27.0 years (including the ages of most frequent childbearing from 23 to 26) and encompassing a little over half the total area of the schedule, followed by a positive half cycle (27.0 to 34.7 years) covering about 20% of the area, and a final negative half cycle (34.7 to 42.4) covering about 10%. The net negative balance is only 0.176, and minimum amplification falls only to .85 (approximately $1/1.176$). Higher frequency cosine terms have still more rapid alternations of positive and negative loops within the range covered by $e^{-ra}\phi(a)$, so at frequencies greater than 15 cycles per century $|c_f| < .01$.

In the 45 net fertility schedules for which c_f and s_f were calculated at frequencies from one quarter of a cycle per century to 100 cycles per century, the period approximating a generation that gives maximum amplification is more closely related to the median than the mean of the schedule. Indeed the period of maximum amplification falls within one

183

year of the median age of the net fertility schedule for all 45, and within 0.3 years (with only two exceptions) of a line defined by 1.17 times the median minus 4.17. The maximum amplification for these schedules at "resonance" ranged from 1.41 to 1.99; most of the variation can be estimated by knowledge of two measures of dispersion: (1) the fraction of net fertility occurring between $3/4$ of the median and $5/4$ of the median — the fraction that would be multiplied by positive values of a cosine function when the period is equal to the median — and (2) the average deviation divided by the median. The multiple correlation between these measures (as independent variables) and amplification at resonance is 0.947.

Birth Sequences Resulting from Large Amplitude Fluctuations in Fertility at a Single Frequency

All of the discussion of amplitude and phase relations between fertility fluctuations of the form $G(t) = \overline{NRR}(1 + g \cos wt)$ and birth fluctuations of the form $B(t) = Be^{rt}(1 + \Sigma(a_n \cos nwt + b_n \sin nwt))$, where a_n is the real part and b_n the imaginary part of h_n, or $a_n = h'_n + h_n^*$, and $b_n = i(h'_n - h_n^*)$, applies only to fertility fluctuations of small amplitude, say g less than 10% of $\overline{NRR}$. The need for this restriction is to permit the neglect of the term $g(t) \cdot z(t)$ in the basic cyclical equation, Equation (6.7):

$$(6.7) \qquad 1 + h(t) = y(1 + g(t)) + z(t)(1 + g(t)).$$

If g is small, not only is $z(t) \cdot g(t)$ of a second order of smallness, it also follows that $y \doteq 1$, so $h(t) = g(t) + z(t)$, and there are variations in h and z only at the frequency contained in $g(t)$. When $g(t)$ is larger, we must consider the harmonics generated by $z(t) \cdot g(t)$, and also the effect of the product $z(t) \cdot g(t)$ on y (defined as $\int_0^\beta e^{-ra}\phi(a)da$. We have already outlined a procedure (employing successive approximation) for determining y, r, c_n, and s_n (n is the order of the harmonic of the basic frequency f), and of the coefficients in the birth sequence of the sine and cosine terms at frequencies f, $2f$, $3f$, etc., in $h(t)$ for a given $g(t)$ and net fertility function $\phi(a)$. The procedure is one of solving a set of simultaneous equations (those listed in Equation (6.17), beyond the first) with provisional values of c_n's and s_n's obtained on the assumption that $y = 1$, calculating a new value of y based on the solution of the equations, a new value of r, new values of the c_n's and s_n's, and thence a new set of simultaneous equations. (One of the conventional methods

184

of calculating Lotka's r is employed when y is assumed equal to 1.0.)

Then, since $dy/dr = -\bar{A} \cdot y$, where $\bar{A} = \int_0^\beta ae^{-ra}\phi(a)da \bigg/ \int_0^\beta e^{-ra}\phi(a)da$,

the change in r resulting from a change in y can be estimated as $\delta r = -2\delta y/\bar{A}(1 + y)$. The calculations are readily programmed on a computer. We have determined the change in r, and the value of the coefficients of the terms at the fundamental frequency and at harmonics up to five times the fundamental for frequencies of varying fertility from one cycle every 400 years to one cycle per year. (With g, the magnitude of fertility fluctuations, set at 0.5, or half the average value of fertility.) The calculations were made by assuming that the coefficients of terms with frequencies six times the fundamental are zero. The absolute value of the term at four times $f(|h_4|)$ never reaches one percent of $|h_1|$ at frequencies above one cycle every 400 years, and the ratio $|h_5|/|h_1|$ never reaches 0.001. Hence for g no greater than 0.5 the solution of three equations in complex coefficients would give essentially the same results as the five equations we used. The net fertility function used in these calculations was compounded of the fertility of Swedish women 1891–1900 and a "West" model life table with $e_0^0 = 70$ years, net fertility adjusted in scale so that $\text{NRR} = 1$, and hence $r = 0$ in the absence of fluctuations. Figure 6.8 shows amplification for this fertility schedule at the fundamental frequency when g is small, and when $g = 0.5$, which is a large value indeed, since the maximum level of fertility is three times the minimum. Also shown is the amplitude of the birth fluctuations at twice and three times the frequency of fertility fluctuations, relative to g (i.e., the amplitude of the first two harmonics), and finally, the value of r (which is zero with no fluctuations in fertility, or with small fluctuations).

We shall discuss two questions about these harmonics and the effect of large fluctuations in fertility on r: (1) how they are related to the frequency response (to small amplitude fluctuations) of a given net fertility function; and (2) what form of distorted output results from the harmonics.

The expression for the complex coefficient of the term at $2f$ was given in Equation (6.17) as:

$$(6.25) \quad h_2' = (g/2)(h_1')(c_1 - is_1) + h_2'(c_2 - is_2) + (g/2)(h_3')(c_3 - is_3).$$

At all frequencies greater than one cycle every 400 years, $|h_3'|$ is less than $0.05|h_1'|$, and $|c_3 - is_3|$ is always less than $|c_1 - is_1|$, so the last term in Equation (6.25) can be neglected with little loss of accuracy.

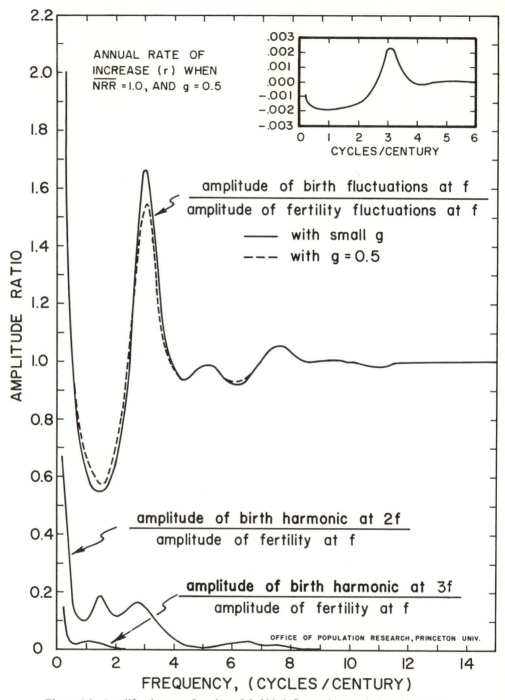

Figure 6.8. Amplification as a function of *f* of birth fluctuations at *f* when fertility fluctuations are small, at *f*, 2*f*, and 3*f* when fertility fluctuates from 0.5 to 1.5 times average fertility; and annual rate of increase, with *g* = 0.5. Net fertility of Swedish women 1891–1900, adjusted so that NRR = 1.0.

The result is:

$$(6.26) \qquad h_2' = \frac{(g/2)(h_1')(c_1 - is_1)}{1 - c_2 - is_2}.$$

The magnitude of h_2' relative to h_1' ($|h_2'|/|h_1'|$) is thus $(g/2)(c_1^2 + s_1^2)^{1/2}/((1 - c_2)^2 + s_2^2)^{1/2}$. This relation can be viewed as follows: the term $x(t)$ in Equation (6.7) ($x(t) = g(t)z(t)$) is the source of frequencies not present in $g(t)$. In particular, $z_1(t) \cdot g(t)$ generates a term at $2f$, as was shown in Equations (6.13) to (6.16), and as can be seen alternatively from the fact that $\cos x \cdot \cos x = (1 + \cos 2x)/2$. The magnitude of the term generated at $2f$ is $(g/2) \cdot |z_1|$, or $(g/2) \cdot |h_1|(c_1^2 + s_1^2)^{1/2}$. This "signal" is then subject to the amplification that applies to any "signal" at $2f$, which is $1/((1 - c_2)^2 + s_2^2)^{1/2}$. Similarly, a term at $3f$ is generated by $z_2(t) \cdot g(t)$; this term is subject to the amplification found at $3f$. These formulations provide estimates of the relation of the amplitude of the harmonics very close to the exact values calculated from the simultaneous equations for coefficients up to $5f$.

The value of y $\left(\int_0^\beta e^{-ra}\phi(a)da \right)$ is affected by the aperiodic component of $z_1(t) \cdot g(t)$, since $y + x_0 = 1$, where x_0 is $(g/2)(z_1' + z_1^*)$, or $(g/2)$ (coefficient of $\cos wt$ in $z_1(t)$). The coefficient of $\cos wt$ in $z_1(t)$ is $(a_1c_1 - b_1s_1)$, a_1 and b_1 being the coefficients of $\cos wt$ and $\sin wt$ in $h(t)$. To get a first approximation to the change in y that occurs with large values of g, we can assume that the relation of $h_1(t)$ to $g(t)$ is the same with large g as with small g; that is, we assume that harmonics are created by a large value of g but that the response at the fundamental frequency is essentially the same. This approximation gives x_0 (the increment in y) as:

$$(6.27) \qquad x_0 \doteq (g^2/2) \frac{(1 - c_1)c_1 - s_1^2}{(1 - c_1)^2 + s_1^2}.$$

Equation (6.27) is a good approximation for moderate values of g (less than 0.25), and for larger values of g (up to 0.5) except at very low frequencies. It neglects the effect of the change in y itself and of the harmonics on $h_1(t)$ and $z_1(t)$. This effect is the last aspect of relations with large g that we shall discuss.

The term at the fundamental frequency in Equation (6.7) can be written:

$$(6.28) \qquad h_1 = y \cdot g + z_1 + (g \cdot z_2)_1,$$

187

where $(g \cdot z_2)_1$ is the component of $(g \cdot z_2)$ at the fundamental frequency. When g is small, y is 1.0, and $(g \cdot z_2)_1$ is negligible, leading to the vector relation $h_1 - z_1 = g$ that was discussed earlier. With large g, the effective signal is $y \cdot g + (g \cdot z_2)_1$ instead of g. Thus the effective signal is modified, when g is large, by: (1) multiplication by y, no longer necessarily equal to 1.0, and (2) addition of the term $(g \cdot z_2)_1$. The magnitude of the effective signal is:

$$g[(y + (1/g) \text{ (coefficient of cos } wt \text{ in } (gz_2)_1))^2$$

$$+ (1/g)^2 \text{ (coefficient of sin } wt \text{ in } (gz_2)_1)^2]^{1/2}.$$

The coefficient of $\cos wt$ in $(gz_2)_1$ is $(g/2)(a_2c_2 - b_2s_2)$; the coefficient of $\sin wt$ is $(g/2)(b_2c_2 + a_2s_2)$, hence the magnitude of the effective signal is

$$g \left[y^2 + y(a_2c_2 - b_2s_2) + \frac{(a_2^2 + b_2^2)(c^2 + s_2^2)}{4} \right]^{1/2};$$

therefore the amplification of the fundamental term in $h(t)$ when g is large is modified by multiplication by the expression under the radical. The phase of the effective signal is changed by

$$\arctan (a_2s_2 + b_2c_2)/(y + a_2c_2 - b_2s_2).$$

The Birth Sequence Resulting from Fluctuations in Fertility at a Single Frequency: Recapitulation

If a population were subject to a fertility sequence consisting of a constant age schedule of fertility whose level at every age changed according to a repetitious sinusoidal pattern, the resultant birth sequence would be the product of an exponential, and a periodic function with the same period as that of the fertility variations. The basic relation is:

(6.7) $$1 + h(t) = y(1 + g(t)) + z(t)(1 + g(t)).$$

When g is small, the fluctuations multiplying the exponential birth sequence are themselves sinusoidal, and at the same frequency as the fertility fluctuations. There is a "response curve" of each net fertility function defining the amplitude and phase of birth fluctuations relative to small amplitude fertility fluctuations as a function of frequency, a response curve characterized by alternate amplification and attenuation of the fertility fluctuations, with maximum amplification at very low frequency, maximum attenuation in the neighborhood of $1/2\bar{a}$, and a convergence of amplification on unity as frequency increases. These properties (and corresponding characteristics of phase differences as a function of frequency) can be explained by the effect on $e^{-ra}\phi(a)$ of $\cos 2\pi fa$ and $\sin 2\pi fa$ in the formation of $z(t)$ — the effective variation in the number of mothers as a contributing factor in birth fluctuations.

If g is large, the fluctuations multiplying the exponential birth sequence are still periodic with the same period of repetition as the fertility fluctuations, but (1) the average rate of increase of births may no longer be the same as in the absence of fertility fluctuations; and (2) the birth fluctuations multiplying e^{rt} are no longer sinusoidal, but contain harmonics of the frequency of the fertility variation, in addition to a sinusoidal component at the same frequency. The harmonics are generated by the term $g(t) \cdot z(t)$ in Equation (6.7); the relation between the component at one frequency and the next depends on the magnitude of $z(t)$ at the lower of the two frequencies and the "frequency response" at the higher.

The effect of harmonics on the "wave form" of the birth sequence is illustrated in Figure 6.9, which shows a sinusoidal $g(t)$ as a reference; then the $h(t)$ that would result if g were small (no harmonics) and if g were large ($g = 0.5$; substantial harmonic at $2f$ and slight harmonic at $3f$ when the frequency is very low). Note that at all frequencies of $g(t)$ shown in Figure 6.9 except about six cycles per century, the $h(t)$ with large g deviates substantially from a sine wave. The exception is interesting: This frequency is a local extremum — a point of minimum amplification; with small g, the birth cycles are only 85% as large as the fertility cycles. The absolute value of z_1 is 17% of h_1; so $g \cdot z_1$ is not completely negligible. However, the amplification of the harmonic is very nearly 1.0, and the birth sequence with $g = 0.5$ is nearly sinusoidal. In contrast, at about 1.4 cycles per century there is the deepest minimum; for small g, h is only about 55% of g, the absolute value of z_1 is nearly 85% of h_1, so $g \cdot z_1$ is substantial. Moreover the harmonic generated by gz_1 occurs at a frequency where amplification is about 1.5, and the deviation of h_1 from sinusoidal form when $g = 0.5$ is very marked.

Almost all of the relations between fertility fluctuations at a single frequency are encompassed in Figure 6.10, which shows an equivalent electrical circuit in block diagram form. The conversion of fertility fluctuations into birth fluctuations is represented as the action of a feedback amplifier with a unit amplification factor at all frequencies. The frequency response of the whole network is determined by the feedback path; the feedback varies both in amplitude and phase. For

189

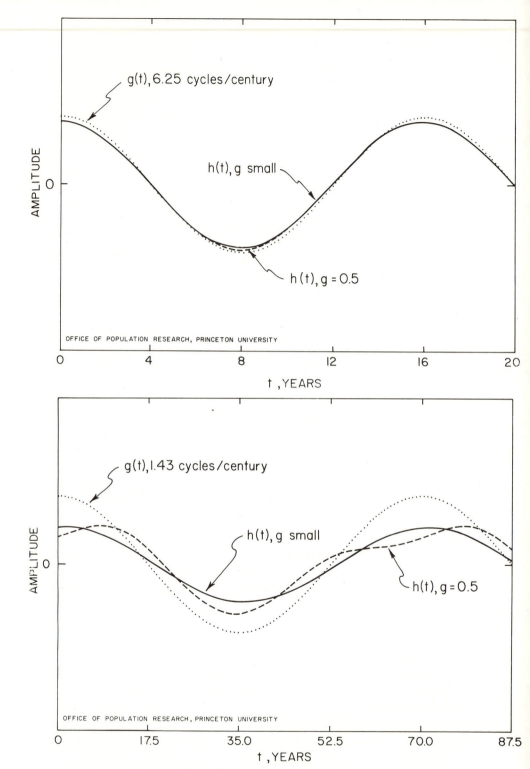

Figure 6.9. Relation of $h(t)$ to $g(t)$, when g is small and when $g = 0.5$, at frequencies of 6.25, 3.03, 1.43, and 0.25 cycles per century. Net fertility of Swedish women, 1891–1900, adjusted so that NRR = 1.0.

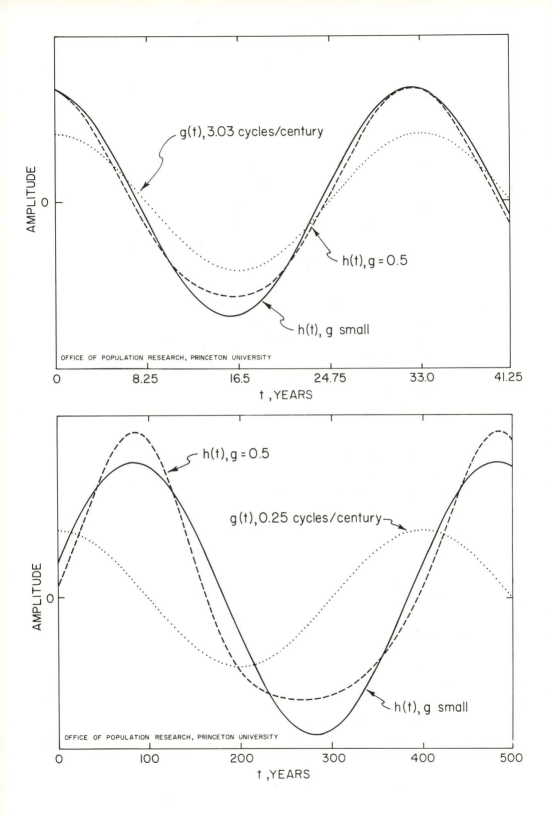

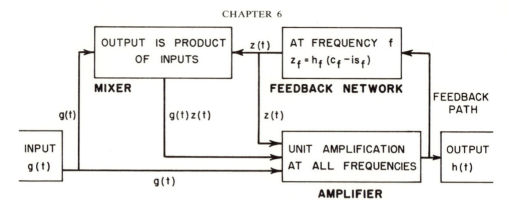

Figure 6.10. Block diagram of equivalent circuit that would produce an output of $h(t)$ from an input of $g(t)$.

small amplitude input, the equivalent circuit is a precise analog. For large inputs, the analogy is still a good one; the generation of harmonics is appropriately represented by the action of a "mixer" that produces a signal equal to the product of the original input and the feedback, that is, $g \cdot z(t)$. The only element not represented is the effect of $z(t) \cdot g(t)$ on y, which alters the effective magnitude of $g(t)$, and changes the response of the feedback network by modifying the set of c_f's and s_f's.

The Age Distribution of a Population with Fluctuating Fertility

It has been shown in Chapter 6 to this point that if fertility follows fluctuations of the form $m(a,t) = m(a)(1 + g(t))$ where $g(t)$ is periodic, the birth sequence follows an exponential of the form

$$(6.29) \qquad B(t) = B(0)e^{\bar{r}t}(1 + h(t))$$

where $h(t)$ is also periodic, with the same cycle length as $g(t)$. Methods for calculating $\bar{r}$ and $h(t)$ have been developed when $g(t)$ is a sinusoidal variation at a single frequency.

We now consider the age distribution of the population when fertility is subject to periodic variation. From Equation (6.29) we find

$$(6.30) \qquad B(t-a) = (B(0)e^{\bar{r}t})e^{-\bar{r}a}(1 + h(t-a)).$$

Since $h(t' - a)$ is a function of a that is simply $h(t)$ written backwards from the point t', $B(t - a)$ for a given value of t is the product of a constant $(B(0)e^{\bar{r}t}(1 + h(t))$, an exponential in $a(e^{-\bar{r}a})$, and a section of a periodic function of a $(1 + h'(a))$ a function with the same period and range of variation as $1 + h(t)$. The age distribution of any closed

192

population with fixed mortality is $c(a) = B(t - a)p(a) \Big/ \int_0^\omega B(t - a)$ $p(a)da$, and thus the age distribution of a population with fluctuating fertility is:

(6.31)
$$c_{ff}(a) = \frac{e^{-\bar{r}a}p(a)(1 + h'(a))}{\int_0^\omega e^{-\bar{r}a}p(a)(1 + h'(a))da},$$

or, since $b_{ff} = (1 + h'(0)) \Big/ \int_0^\omega e^{\bar{r}a}p(a)(1 + h'(a))da$,

(6.32)
$$c_{ff}(a) = \frac{(b_{ff}/b_s)(1 + h'(a))}{(1 + h'(0))c_s(a)}.$$

where $c_s(a)$ is the proportion at age a in the stable population incorporating the given mortality schedule and the rate of increase $\bar{r}$. In short, the age distribution of a population with fluctuating fertility is the product of a stable age distribution and the periodic fluctuations in the birth sequence induced by the fertility fluctuations.

The only empirical instance in human populations of something approaching genuinely periodic fluctuations in fertility is the occurrence in many populations of a seasonal cycle that is repeated in approximately the same form each year. From Equation (6.19) and the fact that $\int_0^\beta e^{-ra}\phi(a) \cos wa \, da$ and $\int_0^\beta e^{-ra}\phi(a) \sin wa \, da$ are both essentially zero for cycles no more than one year in length, it is clear that when the fluctuation in fertility $g(t)$ is an annual cycle, the proportionate fluctuation of births about the trend is the same as the proportionate fluctuation in fertility about its mean, or that $h(t) = g(t)$. Thus if each year births in September are about 8% above the annual average, and in April about 6% below (as in the United States), the age distribution by month at any point in time would have fluctuations of identical magnitude within each year of age.

Only if fertility fluctuations of much greater cycle length occurred would amplification or attenuation and phase shift affect the consequent variations in the birth sequence, and in age composition.

REFERENCE

[1] Courant, R., *Differential and Integral Calculus*, Vol. I, 2d ed., New York, Interscience Publishers, 1937.

193

CHAPTER 7

The Relation Between the Birth Sequence and Sequence of Fertility Schedules in Any Time Pattern Derived by Fourier Analysis

THE birth sequences and age distributions resulting from periodic fluctuations in fertility at a single frequency derived in Chapter 6 are highly abstract, since (with the partial and scarcely important exception of seasonal variations) such fluctuations have not been recorded in any historical data of which I am aware. In this chapter a method is developed for calculating (by Fourier analysis) the birth sequence resulting from any arbitrary time sequence of fertility change, provided the fertility sequence is of sufficient duration to determine the birth sequence, that the age structure of fertility is fixed, and that mortality is constant.

We may begin with the fact cited earlier that a continuous periodic function of any form can be represented as $\Sigma(u_n \cos nwt + v_n \sin nwt)$ where $w = 2\pi/T$, T being the duration of the cycle of the periodic function. Hence, if fertility followed *any* cycle, no matter how long or how irregular, provided only that it recurred exactly, it could be represented as $G(t) = \bar{G}(1 + g(t)) = \bar{G}(1 + \Sigma(u_n \cos nwt + v_n \sin nwt))$, and the consequent birth sequence as $B(t) = Be^{rt}(1 + h(t))$, where $h(t) = \Sigma(a_n \cos nwt + b_n \sin nwt)$. If we can find a way of determining the a_n's and b_n's from the u_n's, v_n's and $\phi(a)$, it would be a natural extension of the analysis already presented.

Again we must concede that genuine fertility sequences are not periodic, even when we allow a completely arbitrary sequence within each cycle, rather than requiring that the cycles be purely sinusoidal. Nevertheless, the fact that birth sequences "forget" the remote past means that we can usefully make the contrary-to-fact assumption that fertility follows a cyclical pattern with a very long period of repetition, and that an extended segment of the fictitious cycle duplicates the actual sequence of fertility experienced by a given population. To be specific, suppose we assume a cycle of 400 years' duration, the last 200 years of which are an exact duplication of the fertility during the past 200 years of some closed population, the other 200 years consisting of constant fertility at the average level for the later 200 years. Suppose (as we shall see, a correct supposition) that by Fourier analysis we can ascertain the relation between such a fertility sequence and the birth sequence that would result from it. Note that at the end of the 200 year portion of the cycle duplicating an actual fertility sequence the

194

population with a cyclical fertility history would have 200 years of experience precisely the same as that of the actual population. Since the birth sequence "forgets" the remote past, the actual birth sequence in the last portion—perhaps the last 100 years—would be essentially the same in the actual population as in the population that had experienced a fictitious sequence of very long cycles of fertility.

If fertility is cyclical, the relation established in Equation (7.1) for repetitive fluctuations in fertility holds (Equation (7.1) is repeated from Equation (6.7)):

(7.1) $$1 + h(t) = y + y \cdot g(t) + z(t) + x(t),$$

where

$$y = \int_0^\beta e^{-ra}\phi(a)da,$$

$$z(t) = \int_0^\beta e^{-ra}\phi(a) \cdot h(t-a)da,$$

and

$$x(t) = g(t) \cdot z(t).$$

If the functions of time in Equation (7.1) are now expressed in Fourier form, each will contain components at the basic frequency $f = 1/T$ (where T is the duration of the cycle) and at multiples of f. We can write a separate equation for each frequency, as follows:

(7.2)
$$1 = y + x_0$$
$$h_n(t) = y \cdot g_n(t) + z_n(t) + x_n(t),$$

where x_0 is that component of $g(t) \cdot z(t)$ that does not involve time, and $x_n(t)$ is that component of $g(t) \cdot z(t)$ that involves cos nwt and sin nwt. As before, we can make use of the fact that $a \cos x + b \sin x = (\frac{1}{2})(a - ib)e^{ix} + (\frac{1}{2})(a + ib)e^{-ix}$, and write $h_n(t)$ as $h'_n e^{inwt} + h_n^* e^{-inwt}$ with corresponding expressions for $z_n(t)$ and $x_n(t)$. The last term $(x_n(t))$ is the component of $g(t) \cdot z(t)$ at frequency nf.

(7.3)　$$z(t) \cdot g(t) = \sum_{s=1}^\infty \sum_{r=1}^\infty (z'_r e^{irwt} + z_r^* e^{-irwt}) \cdot (g'_s e^{iswt} + g_s^* e^{-iswt}),$$

or

(7.4)　$$z(t) \cdot g(t) = \sum \sum (z'_r g'_s e^{i(r+s)wt} + z_r^* g_s^* e^{-i(r+s)wt}$$

$$+ z'_r g_s^* e^{i(r-s)wt} + z_r^* g'_s e^{-i(r-s)wt}).$$

195

The component of $x(t)$ at frequency nf consists of the sum of all elements in Equation (7.4) where the exponent is $inwt$ or $-inwt$. Hence

$$x_n(t) = \sum_{r=1}^{n-1} (z_r g'_{n-r} e^{inwt} + z_r^* g_{n-r}^* e^{-inwt}) \qquad [r + s = n]$$

$$+$$

(7.5)
$$\sum_{r=n+1}^{\infty} (z'_r g_{r-n}^* e^{inwt} + z_r^* g_{r-n}^* e^{-inwt}) \qquad [r - s = n]$$

$$+$$

$$\sum_{r=1}^{\infty} (z_r^* g'_{n+r} e^{inwt} + z'_r g_{n+r}^* e^{-inwt}) \qquad [s - r = n].$$

Also

(7.6)
$$x_0 = \sum_{r=1}^{\infty} (z'_r g_r^* + z_r^* g'_r).$$

Thus we see that every frequency present in $g(t)$ contributes to all frequencies in $h(t)$, because of the fact that

$$(a' e^{ix} + a^* e^{-ix})(b' e^{iy} + b^* e^{-iy})$$

$$= c' e^{i(x+y)} + c^* e^{-i(x+y)} + d' e^{i(x-y)} + d^* e^{-i(x-y)}.$$

From Equation (7.2), we can obtain an expression equating the coefficients of e^{inwt}, as follows:

(7.7)
$$h'_n = y g'_n + z'_n + \sum_{r=1}^{n-1} z'_r g'_{n-r} + \sum_{r=n+1}^{\infty} z'_r g_{r-n}^* + \sum_{r=1}^{\infty} z_r^* g'_{n+r}.$$

Since at every frequency $z'_n = h'_n(c_n - is_n)$, and $z_n^* = h_n^*(c_n + is_n)$, Equation (7.7) can be converted by making these substitutions into an expression in which the only terms are h'_n's and h_n^*'s (viewed as unknowns), y, g's, c's, and s's. Our ultimate purpose is to determine the a's and b's in $h(t) = \Sigma(a_n \cos nwt + b_n \sin nwt)$ from knowledge of $g(t)$, which can be written as $g(t) = \Sigma(u_n \cos nwt + v_n \sin nwt)$, and knowledge of the age structure and level of $\phi(a)$, which is the average schedule of fertility about which the fluctuations take place. To suit this purpose, we can convert the equations at each frequency (exemplified by Equation (7.7)) into a set of equations for the coefficients (a_n and b_n) of the sine and cosine terms at every frequency in the birth variations; making use of the fact that $a_n = h'_n + h_n^*$, and $b_n = i(h'_n - h_n^*)$. The result of carrying out these substitutions and rearranging terms is:

196

$$w_{11}a_1 + \cdots + w_{1r}a_r + x_{11}b_1 + \cdots + x_{1r}b_r = -2y \cdot u_1$$

$$\cdot \qquad\qquad\qquad\qquad \cdot$$
$$\cdot \qquad\qquad\qquad\qquad \cdot$$
$$\cdot \qquad\qquad\qquad\qquad \cdot$$

(7.8)
$$w_{r1}a_1 + \cdots + w_{rr}a_r + x_{r1}b_1 + \cdots + x_{rr}b_r = -2y \cdot u_r$$

$$y_{11}a_1 + \cdots + y_{1r}a_r + z_{11}b_1 + \cdots + z_{1r}b_r = -2y \cdot v_1$$

$$\cdot \qquad\qquad\qquad\qquad \cdot$$
$$\cdot \qquad\qquad\qquad\qquad \cdot$$
$$\cdot \qquad\qquad\qquad\qquad \cdot$$

$$y_{r1}a_1 + \cdots + y_{rr}a_r + z_{r1}b_1 + \cdots + z_{rr}b_r = -2y \cdot v_r,$$

where the w_{ij}'s, x_{ij}'s, y_{ij}'s, and z_{ij}'s have the values given in Table 7.1.

The nonperiodic equation (Equation (7.6)) can be expressed in terms of a's, b's, u's, and v's, as follows:

(7.9) $$1 = y + \frac{1}{2}\sum \left[(a_r c_r - b_r s_r)u_r + (a_r s_r + b_r c_r)v_r\right].$$

We have now completed the formal statement of how Fourier analysis can be used to determine the relation between any specified sequence of fertility change and the birth sequence that results. The actual steps employed in a concrete application of the process are perhaps obscured in the lengthy formulae we have presented; an explicit description of the steps will make the procedure clearer.

Suppose we are given age-specific mortality and fertility rates of a closed female population during a sequence A years in length, A being a long interval in the order of 150 to 200 years. Suppose we calculate

Table 7.1. Values of the coefficients in Equation (7.8)

Coefficient	$i > j$	$i = j$	$i < j$
w_{ij}	$c_j(u_{i-j} + u_{i+j})$ $- s_j(v_{i-j} - v_{i+j})$	$2(c_j - 1) + c_j u_{2j} + s_j v_{2j}$	$c_j(u_{j-i} + u_{i+j})$ $+ s_j(v_{j-i} + v_{i+j})$
x_{ij}	$-c_j(v_{i-j} - v_{i+j})$ $- s_j(u_{i-j} + u_{i+j})$	$-2s_j + c_j v_{2j} - s_j u_{2j}$	$c_j(v_{j-i} + v_{i+j})$ $- s_j(u_{j-i} + u_{i+j})$
y_{ij}	$c_j(v_{i-j} + v_{i+j})$ $+ s_j(u_{i-j} - u_{i+j})$	$2s_j + c_j v_{2j} - s_j u_{2j}$	$-c_j(v_{j-i} - v_{i+j})$ $+ s_j(u_{j-i} - u_{i+j})$
z_{ij}	$c_j(u_{i-j} - u_{i+j})$ $- s_j(v_{i-j} + v_{i+j})$	$2(c_j - 1) - s_j v_{2j} - c_j u_{2j}$	$c_j(u_{j-i} - u_{i+j})$ $+ s_j(v_{j-i} - v_{i+j})$

$\phi(a,t) = m(a,t)p(a,t)$, and that $\phi(a,t)$ can be decomposed into a fixed average age function $(\phi(a))$ and a varying time sequence $(X(t))$. The value of $\phi(a)$ is the average value of $\phi(a,t)$, or $\phi(a) = (1/A) \int_0^A \phi(a,t)dt$.

We now assume that the A years of recorded net fertility is part of one cycle of an endlessly repetitious pattern of fertility change. We are at liberty to specify the length of cycle as any number of years, T, that we choose, provided $T \geqslant A$. A computationally convenient choice is $T = 2A$, with the assumption that fertility during the A years in the cycle *not* taken up with the recorded variations follows the recorded pattern in reverse, assuring continuity over the whole cycle including the points of junction between recorded and assumed portions. In other words, we may assume that fertility has always followed a cycle of A years of the recorded pattern, A years of the recorded pattern in reverse, A years of the recorded cycle, etc. This pattern implies

$$\phi(a,t) = \phi(a)(1 + g(t)),$$

where $g(t)$ is the repetitive function of period T and with a mean value of zero over each cycle. The next step is to represent $g(t)$ as $\Sigma_{n=1}^N (u_n \cos nwt + v_n \sin wt)$. ($N$ is written as the upper limit of the summation [rather than ∞] because our data typically are provided at finite intervals [such as annually] rather than as a continuous function. As we shall see, if the data are annual, and cover A years, and we assume A years of arbitrary fertility to complete the cycle, N is equal to A.) The standard formulae for calculation of the Fourier coefficients to yield the series $\Sigma(a_n \cos nx + b_n \sin nx)$ when the function fitted is $f(x)$, periodic from $x = -\pi$ to $x = \pi$, are:

$$a_n = \frac{1}{\pi} \int_{-\pi}^{\pi} f(x) \cos nx \, dx,$$

and

$$b_n = \frac{1}{\pi} \int_{-\pi}^{\pi} f(x) \sin nx \, dx$$

(Courant [1].) We set $t = 0$ at the beginning of the A years of recorded fertility; the cycle extends from $-A$ to $+A$ and x is $2\pi t/T$. Hence

(7.10) $$u_n = \frac{1}{A} \int_{-A}^{A} g(t) \cos nwt \, dt,$$

and

198

(7.11)
$$v_n = \frac{1}{A} \int_{-A}^{A} g(t) \sin nwt \, dt.$$

But from $-A$ to A, $g(t)$ has been formulated so that $g(t) = g(-t)$; also $\cos(-nwt) = \cos(nwt)$, but $\sin(-nwt) = -\sin nwt$. Therefore,

(7.12)
$$u_n = \frac{2}{A} \int_{0}^{A} g(t) \cos nwt \, dt,$$

and

(7.13)
$$v_n = 0.$$

By postulating a cycle for $g(t)$ that is symmetrical about $t = 0$, we have generated a convenient Fourier expansion of $g(t)$ that contains only cosine terms. If the number of terms in the Fourier expansion is made equal to the number of years of recorded annual data, the Fourier series expressing $g(t)$ will fit the recorded data exactly, since in employing annual data we approximate the integral in Equation (7.12) by a sum, replace a continuous $g(t)$ by a function defined only at discrete points, and fit a Fourier function only at those points. Since the number of constants we choose equals the number of observations, the fit is exact.

Values of c_n and s_n are calculated ($c_n = \int_{0}^{\beta} e^{-ra}\phi(a) \cos(nwa)da$, $s_n = \int_{0}^{\beta} e^{-ra}\phi(a) \sin(nwa)da$) for $n = 1$ to $n = A$; with u_n's determined over the same range of n, and $v_n = 0$, all of the needed values are at hand to form $2A$ linear equations for $2A$ unknowns (a_n's and b_n's, $n = 1$ to A) that define $h(t)$, the fluctuating component of the birth sequence. Since A should be a large number of years (150 or more), we are faced with finding the solutions of 300 or more linear equations in 300 or more unknowns, an imposing job for all but the largest computers.

At the corresponding point in the discussions of fertility variations at one frequency, the potential number of equations determining the coefficients of oscillatory terms in the birth sequence shrank from a large number to no more than two (only one in complex numbers) when the amplitude of fertility variation was small, and to only a few with fertility variations of substantial magnitude, because harmonics above three or four times the basic frequency are negligible. The same tendency toward simplification may exist when $g(t)$ is an irregular sequence rather than a sine wave at a single frequency. Since $h_n(t) = y \cdot g_n(t) + z_n(t) + (z(t) \cdot g(t))_n$ (cf. Equation (7.2)), the term in $h(t)$ at each fre-

199

quency would be determined solely by the term in $g(t)$ at the same frequency, if $(z(t) \cdot g(t))_n$ were negligible; and the array of simultaneous equations would become a set of equations of equal number, each in one (complex) unknown. But $z(t) \cdot g(t)$ generates a component at frequency nf for every z_r and g_s such that $r - s = n, r - s = n$, or $s - r = n$. So moderate values of z_r at several frequencies and of g_s at several others can combine to generate a nonnegligible term at frequency nf. What is significant is whether the sum of terms of the form $\Sigma z_r g_{n-r}$, $\Sigma z_r g_{n+r}$ (cf. Equation (7.7)) are negligible; when this is so, the Fourier analysis of the birth sequence resulting from a specified sequence of changing fertility takes its simplest form. When the term $(g(t) \cdot z(t))_n$, or $x_n(t)$ in Equation (7.2) is of negligible magnitude, a_n is $u_n(1 - c_n)/((1 - c_n)^2 + s_n^2)$, and b_n is $u_n \cdot s_n/((1 - c_n)^2 + s_n^2)$. Under these circumstances, we determine the Fourier composition of $g(t)$, subject the term at each frequency to the amplification $1/((1 - c_n)^2 + s_n^2)^{1/2}$ and phase shift arctan $(s_n/(1 - c_n))$ characteristic of $e^{-ra}\phi(a)$, and thus determine the term in $h(t)$ at the same frequency.

A sufficient condition that this relatively simple analysis be valid is that fertility fluctuations never be large. Unfortunately, the demographic importance of small changes in fertility is very limited. An interesting particular example of fertility variation that lends itself to analysis without introducing the effects of $g(t) \cdot z(t)$ is an isolated "pulse" of elevated fertility that lasts a very short time. The resultant variation in births is already well known to demographers as the "Progeny of a Population Element" (Lotka [2]). The pulse may be represented as follows: suppose that $NRR = 1.0$ from $t = -150$ to $t = -1$, 2.0 at $t = 0$, and 1.0 from $t = 1$ to $t = 150$. The average value of the net reproduction rate is $301/300$ or 1.0033; $g(t)$ is -0.0033 at all points except $t = 0$; $g(0)$ is .9967. It is clear without Fourier analysis that $g(t) \cdot z(t)$ is negligible, since $g(t)$ is essentially zero at all points except $t = 0$, and since $z(t) = \int_0^\beta h(t - a)e^{-ra}\phi(a)da$, $z(t)$ can hardly have a consequential value at $t = 0$. Hence we can proceed with the simple version of Fourier analysis. Under these circumstances, $u_n = (2/150) \int_0^{150} g(t) \cos nwt \, dt$, or simply $2/150$, and $v_n = 0$. (This formulation treats $g(0)$ as rectangular pulse of unit area and vanishingly short duration.) We have calculated 600 values of u_n, and, using the age pattern of the Swedish fertility schedule of 1891–1900, mortality of the "West" model life table, $e_0^0 = 70$, a set of c_n's and s_n's calculated from this schedule, and finally the a_n's and b_n's in the Fourier expansion of the oscillatory portion of the consequent birth sequence. We set

$$h(t) = \sum_{n=1}^{600} (a_n \cos nwt + b_n \sin nwt),$$

and

$$B(t) = Be^{\bar{r}t}(1 + h(t)).$$

The average value of the NRR is 1.0033, hence $\bar{r}$ is not zero, but (log 1.0033)/32.11. Since $\bar{a}$ for this schedule is 32.11, $r = 0.000104$. The resultant birth sequence is shown in Figure 7.1. If we subtract the births that would result from fertility held constant at NRR $= 1$ (namely, $B'(0)$, the births at $t = 0$ in the absence of fertility change), the resultant sequence generated by changing fertility is indistinguishable from the sequence generated by projecting a population element of suitable size born at $t = 0$. What is remarkable about $B(t)$ calculated in this way is that the sum of a number of sinusoidal terms (each at fixed amplitude) at different frequencies precisely duplicates the sum of a number of *damped* sinusoidal sequences, each with its own annual decrement in amplitude — a sum soon dominated by a diminishing cyclical term with a period about equal to $\bar{a}$.

Note that since the "spectrum" of a "spike" in fertility is flat (the amplitude of the fundamental and of all harmonics is the same), and since all components of such a spike are pure cosine functions (in phase, so to speak, at $t = 0$) it follows that the amplitude of the various components of the resultant birth sequence is proportional to $1/((1 - c_n)^2 + s_n^2)^{1/2}$, and that the component at frequency nf lags the corresponding component in the spectrum of the fertility pulse by arctan $s_n/(1 - c_n)$. Thus the "spectrum" of a population element and its progeny is exactly specified by the amplification and phase curves characteristic of $e^{-ra}\phi(a)da$.

With most actual time patterns of changing fertility, however, the product of $z(t) \cdot g(t)$ is not negligible. To work out an example where allowance is made for this product, we have applied the more complicated form of Fourier analysis to the recorded sequence of fertility change in Sweden for the 155 years from 1808 through 1962. We first estimated NRR(t) for each year, when $\text{NRR}(t) = \int_0^\beta p(a,t)m(a,t)da$; $p(a,t)$ representing the proportion surviving from birth to age a at time t of those born at time $t - a$ and $m(a,t)$ representing the rate of bearing

201

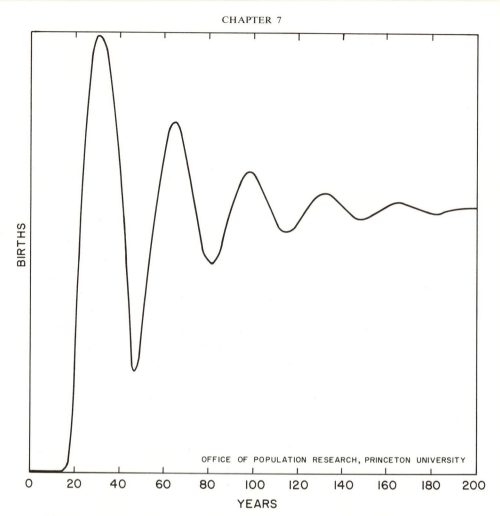

Figure 7.1. Births in excess of those that would be produced by fertility constant at NRR = 1.0 from doubling of fertility during a pulse at $t = 0$; a pulse recurrent once every 300 years. Births calculated by Fourier analysis (net fertility of Swedish women 1891–1900).

female offspring at age a at time t. We began with average estimates of fertility for five-year time intervals given by Keyfitz and Flieger [3], and estimated survival values by employing model life tables with the average infant mortality 25 to 30 years earlier. NRR(t) for single years was then estimated by assuming that within each five-year time interval, NRR$(t)/\overline{\text{NRR}} = b(t)/\bar{b}$, where $b(t)$ is the birth rate in year t and $\bar{b}$ is the average for five years. Supplied with these estimated values of NRR(t), we constructed $g(t) = (\text{NRR}(t) - \overline{\text{NRR}})/\overline{\text{NRR}}$, and then assumed that fertility had been constant at $\overline{\text{NRR}}$ during the 155 years preceding 1808. Thus our fictitious cycle was 155 years of constant fertility followed by 155 years approximating recorded fertility. It was then assumed that the age structure of net fertility remained fixed at the combination of $m(a)$ for Swedish women 1891–1900 and $p(a)$ from 'West" model life tables, level 21. The fictitious cycle was 310 years long; values of u_n and v_n were calculated up to $n = 155$, using as many Fourier coefficients as assumed points in the cycle, assuring that $\Sigma(u_n \cos (n2\pi t/310) + v_n \sin (n2\pi t/310))$ exactly matches variations in $g(t)$.

However, a way was found to avoid solving 310 simultaneous equations to determine the a_n's and b_n's. The basic equation for the birth sequency in cyclical form is $1 + h(t) = y + y \cdot g(t) + z(t) + z(t) \cdot g(t)$. If we assume that $y \left(\int_0^\beta e^{-ra}\phi(a)da \right)$ is very close to 1.0, this equation becomes $h(t) = g(t) + z(t) + z(t) \cdot g(t)$. Solution must be sought for a large number of simultaneous equations because $z(t) \cdot g(t)$ is not negligible relative to the other terms. However, the magnitude of the components of $z(t)$ falls with frequency, since $|z_n| = |h_n| \cdot (c_n^2 + s_n^2)^{1/2}$; and at frequencies above 10 cycles per century (or indeed, five cycles per century) the components of z have very little effect on $h(t)$.

The rapidly diminishing importance of z_n as n increases above a certain point led to the following system of calculations:

(1) Equations (60 in number) of the form shown in Equation (7.8) were used to calculate a_n and b_n for $n = 1$ to 30 (frequencies up to one cycle every 10.3 years) on the assumption that components of $z(t)$ at higher frequencies are negligible. The cosine term in z_n has a coefficient $a_n c_n - b_n s_n$, and the sine term a coefficient of $a_n s_n + b_n c_n$; hence $z(t)$ can be calculated from these 30 a_n's and b_n's, on the assumption that $z(t)$ contains no important components above ten cycles per century. The $z(t)$ obtained from the lowest 30 frequencies is then used to determine $h(t)$ directly, from $h(t) = g(t) + z(t) + z(t) \cdot g(t)$.

An examination of the meaning of the terms in $h(t) = g(t) + z(t) + z(t) \cdot g(t)$ will make it clear why $z(t)$ contains essentially only low frequency components. The term $h(t)$ expresses the variation of births from the exponential sequence that would result if fertility were fixed at its average value; $g(t)$ is the variation in fertility about its average; and $z(t)$ is the weighted average of the variation of births in the parental generation from the exponential. Thus $g(t)$ is the contribution of fertility variation to the variation in births; $z(t)$ the contribution of the variation in the number of parents to the variation in the number of births; and $g(t) \cdot z(t)$ is the contribution of the interaction of the variation of fertility and of the number of births. High frequency components in the birth sequence "average out" during the parental generation; only low frequency components contribute to $z(t)$.

Figure 7.2 shows $g(t)$, $z(t)$, and $h(t)$ calculated in this way. We have compared the births estimated on this basis (as $B(t) = Be^{rt}(1 + h(t))$ with births calculated by projection, assuming that prior to 1808 (our starting point) births had followed a simple exponential consistent with the NRR of 1808. We use projected births rather than actual births in the comparison, because actual births have been strongly affected by migration. The projected births vary from a minimum of 61,000 to a maximum of 174,000; deviations from the exponential from −26% to +38%; but the births calculated as the sum of Fourier components follow the projected births with a maximum discrepancy of less than 0.5%. It is apparent that the procedure works!

It is now clear that the complicated form of Fourier analysis need not be used to establish the relation between fertility sequences and birth sequences except for components at frequencies less than five to ten cycles per century. At such low frequencies the specification of the

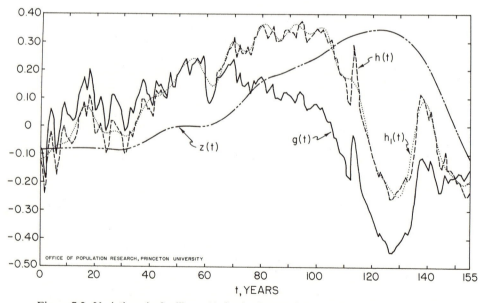

Figure 7.2. Variations in fertility, $g(t)$, in the first 30 frequencies of birth fluctuations, $h_1(t)$, in $z(t)$, and in the first 155 frequencies of birth fluctuations, $h(t)$. Fluctuations in net fertility, $g(t)$, based on annual Swedish records 1808–1962.

204

age schedule of fertility by single years of age, and of the time sequence of fertility by single years in time is redundant. Average values of fertility over five (or even ten) year age and time intervals would be sufficient. (Recall that a fertility schedule concentrated at its mean age would give a close approximation to the frequency response to changing fertility up to frequencies of about one cycle every 70 years.) Thus to employ this method, one could record a sequence of average values of $g(t)$ over ten year time intervals for 15 to 20 such intervals, and find values of u_n (n from one to 15 or 20) instead of the 150 to 200 values suggested earlier, thereby assuming a basic cycle length of 300 to 400 years. Values of c_n and s_n could be calculated from a $\phi(a)e^{-ra}$ given in the form of average values for 15 to 24, 25 to 34, 35 to 44 years. These data would suffice to calculate $z(t)$ based on the low frequencies that in fact constitute $z(t)$. It is too early to say whether many interesting insights into the formation of birth sequences will result from examining in this fashion the consequences of a variety of different forms (and amplitudes) of fertility variation.

REFERENCES

[1] Courant, R., *Differential and Integral Calculus,* New York, Interscience Publishers, 1937.
[2] Lotka, Alfred J., "The Progeny of a Population Element," *American Journal of Hygiene,* Vol. 8, 1925, pp. 875–901.
[3] Keyfitz, N., and Flieger, W., *World Population: An Analysis of Vital Data,* Chicago and London, The University of Chicago Press, 1968.

CHAPTER 8
Conclusion

IT IS evident even to its author that this book may not be an easy one to read. Its difficulty is not caused primarily by the use of advanced mathematics (it rarely goes beyond the level encountered by a college sophomore studying physics), but because the mathematics may be in fields not familiar to the mathematically inclined social scientist, and because from time to time a series of complicated ideas and interrelations are introduced within a short space. This concluding chapter is intended to restate in less technical form, and in a few instances to extend, some of the important points that may be concealed in the complexity of the earlier chapters.

The premise upon which this book is based is the property of human populations that Lopez (borrowing a term from John Hajnal) called "weak ergodicity." This property might be identified as the progressive forgetting of the past; the time structure of the birth sequence of a human population and its age structure at a given moment are dominated by the recent history of fertility and mortality to which the population has been subject. It is not necessary to know anything about the history of a population more than two centuries ago to account for the recent sequence of births, or the present age composition. In fact, the age composition and the birth sequence in a population can be calculated from no more than a specified sequence of fertility and mortality schedules over a moderate interval of time.

The principal purpose of this book is to explain the relationships between specifiable features characterizing sequences of fertility and mortality schedules, and the consequent general structure of the birth sequence or the age composition that result. A number of special cases of particular sequences of variation in fertility and mortality are explored, namely: (1) the birth sequence and age composition that result when fertility and mortality schedules are, and have been, fixed for a long time (the exponential birth sequence and the stable population); (2) the birth sequence that results when fertility and mortality schedules are fixed, starting at a given moment, with arbitrary conditions assumed to prevail prior to this moment (the approach to stability); (3) the birth sequence and age composition that result when mortality is constant and fertility (with a constant age pattern) follows a perpetual trend of constant annual change; (4) the birth sequence and age distributions that occur following a shift of fertility from one constant annual rate of change to another (especially when one of the two trends

206

is a horizontal one); (5) the age distribution that results when fertility is constant and mortality has recently followed a particular pattern of annual change, a pattern closely equivalent to a constant annual change in fertility (in this case, the age pattern of mortality is not considered constant but rather subject to a typical change in age pattern with change in level); (6) the birth sequence and age distributions that result when mortality is constant and fertility, constant in age pattern, is subject to periodic fluctuation.

In the general case of changing fertility and mortality without specification of the time or age patterns of either set of schedules, the birth sequence and age composition can be calculated by standard procedures of population projection applied to any arbitrary initial age distribution assumed in the remote past (weak ergodicity guarantees that the arbitrarily assumed initial age distribution will make no difference if it is postulated at a point sufficiently long ago). However, we cannot visualize the results of population projection. Therefore the formal "explanation" of the current age distribution as the result of applying a long Markov chain of transition matrices to the initial arbitrary population vector (one way of formally representing population projection) does not really help us understand how a particular age structure came about, or help us to see by inspection what age structure would result from a specified sequence of fertility and mortality schedules.

In Chapter 7, another method of relating an arbitrary fertility sequence to the resultant birth sequence is described. (Note that this chapter does not examine the completely general case; it is assumed that mortality is fixed, and that the age pattern of fertility does not change; however, there is no restriction placed on the sequence of fertility changes analyzed.) It is shown in Chapter 7 that a fertility sequence over a long period of time can be fitted by a Fourier series, utilizing a contrary-to-fact assumption that the sequence observed over an extended period—say two or three centuries—is one cycle of an endlessly repeated set of cycles of the same pattern. The birth sequence that would result from such a fertility sequence can be calculated, and the part of the calculated birth sequence during a recent subinterval (e.g., the last century) is essentially the same as the actual births caused by the given sequence of fertility schedules. Thus a solution for the relationship between varying fertility in *any* time pattern and the consequent birth sequence and age composition is apparently at hand. However, this solution has a discouraging feature: In the ap-

207

proach through Fourier analysis an interaction of terms at different frequencies is encountered, necessitating the solution of a large number of simultaneous equations to determine the coefficients of terms at different frequencies in the birth sequence. In consequence there is no readily visualizable relationship between the "spectrum" of the variations in fertility and the resultant spectrum of the variations in births around an exponential trend. In the end, we find that the Fourier solution has the same lack of heuristic value as the already existing solution of the general case through standard techniques of population projection. It is quite possible that there is a general principle at work here: The age distribution effects of certain simple specified sequences of fertility or mortality changes can be visualized, but the general case will always remain merely calculable, but not readily understandable at an intuitive level.

The Stable Population and the Approach to Stability

The stable population—the population that would result from the indefinite continuation of given schedules of fertility and mortality—incorporates in simplest and most easily comprehensible form the effects on age distribution of fertility and mortality. In this book, we have proposed a few simplified expressions showing certain interrelationships among age compositions in the stable population, the fertility and mortality schedules upon which it depends, and its birth and death rates. One of these expressions is:

$$(2.18) \qquad r \doteq \frac{\log (\mathrm{GRR} \cdot p(\bar{m}))}{\bar{m} - \sigma^2(\log \mathrm{GRR}/2\bar{m})}.$$

This equation shows the dependence of the rate of increase in a stable population on the level of fertility (GRR), the mean age of fertility ($\bar{m}$), the variance in age of fertility (σ^2), and the level of mortality ($p_{\bar{m}}$), represented by the probability of surviving to the mean age of childbearing. Another expression is:

$$(2.31) \qquad b \doteq \mathrm{GRR} \cdot c(\bar{m});$$

showing the dependence of the birth rate on fertility and a feature of the age distribution in the stable population. The most intriguing new feature of stable populations described is

$$(2.38) \qquad \frac{dG}{dr} = G (\bar{a} - \bar{a}_g),$$

in which G stands for the proportion of the population with a given characteristic (or experiencing a given event), $\bar{a}$ is the mean age of the stable population, and $\bar{a}_g$ is the mean age of persons with the given characteristic. The proportion with the characteristic g may be, for example, the proportion in a given age interval in the stable population (20 to 25 or over 85), the proportion of married women according to a specified schedule of proportions married by age, or the overall proportion dying (the death rate) according to the mortality schedule underlying the stable population. In all such instances, the extreme proportion (if one exists) occurs when the mean age of the persons with the characteristic is the same as the mean age of the whole population, and consequently the same as the mean age of the persons *without* the characteristic. Thus the minimum death rate with a given mortality schedule occurs in the stable population when the mean age at death and the mean age of the population are the same.

When the imposition of constant fertility and mortality is visualized as occurring following arbitrary initial conditions, the approach of the population to a stable form occurs within ω years after the birth sequence has changed from whatever initial irregular form it may have to a simple exponential function. This approach to an exponential can be calculated either by projecting the initial population using fixed schedules, or by finding the complex roots of

$$(3.3) \qquad \int_0^\beta e^{-ra}p(a)m(a)da = 1$$

and expressing the birth sequence as

$$(3.4) \qquad B(t) = \sum_{i=0}^\infty Q_i e^{r_i t}$$

after finding the real and complex roots of Equation (3.3) and their coefficients. The latter mode of visualizing stabilization depends on the fact that the complex roots (which generate oscillatory terms at different frequencies, each oscillation multiplied by its own exponential that causes a constant rate of change in amplitude) incorporate real exponential terms with a smaller exponent than that of the single component of the birth sequence that is nonoscillatory. In other words, the oscillations all fall in magnitude relative to the exponential birth sequence, ultimately becoming of negligible magnitude compared to this sequence, whatever quantitative criterion (other than zero) of "negligible" is utilized. When the factors determining the rate of damping and

209

the frequency of the complex roots are examined, it is seen that the lowest frequency root has a period about the same as the mean length of generation, and that higher frequency roots are very much more highly damped (i.e., fall much more rapidly with time) than the low frequency oscillatory term. In fact, with actual human net fertility functions and any arbitrary initial conditions, the low frequency term is the only complex (oscillatory) component of any consequence a few years more than the mean age of childbearing past the initiation of constant fertility and mortality. Thus the process of convergence of the birth sequence to an exponential is often best visualized by picturing the result of projecting the difference between a stable age distribution and the initial age distribution for 25 or 30 years, then calculating the approximate magnitude, phase, and rate of decrement of the lowest frequency oscillation, and splicing the projection with this continuing damped oscillatory component.

Damping of the low frequency term relative to the real exponent is almost wholly determined by the fraction of the net fertility function that is included between the limits $3/4$ of the mean age and $5/4$ of the mean age on the one hand, and by the skewness of the net fertility function on the other. The less the fraction of net fertility between these age limits, and the more skewed the distribution, the more rapid is the damping of this component.

In Chapter 4, the convergence of a birth sequence to a second order exponential when fertility is constantly falling is compared to convergence to a first order exponential when fertility is constant. The same age pattern of fertility is assumed, and the same initial deviation of the age distribution from its long range form. The sequence of fluctuations about the long range trend is virtually identical in the two cases. Thus the erasure of the effect of an initial arbitrary set of conditions is much the same whether one is dealing with convergence to stability or convergence to the age composition dictated by some other specified sequence of fertility and mortality schedules.

The dependence of the relative decrement of the low frequency oscillations on the fraction of net fertility between $3/4$ and $5/4$ of the mean age of childbearing and on the degree of skewness was inferred from general considerations of what causes complex roots to have a real component less than the real root of Equation (3.1). Note that the expression of the degree to which the damping of the low frequency term depends on these factors (in Equation (3.37)) is based purely on empirical observations of a number of recorded net fertility functions. On the other hand, the age structure of human fertility is determined by virtually universally operative factors illustrated in Figure 1.1: The shape of the rising portion of age-specific fertility rates is dominated by the rate at which women enter regular cohabitation as a function of age, and the shape of the declining part of the curve by the degree to which fertility is affected by the practice of contraception or abortion. Thus one can predict with fair accuracy the general structure of age-specific fertility in a population where marriages are concentrated soon after puberty and little birth control is practiced, on the one hand, or on the other, in populations where marriage begins at 17, occurs at a mean age of 25, and where the fertility of married women is sharply curtailed by contraception and abortion. One can be confident that the observed fertility functions upon which Equation (3.37) is based are representative of the variations in the age structure of fertility in other human populations.

Birth Sequences and Age Composition When Mortality Is Constant and Fertility Follows a Trend of Constant Annual Change

If mortality were constant and fertility (with a constant age structure) changed by the same relative amount each year, the sequence of births would closely resemble a second order exponential. The second order exponential is approximated by the solution to a difference equation derived on the assumption that all births occur at the mean age of childbearing. The approximation can be made very close indeed by modifying the difference equation to allow for the fact that births are *not* concentrated at the mean age.

The reason the difference equation leads to a good approximation (and the modified version to a better one) is that when fertility is constantly changing, the births at the mid-point of the preceding generation differ only slightly from an appropriately weighted average of the births a generation earlier. The basic equation that is satisfied by the sequence of births when fertility is constantly changing in magnitude but not in age structure is

$$(4.3) \qquad B(t) = R(0)e^{kt} \int_{\alpha}^{\beta} B(t-a)f(a)da.$$

In this equation $R(0)$ is the net reproduction rate at time 0 and $f(a)$ is the net fertility at age a divided by the net reproduction rate. Since the age pattern of fertility is assumed constant, $f(a)$ does not change with time. It is a function whose aggregate value from α to β is 1.0. Under these circumstances the equivalence of $B(t - T)$, T constant, and $\int_{\alpha}^{\beta} B(t - a)f(a)da$ is almost exact (and still more so if T is assigned a gradually changing value). The reason for near equality is that $B(t)$ is a second order exponential, and since the term in t^2 has a small coefficient, there are only minor deviations from a first order exponential over a range of β to α years. Since the assumption that all births occur at a single age works so well in finding the relationship between fertility sequence and birth sequence when fertility is constantly changing, there is a natural tendency to use such an assumption in instances where the fertility sequence is subject to more complex variation. However, such a procedure is not, in fact, feasible. If, for example, fertility is subject to second order exponential variation, the birth sequence can have segments of substantial curvature, and different curvature over different segments. Under these circumstances $B(t - T)$, T constant, would be a very poor approximation to $\int_{\alpha}^{\beta} B(t - a)f(a)da$. Thus the results of Chapter 4 and the methods utilized there must be restricted to constantly declining fertility. Nevertheless, the age compositional effects of a period of constant fertility, an interval of declining fertility, and then a period of constant fertility at a low level — all analyzed in Chapter 4 — are of general demographic interest, since this is a rough outline of the fertility change characteristic of modernization.

When constantly decreasing net fertility passes from well above to well below the level that would, if maintained, just insure replacement, the second order exponential birth sequence must move from a phase in which the number of births is annually increasing to one in which births are annually decreasing, and hence must attain a maximum. The maximum number of births is reached half a generation before the intrinsic rate of increase is zero. The population reaches a maximum $\bar{a}_t$ years after births do, where $\bar{a}_t$ is the mean age of the population at time t; about 20 years after the intrinsic rate of increase is zero, if mortality is low. Hence if fertility were continuously declining, the population would increase consequentially after the intrinsic rate of increase passes below zero. Of course, the increase in population after the intrinsic rate of increase reaches zero would be still greater in a population in which fertility leveled off on reaching the replacement level. The amount of further increase in such a population depends upon the rate at which fertility has been declining, the mean length of generation, and the mean age of the stationary population. If fertility has been falling at 2% annually, e_0^0 is 70 years, and the mean length of generation is 28 years, the further increase after reaching replacement would be about one third.

The rate of increase in a population with a history of constantly changing fertility is

$$(4.47) \qquad r_k = r_s + \left(\frac{1}{2} - \frac{\bar{a}_k}{T}\right) k,$$

where r_s is the rate in increase in the stable population, $\bar{a}_k$ is the mean age of the population, T is the mean length of generation, and k is the annual rate of change in fertility. In all but extremely high fertility populations, $\bar{a}_k/T$ is greater than one half, and hence the rate of increase of a population with constantly changing fertility is typically greater than the stable rate of increase when k is negative, and less than the stable rate of increase when k is positive.

Age Composition When Fertility Is Constant and Mortality Has Been Declining

The effect on age composition of a history of declining mortality is analyzed by making allowance for the age pattern of mortality change that characterizes most instances of substantial decrease in mortality experienced by human populations. The typical change in age-specific mortality rates includes very large declines in mortality under age five, with a difference in rates that is a maximum at age zero and a minimum not much past age 5, very gradually increasing differences in mortality rates from 5 to age 45 or 50, and increasing differences beyond age 50. This age pattern of changing mortality can be approximated as the sum of three components, a minimum change in age-specific mortality that is assumed shared by all ages, and components in excess of this minimum under age 5 and over age 45. The change in mortality rates shared by all ages has no effect whatsoever on age composition, and the decline in mortality under age 5 has an effect on age composition much like an increase in fertility. As a result of these relations, the age composition of a population with a history of declining mortality during the preceding t years can be related to the age composition of a population with an appropriately selected rate of increase in fertility during the preceding t years. The age distribution of a population with a history of declining mortality is shown relative to the age distribution of a stable population in Figure 5.2.

213

Birth Sequences and Age Composition When Fertility Follows Cyclical Fluctuations

If fertility were subject to cyclical fluctuations of a perfectly repetitious character (no matter what the form and duration of cycle), the property of weak ergodicity implies that the age distribution would also follow a repetitious cycle of the same duration as the cycle in fertility. This inference follows from the fact that if fertility (or for that matter fertility and mortality) follows a wholly repetitious pattern, the history of fertility and mortality is the same at corresponding points in two consecutive cycles. Since populations with the same history of fertility and mortality must have the same age composition, it follows that the age composition of a population with periodic fluctuations in fertility, or in fertility and mortality, must have the same periodicity. Another implication of periodic fluctuations in fertility is that the birth sequence is the product of an exponential function and a periodic function.

If cyclical fluctuations in fertility were small amplitude variations at a single frequency, the birth sequence would be an exponential multiplied by a cyclical function with variations at the same frequency as the fertility variations. However, in general, the amplitude of the birth cycles would differ from those of the fertility cycles, and the birth cycles would reach maxima and minima at points different from the maxima and minima in fertility. In other words, cyclical fluctuations in births are subject to amplification or attenuation, and to phase shift, relative to fluctuations in fertility. The degree of amplification or attenuation and the extent of the shift in phase is shown as a function of frequency in Figure 6.1 and as a function of the duration of the cycle in Figure 6.2. Note that at very low frequencies (very long cycles) the birth cycles are much amplified relative to fertility cycles. This large amplification can be readily understood by noting that when cycles are very long—many generations in length—fertility would remain above average for several generations during the positive half cycles and below average for many generations during the negative half cycles. Thus the positive swing of births would be accentuated by a greater-than-average growth of population during the positive half cycles, and the negative swing by a less-than-average growth.

On the other hand, when fertility is subject to high frequency oscillations (oscillations of very short duration), the relative fluctuation in births exactly follows the relative fluctuation in fertility, without ampli-

214

fication, attenuation, or phase shift. This result is intuitively under-standable on the grounds that rapid fluctuations in fertility do not affect the age composition of the population in a way that influences the annual production of births. That is to say that alternating increases and decreases of persons within a short interval of ages have offsetting effects on the production of births. There is no interaction between the induced age distributional effects of fluctuating fertility and the age structure of the fertility function.

On the other hand, if fertility fluctuations had a period about one generation in length, the amplitude of the resultant birth cycles would be substantially greater than the amplitude of the fluctuations in fer-tility. The reason is again readily understood, since at each fertility maximum the women at the central childbearing ages would have been born during a preceding maximum, and the peaks in fertility would coincide with peaks in the number of mothers. Thus the age distribu-tion effects of fertility variation would reinforce the fertility variations themselves. Amplification in the neighborhood of one cycle per genera-tion (calculated for 45 net fertility functions) ranged from 1.41 to 1.99. Roughly speaking, the broader the fertility function relative to the mean length of generation, the less the amplification, and the narrower the function the greater the amplification. (If fertility were concen-trated at a single age, the amplification of periodic fluctuations of dura-tion equal to that age would be infinite.)

If, on the other hand, fertility variations had a duration about equal to twice the mean length of generation, the amplitude of fluctuations in births would be substantially less than the fluctuations in fertility, because under these circumstances fertility would be at a maximum when the number of mothers would be at a minimum. Attenuation at this frequency is such that birth cycles have only about 55% of the amplitude of fertility cycles.

When fluctuations in fertility at a single frequency are of more than very small amplitude, the resultant birth fluctuations about an exponen-tial trend no longer follow the same basic form as the fertility fluctua-tions. In addition to amplification (or attenuation) and phase shift, the birth cycles now contain harmonics—fluctuations at multiples of the frequency of the fertility fluctuations. The wave form of the birth fluctuations is distorted relative to the wave form of fertility. This dis-tortion is a result of a nonlinear term in the equation expressing the relationship between birth fluctuations and fertility fluctuations. This nonlinearity also implies that if fertility fluctuations contain more than

215

one frequency, the birth fluctuations at various frequencies are affected by interaction between components at different frequencies in the fertility fluctuation. It is this fact that makes it impossible to derive a simple relationship between the Fourier components of fertility fluctuations and the Fourier components of the consequent birth fluctuations.

As a final point we shall mention aspects of the analysis in this book that depend on empirical properties of human populations, and that cannot, therefore, be extended to other self-renewing aggregates. The mortality schedules to which human populations are subject have characteristic forms at different levels of mortality, and human fertility schedules have age structures constrained by human biology and by the limited variability of social behavior. Many of the results elaborated in the earlier chapters depend on the limited range of variability of human mortality and fertility schedules; and various formulae for estimation of parameters, and various relationships described are valid only for human populations and cannot be accurately attributed to other animal species or to a population of automobiles, for example.

An example of a result that depends upon empirical properties of schedules of fertility and mortality in human populations is the limited variability in the age structure of stable populations incorporating the same fertility schedule but different schedules of mortality. One can imagine a hypothetical schedule of mortality that would produce a vastly different age distribution. Similarly, the small influence of the second moment (and the negligible influence of third and higher cumulants) of the net fertility function on the rate of increase of stable populations is a consequence of the limited variability of the age schedules of net fertility in human populations. Again, it is possible to imagine schedules—for example, strongly bi-modal distributions of net fertility—where the effect of higher moments would be much more important.

An extreme instance of dependence on properties peculiar to human populations is the analysis in Chapter 5 of the effect of changing mortality on age composition. This analysis rests entirely on the existence of a typical pattern of mortality change by age. The analysis would not be applicable at all to aggregates in which mortality change followed a quite different pattern.

The contrast between general relations that would apply to any self-renewing aggregate and particular relations dependent on properties of human populations is illustrated in the analysis of the approach to stability in Chapter 3. The procedure of successive approximation for finding complex roots is applicable in examining the approach to stability of any self-renewing aggregate. However, the dominance after a few years of the low frequency oscillatory term and the relations found among the frequencies and relative attenuations of the other oscillatory terms would not necessarily characterize any population other than the human. The use of regression analysis to determine characteristics of the lowest frequency oscillatory term is justifiable only because of the limited range of social and biological factors influencing the age structure of human fertility. Thus, fertility schedules for recent years in Hungary have a very early peak and are highly skewed, with a curve above the age of maximum fertility that is very concave upward. A fertility schedule of this form could be predicted from the early age at marriage found in Hungary and the high degree of fertility control. The general form is surprisingly similar to the fertility schedule in the United States where early nuptiality and extensive fertility control are also found.

In short, this is a book about fertility, mortality, and age composition in human populations, and applications to other populations must be attempted only with caution.

GLOSSARY OF MOST SIGNIFICANT SYMBOLS

THE symbols that appear most frequently, and especially those employed at some distance in the text from their definition, are listed and briefly defined below. A page reference is supplied to the first appearance of each symbol. There has been some effort to achieve consistency, but there remain instances in which the same symbol is employed for quite different concepts in different chapters. The most conspicuous example is the use of T to designate both the mean length of generation in the stable population and the duration of a cycle in periodic fluctuations of fertility. Both usages are well established conventions, and since the mean length of generation plays no significant role in Chapters 6 and 7, T was retained for this double duty.

Symbol	Definition	First Appearance
$\bar{A}$	Mean age of childbearing in the stable population	p. 19
	$\bar{A} = \dfrac{\displaystyle\int_{\alpha}^{\beta} ae^{-ra}p(a)m(a)da}{\displaystyle\int_{\alpha}^{\beta} e^{-ra}p(a)m(a)da}$	Equation (2.11)
$\bar{a}$	Mean age of the stable population	p. 28
	$\bar{a} = \dfrac{\displaystyle\int_{0}^{\omega} ae^{-ra}p(a)da}{\displaystyle\int_{0}^{\omega} e^{-ra}p(a)da}$	Equation (2.42)
$\hat{a}$	Age at which the age distributions of two stable populations with the same mortality schedules intersect	p. 60
	$\hat{a} = \dfrac{(\bar{a}_1 - \bar{a}_2)}{2}$	
$\bar{a}_d$	Mean age of deaths in the stable population	p. 51
	$\bar{a}_d = \dfrac{\displaystyle\int_{0}^{\omega} ae^{-ra}p(a)\mu(a)da}{\displaystyle\int_{0}^{\omega} e^{-ra}p(a)\mu(a)da}$	
$\bar{a}_g$	Mean age of persons experiencing an event g (or possessing a characteristic g) in the stable population	p. 49
	$\bar{a}_g = \dfrac{\displaystyle\int_{0}^{\omega} ae^{-ra}p(a)g(a)da}{\displaystyle\int_{0}^{\omega} e^{-ra}p(a)g(a)da}$	Equation (2.43)
$\bar{a}_k, \bar{a}_s$	Mean ages of a population with a history of constantly declining fertility and of a stable population	p. 131

219

Symbol	Definition	First Appearance
	based on the same mortality and the prevailing fertility schedules	
b	Intrinsic birth rate: birth rate in the stable population	p. 17
	$$b = \frac{1}{\int_0^\omega e^{-ra}p(a)da}$$	Equation (2.3)
b_f, b_m, b_t	Birth rate in a female stable population; and birth rates in a male stable population and in a two-sex stable population defined by fertility schedules of women (children of both sexes) and by female and male mortality schedules	p. 54
b_{ff}	Birth rate in a population with a history of fluctuating fertility	p. 193
	$$b_{ff} = \frac{(1 + h'(0))}{\int_0^\omega e^{\bar{r}a}p(a)(1 + h'(a))da}$$	
b_k, b_s	Birth rates in a population with a history of constantly declining fertility and in a stable population based on the same mortality and the prevailing fertility schedules	p. 132
	$$b_k = \frac{1}{\int_0^\omega e^{-(k/2)a+(k/2T)a^2}e^{-ra}p(a)da}$$	Equation (4.38)
$C(a)$	Proportion under age a in the stable population	p. 30
$c(a)$	Proportion at age a in the stable population	p. 16
	$c(a) = be^{-ra}p(a)$	Equation (2.1)
$c_{dm}(a)$	Proportion at age a in a population with a history of constantly declining mortality	p. 163
$c_{ff}(a)$	Proportion at age a in a population with a history of fluctuating fertility	p. 193
	$$c_{ff}(a) = \frac{e^{-\bar{r}a}p(a)(1 + h'(a))}{\int_0^\omega e^{-\bar{r}a}p(a)(1 + h'(a))da}$$	Equation (6.31)
$c_k(a)$, $c_s(a)$	Proportions at age a in a population with a history of constantly declining fertility and in a stable population based on the same mortality and the prevailing fertility schedule	p. 121
$c_m(a)$	Proportion at age a in a male stable population defined by fertility schedules for women (children of both sexes) and by female and male mortality schedules	p. 54
$c(\bar{m})$	Proportion at the mean age of the fertility schedule, $\bar{m}$	p. 43
c_f	Element helping to determine frequency response of net fertility function	p. 170

Symbol	Definition	First Appearance
	$$c_f = \int_\alpha^\beta e^{-ra}\Phi(a)\cos(2\pi fa)da$$	
c_n	Element helping to determine amplitude of harmonics in a birth sequence with fluctuating fertility	p. 168
	$$c_n = \int_\alpha^\beta e^{-ra}\Phi(a)\cos(nwa)da$$	
d	Intrinsic death rate: death rate in the stable population	p. 50
	$$d = \int_0^\omega be^{-ra}p(a)\mu(a)da$$	Equation (2.47)
d_0	Death rate in a stationary population	p. 51
d_f, d_m, d_t	Death rate in a female stable population; and death rates in a male stable population and in a two-sex stable population defined by fertility schedules of women (children of both sexes) and by female and male mortality schedules	p. 54
d_k, d_s	Death rates in a population with a history of constantly declining fertility and in a stable population based on the same mortality and the prevailing fertility schedules	p. 135
e_0^0	Average expectation of life at birth	p. 9
F	Fraction of net fertility, $\Phi(a)$, encompassed between $(3\mu_1/4)$ and $(5\mu_1/4)$, where μ_1 is the mean age of the net fertility schedule	p. 73
f	Frequency of fertility fluctuations	p. 167
$f(a)$	Frequency distribution of the net fertility function, $\Phi(a) = m(a)p(a)$	p. 118
	$$f(a) = \frac{p(a)m(a)}{\int_0^\beta p(a)m(a)da}$$	
G	Overall rate (or proportion) of an event (or characteristic), g, in the stable population	p. 49
	$$G = \int_0^\omega g(a)c(a)da$$	Equation (2.37)
G_0	Overall rate (or proportion) of an event (or characteristic), g, in the stationary population	p. 50
$g(a)$	Rate (or proportion) of an event (or characteristic), g, at age a	p. 49
$g(t)$	Periodic fluctuations in fertility around the mean value of fertility, with aggregate value of zero for each cycle	p. 166
$h(t)$	Periodic fluctuations of births, with aggregate value of zero for each cycle	p. 166
$h_n(t)$	Component of $h(t)$ at frequency $n.f$	p. 167

221

Symbol	Definition	First Appearance
$m(a)$	Rate of bearing female children at age a	p. 18
$\bar{m}$	Mean age of the fertility schedule, $m(a)$	p. 18

$$\bar{m} = \frac{\int_\alpha^\beta am(a)da}{\int_\alpha^\beta m(a)da}$$
Equation (2.9)

| $p(a)$ | Proportion surviving to age a, given the mortality schedule $\mu(a)$ | p. 16 |

$$p(a) = e^{-\int_0^a \mu(x)dx}$$
Equation (2.2)

| $p(a,t)$ | Proportion surviving to age a in the cohort reaching age a at time t | p. 156 |

$$p(a,t) = e^{-\int_0^a \mu(x,t-a+x)dx}$$

| $p(\bar{m})$ | Proportion surviving to age $\bar{m}$, the mean age of the fertility schedule, $m(a)$ | p. 18 |

| Q_i | i'th coefficient of $e^{r_i t}$ in the solution $B(t) = \sum_{i=0}^\infty Q_i e^{r_i t}$ (Equation 3.4) of the integral equation, $$B(t) = \left[F(t) + \int_0^\beta B(t-a)p(a)m(a)da \right]$$ (Equation 3.1) | p. 64 |

$$Q_i = \frac{\int_0^\beta F(t)e^{-r_i t}dt}{\int_0^\beta ae^{-r_i a}\Phi(a)da}$$
Equation (3.18)

| $Q_i(a)$ | Value of Q_i that would be produced by a unit population element at age a | p. 68 |

$$Q_i(a) = \frac{\int_0^{\beta-a} e^{-r_i t}\Phi(a+t)dt}{p(a)\int_0^\beta ae^{-r_i a}\Phi(a)da}$$
Equation (3.20)

| R | Net reproduction rate | p. 123 |

$$R = \int_\alpha^\beta p(a)m(a)da$$

| $R(t)$ | Net reproduction rate defined by age-specific fertility rates at time t and by survival to age t of cohorts born a years ago | p. 118 |

$$R(t) = \int_0^\beta p(a,t)m(a,t)da$$

| r | Intrinsic rate of increase: rate of increase in the stable population | p. 16 |
| r_f, r_m | Rates of increase in the female and male stable populations | p. 55 |

222

Symbol	Definition	First Appearance
r_i	i'th root of the equation $\int_0^\beta e^{-ra}p(a)m(a)da = 1.0$. r_0 is real; all others are complex and their real parts are less than r_0	p. 64
s_f	Element helping to determine frequency response of net fertility function $$s_f = \int_0^\beta e^{-ra}\Phi(a)\sin(2\pi fa)da$$	p. 170
s_n	Element helping to determine amplitude of harmonics in a birth sequence with fluctuating fertility $$s_n = \int_0^\beta e^{-ra}\Phi(a)\sin(nwa)da$$	p. 168
T	Length of cycle in cyclically changing fertility	p. 165
T	Mean length of generation in the stable population $$e^{rT} = \text{NRR}$$	p. 18 Equation (2.8)
T_0	Mean length of generation in the stationary population; or more precisely, mean length of generation as r approaches zero $$T_0 = \frac{\int_\alpha^\beta ap(a)m(a)da}{\int_\alpha^\beta p(a)m(a)da}$$	p. 120 Equation (4.5)
T_f, T_m	Mean lengths of generation in the female and male stable populations	p. 56
V	Ratio of the median age of the net fertility function $\Phi(a)$ to the mean age of $\Phi(a)$	p. 74
x_i	Real part of the i'th complex root of the equation $\int_0^\beta e^{-ra}\Phi(a)da = 1.0$	p. 65
$x(t)$	Cyclical fluctuations in births arising from interaction of cyclical variation in fertility and cyclical variation in the number of women one generation earlier $$x(t) = g(t).z(t)$$	p. 167
$x_n(t)$	Component of $x(t)$ at frequency n.f	p. 167
y_i	Imaginary part of the i'th complex root of the equation $\int_0^\beta e^{-ra}\Phi(a)da = 1.0$	p. 65
$z(t)$	Weighted average of the fluctuations in number of births one generation before time t $$z(t) = \int_0^\beta e^{-ra}\Phi(a)h(t-a)da$$	p. 167

223

Symbol	Definition	First Appearance
$z_n(t)$	Component of $z(t)$ at frequency $n.f$	p. 167
α	Lowest age of fertility	p. 11
β	Highest age of fertility	p. 11
δ_i	i'th cumulant of the age distribution of a given event (e.g. death), or characteristic, in the stationary population	p. 51
θ_i	Initial phase of the i'th damped oscillatory component of the birth sequence	p. 96
$\theta_i(a)$	Initial phase of the i'th damped oscillatory component of the birth sequence resulting from a population element at age a	p. 69
λ_i	i'th cumulant of the age distribution of the stationary population	p. 50

$$\lambda_1 = \text{mean age of the stationary population}$$

Symbol	Definition	First Appearance
$\mu(a)$	Death rate at age a	p. 16
μ_n	n'th cumulant of the net fertility function, $\Phi(a) = p(a)m(a)$	p. 19

$$\mu_1 = \frac{\displaystyle\int_\alpha^\beta ap(a)m(a)da}{\displaystyle\int_\alpha^\beta p(a)m(a)da}, \text{ mean age of fertility in the}$$

Equation (2.10)

stationary population

$$\mu_2 = \text{age-variance of fertility in the stationary population}$$

Symbol	Definition	First Appearance
σ^2	Age-variance of the fertility schedule, $m(a)$, or of the net fertility schedule $\Phi(a) = m(a)p(a)$	p. 19 / p. 123
$\Phi(a)$	Net fertility schedule	p. 19

$$\Phi(a) = p(a)m(a)$$

Symbol	Definition	First Appearance
ω	Highest age attained	p. 1